Carlo Scarpa Architect

INTERVENING WITH HISTORY

NICHOLAS OLSBERG

GEORGE RANALLI

JEAN-FRANÇOIS BÉDARD

SERGIO POLANO

ALBA DI LIETO

MILDRED FRIEDMAN

PHOTOGRAPHS BY
GUIDO GUIDI

CANADIAN CENTRE FOR ARCHITECTURE • THE MONACELLI PRESS

Published by the Canadian Centre for Architecture and The Monacelli Press to accompany the exhibition *Carlo Scarpa, Architect: Intervening with History*, presented at the Canadian Centre for Architecture (CCA) in Montréal from 26 May to 31 October 1999. Guest curator: Mildred Friedman.

ISBN 0-920785-61-1 (CCA)
The Canadian Centre for Architecture
1920 Baile Street, Montréal, Québec, Canada H3H 2S6

ISBN 1-58093-035-2 (Monacelli)
The Monacelli Press, Inc.
10 East 92nd Street, New York, New York 10128

Printed and bound in Canada

Legal Deposit:
National Library of Canada, 1999
Bibliothèque nationale du Québec, 1999

Also published in French under the title *Carlo Scarpa, architecte: Composer avec l'histoire*

PHOTO CREDITS

François Bastien, Michel Boulet, CCA Photographic Services: 63, 65, 87, 90, 91b, 91c, 93, 106, 114, 116, 117, 119–23, 128, 130–33, 135, 137, 139–43, 145–48, 150, 151, 213, and 15a, 60, 62, 64 (copy prints); Sergio Benaglia: 241b; Maria Ida Biggi: 102; Tom Bonner: 245a; Maurizio Brenzoni: 227; Michele Buda: 17, 91a, and 11, 12, 13, 15b (copy prints); Dario Busato: 110; James Dow: 246b; Umberto Ferro: 104, 105; Allan Forbes: 240; Jeff Goldberg/Esto Photographics Inc.: 242b, 243a; Anton Grassl Photography: 239b; Guido Guidi: cover, frontispiece, 21, 22, 24–29, 31, 33–36, 107, 111, 113, 155–63, 165–95, 197–201, 203, 206, 209; John Hall: 244; Paolo Monti: 97, 99, 112; Michael Moran: 241a; Jayme Odgers: 246a; Alessandro Paperni, Udine: 149; Publifoto, Palermo: 47, 49–51, 53–57, 220, 221; RIBA, London: 126; Umberto Tomba: 71, 73–75, 77–85, 219, 223, 225, 228, 233, 235, and 68, 229, 231 (copy prints); Luca Vignelli: 242a; Paul Warchol Photography: 243b; Kim Zwarts: 239a.

The Canadian Centre for Architecture is grateful to the Parnassus Foundation (Courtesy of Raphael and Jane Bernstein) for generous support of the photographic commission.

The CCA thanks the J.W. McConnell Family Foundation, Tourisme Montréal, Bank of Montreal, Royal Bank, and Omni The Outdoor Company for their support of the exhibition and the accompanying public programs.

The CCA gratefully acknowledges the support of the Department of Canadian Heritage, the Ministère de la Culture et des Communications du Québec, the Canada Council for the Arts, and the Conseil des arts de la Communauté urbaine de Montréal.

Library of Congress Cataloging-in-Publication Data
Scarpa, Carlo, 1906–1978.
Carlo Scarpa, architect : intervening with history / Nicholas Olsberg ... [et al.] ; photographs by Guido Guidi.
p. cm.
Catalog of an exhibition held at the Canadian Centre for Architecture, Montreal, Canada.
Includes bibliographical references and index.
ISBN 1-58093-035-2
1. Scarpa, Carlo, 1906–1978 Exhibitions. 2. Architecture, Modern–20th century–Italy Exhibitions. I. Olsberg, R. Nicholas. II. Guidi, Guido, 1940– . III. Centre canadien d'architecture. IV. Title.
NA1123.S35A4 1999 720'.92–dc21 99-26887

CONTENTS

The Centre Canadien d'Architecture/ Canadian Centre for Architecture (CCA) is a study centre and a museum devoted to the art of architecture and its history. It is founded on the conviction that architecture, as part of the social and natural environment, is a public concern. The CCA's activities are international in scope and are based on a unique collection of works of art and documentation from all areas – architecture, urban planning, and landscape design – that are part of the built environment.

ACKNOWLEDGMENTS

This publication accompanies an exhibition that has developed over a number of years with the encouragement and support of many generous people. Foremost among them were Tobia and Afra Scarpa, who opened the family archives to us with boundless hospitality and supported our efforts to draw from it the essence of Scarpa's critical work in historical settings.

Despite the heroic work of Francesco Dal Co, Sergio Polano, and their colleagues in *Carlo Scarpa: Opera completa* (published in 1984 but still the indispensable key) and such reconstructive analyses as Richard Murphy's studies of the Castelvecchio and the Fondazione Querini Stampalia, much of Scarpa's work remains to be elucidated. Scarpa could take nine years on the interior of a small house, work through the night with his artisans drawing and testing models, and adjust what he pleased on site. At the same time, he appears to have treated his own history casually. "Unknown" projects regularly emerge from the shadows; cartons of project correspondence lie unexamined; sketchbooks, student drawings, and cigar-box studies appear in profusion. Drawings – many dispersed by Scarpa himself – suddenly come to light for the first time, while others, long recorded, have vanished. The drawings that survive are almost invariably undated, drawn over, re-used as sketch paper, layered not only with the evolving design but with months and even years of second thoughts. His own texts, project notes, and lectures gradually appear, more prolific than we imagined, and the bibliography of his works expands with every visit to the journals of his day. Meanwhile, buildings change, decay, or even burn before being measured, and fallible memory generates dispute as to what is Scarpa's work and what was done by clients and collaborators before, during, or after his intervention.

Thus we are at that not uncommon point in the afterlife of an architect when the sources and structures alike await the patient work of analysis and the unraveling of legends. It is thanks to Tobia and Afra Scarpa's tenacious stewardship that this can go forward.

We are especially grateful to Francesco Dal Co, for his guidance in the critical, early stages of this project, and to the many collaborators and clients of Scarpa who worked with us at that time. Scarpa worked so closely with certain artisans that they became virtual collaborators; those who generously assisted us include the Anfodillo brothers, Francesco and Paolo Zanon, Eugenio and Jasminka de Luigi, Luciano Zennaro, and Paolo Morseletto. We are also indebted to several of Scarpa's patient and knowledgable clients who gave us invaluable insights into their long association with Scarpa: Gianantonio Schiaffino and Carlo de Benedetti of Olivetti, the family of Onorina Brion, and Loredana Balboni. We also received valued help from the architects Giuseppe Davanzo (who meticulously restored Scarpa's Olivetti showroom), Giorgio Vigni (who worked with him at Abatellis), and Arrigo Rudi (who assisted Scarpa on projects including the Castelvecchio and the Banca Popolare di Verona).

In the Scarpa family archive, Nozumi Shinoda has been an indispensable, cheerful, and informed resource. At the Museo di Castelvecchio, director Paola Marini and curator and architect Alba Di Lieto spent many hours with us as we selected drawings from their great collection, while museum architect Eleanora Boaro assisted in acquiring transcriptions of interviews with Scarpa from Radiotelevisione Italiana (RAI). Dr. Vicenzo Abbate and Francesco Orecchio of the Palazzo Abatellis, and Dr. Giorgio Busetto, director of the Fondazione

Querini Stampalia, were extremely generous in providing loans for the exhibition and in sharing their knowledge of Scarpa's working method. Additional help with loans and images was provided by Maria Ida Biggi, Stefan Buzas, Antonia Mulas, and Giancesare Rainaldi of the Istituto di fotografia Paolo Monti.

We are very grateful to Guido Guidi for his discerning response to the photographic commission initiated and directed by our late colleague and friend, Paolo Costantini. Richard Pare later assisted Guido Guidi in the selection of his works for both book and exhibition. The photographic commission was generously supported by the Parnassus Foundation (Courtesy of Raphael and Jane Bernstein).

With the assistance of the Dunard Foundation, the CCA was able to work with Murray Grigor, the gifted Scottish filmmaker, to make his film on Carlo Scarpa a significant part of our exhibition. Thanks are also due to Murray Grigor, Allan Irvine, Richard Murphy, Sandro Giordano, Alberto Mozzato, and Sergio Polano, as well as RAI for making study material available to us, and to the many architects who shared their thoughts on the impact and significance of Scarpa's work today. Ceil Cordioli worked with us on our first visits to the Scarpa archive and has provided assistance with translations.

Roger Thomson undertook measured drawings of the Canova plaster cast gallery to assist in the construction of the model. The exhibition's installation and models were designed by the architect George Ranalli, working in consultation with Phyllis Lambert, Founding Director and Chair of the CCA Board of Trustees. Construction of the models was carried out by Price Harrison and Fran Leadon. George's profound understanding of the process and form of Scarpa's designs has been indispensable to us in developing the project analyses that structure this publication and the exhibition it accompanies. Robert Anderson has coordinated the exhibition's installation with great skill.

Jean-François Bédard was an indispensable member of the curatorial team throughout the project. Others at the CCA and elsewhere who worked diligently throughout the process of preparing the publication and the exhibition include André Bernier, Nadia di Fiore, Renata Guttman, Helen Malkin, and Anne Troise.

The Canadian Centre for Architecture thanks the J.W. McConnell Family Foundation, Tourisme Montréal, Bank of Montreal, Royal Bank, and Omni The Outdoor Company for their support of the exhibition and the accompanying public programs.

The CCA gratefully acknowledges the support of the Department of Canadian Heritage, the Ministère de la Culture et des Communications du Québec, the Canada Council for the Arts, and the Conseil des arts de la Communauté urbaine de Montréal.

MILDRED FRIEDMAN
Guest Curator

NICHOLAS OLSBERG
Chief Curator, CCA

PRINCIPAL LENDERS

Collection Archivio Carlo Scarpa, Trevignano
Coll. ACS

Collection Canadian Centre for Architecture, Montréal
Coll. CCA

Collection Fondazione Querini Stampalia, Venezia
Coll. FQS

Collection Galleria Regionale della Sicilia, Palermo
Coll. GRS

Collection Museo di Castelvecchio, Verona
Coll. MDC

Nicholas Olsberg

INTRODUCTION

IN HIS LAST TWENTY-FIVE YEARS, Carlo Scarpa constructed a series of works, each astonishingly unlike the other, that challenged our notions of what modern architecture might be. While maintaining a passionate allegiance to the modern vocabulary of form, Scarpa, in his late work, showed that it was possible to incorporate within it a highly wrought sense of craft, detail, color, ornament, and materiality. He revived the ideas of an articulated urban wall and the primacy of the connector and the opening – stairs and bridges, doors and windows – as central questions in building design. He taught architects, by his example, to look more respectfully at the banalities and less solemnly at the monuments of the past, and to weave new work into the ongoing dialogue of an evolving fabric. At the same time, he reopened the possibility of an architecture constructed like painting or poetry around questions of memory, allegory, narrative, and metaphor. Together, these innovations helped to liberate younger architects from the rationalist severity of their modernist training, to generate a new historical sensibility that lay outside the sentimental agendas of restoration and revival, and to reawaken architecture to its lyric potential – its capacity to write, on the ground, a sort of civic poetry.

Eight built works from Scarpa's architectural maturity are examined here. Three of these – the Olivetti showroom and the reorganization carried out for the Fondazione Querini Stampalia, both in Venice, with the Banca Popolare di Verona – respond in different ways to a dense, history-laden urban context (further illustrated by two lesser works: the renovation of the Balboni house in Venice and the Gavina showroom in Bologna). Three more – the Palazzo Abatellis in Palermo, the Canova plaster cast gallery at Possagno, and the restoration and reorganization of the Museo di Castelvecchio, Verona – rework or add to historic structures to accommodate carefully planned visual narratives in which light, space, and structure come into dialogue with works of art. The transitional work of the Veritti house in Udine introduces a similar sense of narrative through new architectural forms freshly conceived by Scarpa. The last of the eight – Scarpa's addition to a public cemetery in the landscape of the Veneto to accommodate a tomb commissioned by the Brion family – constructs a visionary landscape for the dead along the perimeter of a conventional civic burial ground. Forms of Scarpa's own devising are arranged there as if the elements of an installation or the components of a new city, drawing a dense symbolic poetry out of their shapes and siting.

These projects are marked throughout by immensely complex relationships of new to old, of the everyday to the monumental, of the familiar to the unexpected. They all express Scarpa's fanatical discipline: his intensive research into the function and conjunction of materials; his belief in the expressive power of details; his meticulous calculation of the accidents of light, reflection, and shadow; and his almost archeological analysis of existing site conditions. Above all they demonstrate his relentless concern with context, in its broadest sense: time past, present, and future; the common sense of a place and the careful reading of its visual character; the methodological traditions of design; and artisanal techniques in building.

Toward the end, Scarpa was openly identifying this question of context and materiality as "the crisis of modern architecture."[1] He recognized the need to reconcile a wholehearted embrace of the new with the longstanding traditions of local craft and of universal practice, to create an architecture that would clearly express its own machine-driven times without abandoning the psychic and sensual forces of place, material, and memory. These projects constitute Scarpa's effort to achieve that reconciliation, and they remain subtly but powerfully pertinent to an environment increasingly concerned with adapting, rather than revolutionizing, the fabric of the built world.

Scarpa was born in 1906 in Venice and grew up in Vicenza. At thirteen he moved back to Venice and entered the fine arts academy, pursuing general courses in painting, sculpture, architecture, and design until 1922, when he chose the four-year architecture course as his specialty, working under Guido Cirilli. Recalling childhood games under the columns and "attic bases" of Palladio's Vicenza, he claimed to have come to architecture "as a given," recognizing from the start that it was "deadly serious,... not a game ... but a very difficult ... very serious matter."[2] Scarpa's student drawings show him following the curriculum's traditional Beaux-Arts structure with a twist of eclecticism: freehand sketches of ancient, medieval, and Baroque buildings; measured *rilievi* of brickwork and ornament; projects for a Neoclassical *nymphaeum* and a neo-Baroque embassy.

For a number of years after 1926 he continued to work with Guido Cirilli, and during the 1930s gradually developed a wide-ranging design practice of his own, renovating domestic and commercial interiors and redesigning portions of the medieval Ca' Foscari (1935–37) for the University of Venice. He designed art glass for the Venini firm in Murano and from 1941 onward worked regularly on the redesign and installation of exhibition spaces, in particular at the *Venice Biennale* and the Gallerie dell'Accademia. Though he remained unlicensed, Scarpa left Venini in 1947 to broaden his architectural practice, working with the young architect Angelo Masieri on projects for banks, churches, tombs, and private houses, and rapidly expanding his work in installation design. At the same time, Scarpa never lost his devotion to painting and sculpture. He was exhibiting oils as late as the 1940s, worked with Mario De Luigi on mosaics, and designed an abstract sculpture in metal for the Olivetti showroom (1957–58) and the Venice pavilion for the exhibition *Italia '61* in Turin.

By 1950, with the construction of such works as the book pavilion at the *Venice Biennale* and the TELVE public telephone facility in Venice, Scarpa's work was widely noticed. When in 1953 he began work on the Galleria nazionale della Sicilia at Palazzo Abatellis in Palermo, his was a busy practice with a series of major public, private, and commercial commissions. Yet it remained highly personal and essentially idiosyncratic. Scarpa worked with only a very few assistants and remained deeply tied to local craft and construction traditions. Many of the design possibilities were explored and completed on site or in the artisans' workshops. While most of his freestanding projects went unbuilt, the realized work remained focused on what had engrossed Scarpa from the beginning: relatively small-scale interventions, additions, and redesigns, and the organization and presentation of works of art.

Each of Scarpa's later projects seems to be invented *de novo*. Distinctively new forms and ideas develop to match each new situation, but certain key themes and motifs link them: the play of levels and the idea of bridging; the use of water and its sport with light; the

Restructuring of Ca' Foscari (1935–37), Venice. Coll. ACS

Restructuring of Ca' Foscari (1935–37), Venice. Coll. ACS

concept of semi-transparency through perforation, screen, and layer; the notion of composing with light and shadow and even with the void of the sky itself; and an evolving fascination with circular forms. Many of these represent the maturing of ideas that Scarpa had explored since the mid 1930s. For example, in his first major project, the renovation at Ca' Foscari (1935–37), Scarpa finds the strategies that will govern his work at Palazzo Abatellis, Querini Stampalia, and Castelvecchio: the deliberate juxtaposition of old and new, heightening the differences between aspects of a single building, showing the change of materials, and exploring the relationship with the outside world by screening new windows against the old. In his gallery of modern art "Il Cavallino" (1941) and the boutique he designed for Ferdinando Ongania (1950), one finds the confrontation with the Venetian street and *campo* that he develops so richly at Olivetti. The use of the sky as a compositional device at Possagno (1955–57) appeared earlier in the *Biennale* book pavilion (1950), just as Possagno's draped windows had made an appearance at the Venezuela Pavilion (1954–56). The broken circles that lead one into the chapel and open up the lawn at the Brion tomb are clearly anticipated in his design for the Veritti tomb at Udine (1951), while projects from the Giacomuzzi house (1947–50) onward begin to explore the sculptural qualities of garden space and the play between land and water – investigations that become increasingly refined at Querini Stampalia, Castelvecchio, and Brion. A dazzling set of alternatives for a new church at Fiorenzuola (1956) prefigures the kind of complex mental exercise he was to undertake in accommodating urban site and context in the Veritti house, the Gavina showroom, and the Banca Popolare di Verona.

Scarpa disliked words, eschewed rhetoric and theory, and disavowed an interest in the architectural debates of his day. But there is a forceful polemic in his work, and, while reticent of theoretical issues, he repeatedly, if quietly, set forth his differences with the pragmatic climate of post-war modernism. His fundamental loyalty to the modern movement was unshakable. He decried the rigid traditionalism and eclectic stylism of his schooling, wryly identifying himself as a direct descendant of the makers of that *bête blanche* of modernism, the Victor Emmanuel monument in Rome. Although he came to value the methodological discipline and precision the academy taught him, he believed its finest legacy was in being so fiercely provincial and constricted that it forced him to look for the most radical alternatives: "We had to detach ourselves from our own pedagogical training."[3]

"Il Cavallino" art gallery (1941), Venice. Coll. ACS

Window of the Ongania showroom (1950), Venice. Coll. ACS

His own need for such a cultural reaction was answered in the year of his graduation, 1926, when he came across the recently published *Vers une architecture*, which he greeted as a revelation. Scarpa never lost his debt to Le Corbusier and especially his invitation to seek new forms in the techniques, materials, and structural discipline of industrial culture. Even when most disdainful of the formulaic functionalism of post-war modernists, Scarpa continued to find in Le Corbusier's late work, as in Kahn's, the most fertile ground in which to grow a new and more poetic modernism. His passion for the pioneers of modern thought was equally strong. He had met Josef Hoffmann in the 1930s, discovering an immediate fellowship with this architect-craftsman from a city that, like Venice, had spent much of its history looking east. The impact of Frank Lloyd Wright – reinforced by a friendship that began with Wright's visit to Venice in 1951 – was even stronger. Scarpa referred to his first encounter with Wright's work as a *coup de foudre*,[4] and critics have noted the appearance in Scarpa's work of quite disparate elements of Wright's formal investigations: the prairie houses in the Banca Cattolica del Veneto (1947–49) and the Giacomuzzi house (1947–50), both at Tarvisio (Udine); Wright's late desert houses, especially that for Jorgine Boomer, in the Veritti house (1955–61); and the Nakoma and Lake Tahoe projects in the Brion family tomb (1969–78).

In embracing Wright's organicism with such enthusiasm and in discovering what he called a certain "Byzantine" kinship with the "orientalism" and polychromy of the Vienna school, Scarpa appeared to distance himself from the rational and functionalist mainstream of the modern movement. But from the thirties onward, he consistently listed Le Corbusier, Alvar Aalto, and Mies van der Rohe, along with Wright and the Viennese, as his great models, although he came to renounce certain works (his early houses in particular) in which Wright's example was too strongly evident. He was also careful to pose his challenge to the increasingly dispirited modern movement of the 1960s and 1970s as a set of correctives that would make it relevant rather than an assault on its fundamentals.

But that challenge was sweeping. Scarpa called for a return to the "ancient" discipline of drawing as the generative force of invention, and with it the recovery of the poetic independence of design, with "a distinctive personal character that would lend each work the moral authority that everyone in the world of art must strive for."[5] Beginning with a famous lecture in 1963, he strenuously defended decoration, arguing – with the example of the microphone stem's tubular column before him – that forms remain 'un-finite,' and thus inexpressive, without it. He believed that a syntax of color and ornament becomes inevitable in an architectural project from the moment the designer makes the first choice of a material – resist as one might.

Scarpa also advocated a return to the sensory delight that comes from what can be touched and felt in each material, to the intellectual

Ceiling in the book pavilion (1950), *Venice Biennale*. Coll. ACS

Windows in the Pavilion of Venezuela (1954–56), *Venice Biennale*. Coll. ACS

excitement that derives from exploring and unveiling its structural characteristics, and to the logical pleasures of seeing how distinctive materials with different properties can be wed. He asked us to re-acknowledge the potential of materials to drive the generative process and produce a ruling idea for the larger work: "It is a curious faculty this, which enables us to sense that a certain dimensional factor, a thickness for instance, can become the determining characteristic of the physical value of things."[6] Above all, he insisted that the building of a vocabulary of material and ornament was a critical step in capturing those senses – tactile, psychological, and mnemonic – that open a work of architecture to "maximum expression and meaning."

There are two areas in which these fragments of a theory of design become most subtle and extended. Perhaps the most provocative of Scarpa's positions, they are clearly related. First is his call for the restoration of a sense of humility in the face of history, context, and tradition. Second is his prohibition of the easy read, the central point of view, the ready unveiling of the visual logic that lies behind a design. The first of these ideas moves him far from the principles of both Wright (pleading for the absolute originality of the moment) and Kahn (seeking a kind of transcendental universalism through the recovery of primal forms). The other takes him equally far from those rationalists in the modern movement who held to the ideal of a transparent display of structure, which he felt to be illusory.[7]

History meant two things to Scarpa: the traditions of the architectural discipline and its craft, and the evolving fabric of the built world. "Architecture is a craft like any other," he claimed. "It has its techniques, its ways of working...."[8] At the same time he decried as anachronistic the mimicry of motifs and materials from the past, especially in projects of renovation and re-use. "I have always had ...," he once said, "an immense desire to belong to tradition, but without having capitals and columns."[9] He despised the false "certainty" with which nineteenth-century positivists approached restoration and rebuilding. And he saw integrity not in the return of a building to some original state but in respect for the gradual accretion of changes that made it "whole." Citing his window at Ca' Foscari as an example, Scarpa stressed that since windows had changed their meaning and function, they must now be expressed in materials and forms that reflected present needs and technologies. For Scarpa, then, it was not the solutions that belonged to tradition but the problems, what he called the "basic questions" – the opening, the door, the stair. Scarpa insisted that these elements were not "details" but fundamentals, the essence of the built form and the thread that connected us to the past. It was here that "the artisan had to show his mastery, autographing ... the critical moments of the building."[10] Further, we should return not to traditional ways of resolving these elements, but rather to the orthodox *techniques* of addressing architectural problems: the pencil, the analysis of structure and joint, and the application of artisanry. From these, new and timely solutions would emerge.

In eschewing the idea of a single, unified form as the central, governing composition by which a building could be read, Scarpa forced the visitor into a circuit of looking, made him shift and turn his gaze, and offered no decisive focal point. He learned much about this from his work in museums, where he took such pains to move the visitor around the works of art and to see the relationships between them. Describing the arrangement of the long suite of galleries at Castelvecchio, Scarpa explained how the sculptures are positioned to face in different directions. "I could have turned them ... but it seems to me that this is the visitor's duty ... to look to right and left ... come back to see it again, and walk around it."[11] Castelvecchio moves the visitor through a single space three times, and Palazzo Abatellis brings him back to the same point twice.

Learning from his installation strategies, Scarpa extended this fluidity into works where the viewing of art is not involved. Brion allows for many different itineraries, and in few of the late works is there a set moment or a standard viewpoint. In some, like the Banca Popolare (where windows are designed to frame reflections of its surroundings) or the Canova gallery at Possagno (where Scarpa intended the geometric design of the "azzura" in the high windows to focus the form), it may be the reflection in the window or the void beyond, far more than the fabric of the building, that organizes the composition. At the same time, Scarpa may be as ready to conceal the structure, and deceive the visitor, as he is to stress or aestheticize a technical passage. He constructs the windows at Possagno around a series of hidden joints that, from within, give the illusion of the sky simply floating in the concrete, as if "the blue of the sky seemed to be cut into pieces,"[12] while its exterior face, visible only from the little street behind, emphatically reveals how the windows are put together.

As Scarpa pointed out, arguments about the circularity of space are also reflections on the uncertainty and circularity of time – reflections elaborated most eloquently in such built works as the Museo di Castelvecchio and the Brion tomb, where they are expressed through a kind of disharmony. Here Scarpa's readiness to focus on the particle, to treat an intervention as the disposition of discrete parts rather than a single form, amounts to a species of urbanism, since it lays as much emphasis on what is left between them as on the objects themselves. At the same time, his insistence on displaying the seams between the fabric and the intervention, on layering an asymmetrical form of his own behind an existing order, and on forcing fiercely new dimensions or materials against the texture of the old – like the great black steel girder that runs along the ceiling in the Museo di Castelvecchio – sets up a conspicuous dialectic, at times a confrontation, between old and new.

This apparently reckless and arrogant procedure in fact reflects a certain humility in the face of the future. For Scarpa was working with an absolute confidence in the power of time to patinate a work and give its disparate parts a sort of common persona. "See how a building inevitably establishes new identities over time," he once said, looking at the campanile on the Venetian island of Torcello. "Once acknowledged, this basic principle makes it fundamental for the architect to leave conspicuous and characteristic evidence of his own era within the historic fabric, trusting time to fuse it into a comfortable whole." In thus reconceiving preservation as a dialogue between what is there and what might be, the architect could set up what Scarpa called a "speculative tension" in which anticipation was as important as memory.

Much has been written about this, the fragmentary nature of Scarpa's work and the tactics of tension, disjunction, and discomfiture that govern aspects of his later projects. Rafael Moneo says that the work is "indefinable and is elusive, capable of revealing its true and full significance only by being fragmented and shattered."[13] Manfredo Tafuri speaks of "an open organization of broken phrases" that refers at once to "an irreparably lost whole" and to a "different mode of completion."[14] On these topics, Scarpa himself is terse but quite explicit. He insists, for example, that architecture must embrace "uneasiness" and "anxiety." Citing examples of these moments of incompleteness or disquieting unfamiliarity – he calls them "ruses" – Scarpa describes the unsettling descent to the garden at Possagno, the disequilibrium

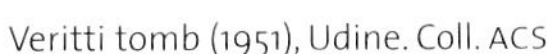
Veritti tomb (1951), Udine. Coll. ACS

Giacomuzzi house (1947–50), Udine. Coll. ACS

suggested there by hiding the joints of vitrines, the arbitrary installation of a step in the midst of its square room, and his "thieving" of this stepped space by straddling it with a sculpture.

As Scarpa's work matures, these points of surprise become more frequent but less theatrical. They move from the enthralling drop across which the visitor greets the *Triumph of Death* at the Palazzo Abatellis to the more quietly troubling incidents at the Banca Popolare (with its bridge as tunnel and its staircase to nowhere) to the disquieting overhang above the Brion family graves and the suggestion that the gravestones have been scattered at random. Speaking of Alberti, Scarpa regretfully finds his plea for "harmony," for "coherence and unity of form," out of tune with modern times. Confronting the great Tuscan architects of the Renaissance, he finds he cannot "embrace that sort of sureness, that sort of certitude."[15] Instead, as Francesco Dal Co explains, Scarpa increasingly asks us to reject the "familiar, gracious, and trusted" and to accept "the impossibility of shaping life according to the values of stability."[16]

This idea of tension also illuminates Scarpa's relationship to history. His dialogue is never with the past, but with the presence of the past in the present, with the fabric around him, with "continuity," and most frequently with the specific continuities of Venice and the Veneto. He recalls his fondness for the *callette,* the narrow city streets, in the void between the old building and the new at Possagno. His admiration for the way the walls enclosing the town of Asolo join each other – their "profound and unconscious wholeness"[17] – is seen in the corner device at Brion. The ubiquity of Venice's bridges is recollected in the Veritti house, Castelvecchio, and the Palazzo Querini Stampalia, while Querini, the Olivetti showroom, and the Balboni house all delight in the reminiscence of Venice's shifting floor planes, its countless steps, stairs, and loggias. The way Venice doubles images in the reflections of its canals is used most profoundly in the bodies of water at Brion, where reflections are given a symbolic purpose. Throughout Scarpa draws upon something that he describes as peculiarly Venetian: a "passion for the particular" and a readiness to let things of different ages, scales, materials, styles, and hues work together.

Out of this Venice and its "Byzantine" sense of color, texture, and detail, Scarpa begins to assemble an essentially poetic language, in which personal history and private fascinations – from the textile samples of his mother (a dressmaker) to the aging brickwork on the Venetian island of Torcello – are given public meaning. Scarpa took pride in the diversity of his career and drew upon its memories as sources. He saw his glass designs as integral to his work in architecture and his "critical" study of painting as a source for the invention of form and symbol. Thus we find him referring to Titian and Tintoretto in the palette of his plasterwork or to Piet Mondrian and Paul Klee in his choice of geometries; to his mother's sensitivity to fabrics in his selection of the backing for the famous *Annunciation* by Antonello at the Palazzo Abatellis; to his love for the woman's form in designing the apartment of Loredana Balboni "as a stage-set for her doll-like beauty;"[18] to Egyptian myths of death, regeneration, and time at the Brion tomb. It is in this territory – where the tactile and the visual join, where references to the everyday can lead to the uncommon, and the old and new confront each other with wary sympathy – that a visible poetry can arise, and it is ultimately in its poetic values that Scarpa's work has its greatest force.

Church at Fiorenzuola, axonometric, plans, and sections, 1956. Graphite on paper, 29.7 x 21 cm. Coll. ACS

Church at Fiorenzuola, context studies, 1956. Graphite on paper, 29.7 x 21 cm. Coll. ACS

THREE MUSEUMS

PHOTOGRAPHS BY GUIDO GUIDI

Portfolio photographs:
chromogenic color prints,
19.5 x 24.6 cm (horizontal),
24.6 x 19.5 cm (vertical).
Coll. CCA

Sala Laurana, Palazzo Abatellis, 19–20 March 1997 (morning).

Sala dei crucifice, Palazzo Abatellis, 20 March 1997 (afternoon).

Canova plaster cast gallery, 12 July 1996.

Canova plaster cast gallery, 12 July 1996.

Canova plaster cast gallery, 12 July 1996.

Canova plaster cast gallery, 12 July 1996.

Canova plaster cast gallery, 12 July 1996.

Canova plaster cast gallery, 12 July 1996.

Museo di Castelvecchio, 14 March 1997.

Museo di Castelvecchio, 1 March 1997.

Museo di Castelvecchio, 11 February 1998.

Museo di Castelvecchio, 11 February 1998.

Museo di Castelvecchio, 8 July 1997.

George Ranalli

Project and portfolio notes: Jean-François Bédard

HISTORY, CRAFT, INVENTION

IN THE WORK OF CARLO SCARPA
'BEAUTY'
THE FIRST SENSE
ART
THE FIRST WORD
THEN WONDER
THEN THE INNER REALIZATION OF 'FORM'
THE SENSE OF THE WHOLENESS OF INSEPARABLE ELEMENTS.
DESIGN CONSULTS NATURE
TO GIVE PRESENCE TO THE ELEMENTS.
A WORK OF ART MAKES MANIFEST THE WHOLENESS OF 'FORM'
THE SYMPHONY OF THE SELECTED SHAPES OF THE ELEMENTS.

IN THE ELEMENTS
THE JOINT INSPIRES ORNAMENT, ITS CELEBRATION.
THE DETAIL IS THE ADORATION OF NATURE.[1]

LOUIS I. KAHN

BY THE LATE 1950S, TWO ARCHITECTS – Louis I. Kahn in the United States and Carlo Scarpa in Italy – had begun to distance themselves decisively from the functionalist aesthetic and machine technology of the modern movement. They commenced what was essentially an alternative discourse – establishing a dialogue with the history of architecture, entering a new realm of thinking about interventions into the historic fabric, and returning to the idea of craft, construction method, and on-site invention as the ultimate creative acts in architecture. Both Kahn and Scarpa were grounded in the modernist aesthetic, and this return to the origins of building was shared in spirit with Ludwig Mies van der Rohe, the reigning master builder of the mid-twentieth century. But they gradually developed a different sensibility, in which chance, mythology, and the irrational were permitted to have a role. They argued for the persistent force of ancient forms and structures and of the classic fundamentals of design – as Scarpa listed them, "the wall, the joint, the window, stair, and door." At the same time, they countered the prevailing emphasis on transparency and ephemerality with a new emphasis on materiality. In proposing an alternative to the post-war doctrine of light construction and mass-production techniques and in rejecting the prevailing assumption of architectural transience – short life-cycles for new buildings – they initiated, in tandem with Frank Lloyd Wright, one of the most radical shifts in architectural thought since the origins of the modern movement.

It is clear that Kahn and Scarpa recognized a kinship of purpose. Each wrote in admiration of the other, and the two sustained an ongoing dialogue. But their approaches were markedly different. Where Kahn tried to rethink the question of permanence through inventing new monumental forms, Scarpa chose to weave new work into its historical setting. Unlike Kahn's rigorously geometrical organization of form, Scarpa's projects seem casually organized and based on an experiential method. Spatial cohesion results from a procession of discrete ideas held together by an uncanny ability to judge the essence of each part and orchestrate its relation to a whole. This approach evolved from Scarpa's long association with traditional artisanship and depended on his readiness to push the boundaries of the maker's craft. To achieve his effects he delved into extreme methods of construction, often demanding radical adaptations of established craft techniques. In effect, Scarpa reinvented traditional technology by returning to a dialogue with craftsmen, who worked with him in close and constant communication on every project. The idea of an architecture that was rooted in artisanal traditions, involved in transforming those traditions into a contemporary language, stood in opposition to other modernist work being produced at the time, centered around a belief in mass-production methods appropriated from industrial-design practice. In opposition to the quest for lightness and the recognition of ephemerality that marked the orthodoxies of post-war modernism, Scarpa proposed textured, solid, often opaque and sculptural structures that would take their place in the continually changing fabric of the city. At the same time, his meticulous creation of a dialogue between an architectural intervention and its setting opened up a new sense of the relationship between old and new. Together, this recombination of history, craft, and invention, applied to the conditions of the latter half of the twentieth century, marks Scarpa's major contribution to the discipline of architecture.

In all of this work, the relationship between artisanry and drawing, design, and construction is indivisible. Scarpa's formative works were glass objects produced for the Venini firm in Murano. These designs show an experimental approach that still respected the conventions established by the glassmakers. Communicating with the artisans was essential, as it informed Scarpa of the limitations of methods and materials. The intricate balance between drawing upon craft traditions and the necessity to explore new territory in design would later become Scarpa's architectural working method.

Scarpa looked to several architects whose built works exemplified a close involvement with both artisans and construction techniques. The most important of these was Frank Lloyd Wright. Wright's Southern California concrete-block buildings of the early 1920s – the Millard, Storer, Freeman, and Ennis houses, in which Wright began to explore the complete integration of decoration and form – were seminal works for Scarpa. Cast concrete, which Wright had used in the Unity Temple, re-emerged in these California projects as a precast material. Scarpa must also have looked closely at Wright's A.D. German warehouse in Wisconsin, of 1915, whose frieze shows a use of concrete casting startlingly similar to that found in the Brion family tomb. These themes in Wright's work were observed and studied by Scarpa, who developed them from the 1950s onward to culminate in a remarkable transformation away from the original source. Scarpa was able to develop a working method with artisans that tempered the reference to Wright and made it more directly applicable to his own intentions. Unlike Wright, who moves on from arts and crafts research to embrace the machine and to explore mass production, Scarpa remains in the manual craft tradition and works with the same artisans all his life. As a result, each work represented new research into the joining of materials in an astonishing set of "interdisciplinary" relationships that revealed new ways of making architecture.

This is borne out in interviews with artisans, many of whom had an intense working relationship with Scarpa that spanned more than twenty-five years. Each spoke of long conversations with the architect even before projects began, dialogues that often focused on a material to be used or a problem Scarpa had anticipated. Scarpa worked consistently with three Venetian firms: Zanon for iron and other metal work, Anfodillo for woodwork, and De Luigi for plasterwork. These craftsmen contributed to Scarpa's projects in ways that move them into the role of collaborators rather than simply fabricators of architectural detail. Scarpa turned to them as experts in the realm of what was possible, as sources of knowledge used to attain specific ends.

At the Museo di Castelvecchio, for example, on many of the iron and metal brackets a small circle appears at the point where the metal changes shape or direction. In discussions with Zanon about how the steel was to be cut, Scarpa realized that when the saw ran into the metal there would be no place to stop and achieve a clean cut; drilling a hole first would give the saw blade a stopping point, permitting a neat crosscut from two directions. This analysis of the artisan's working method provided a basis from which to create form.

Throughout his research, Scarpa's drawings were a vivid representation of his ability to visualize form and material. His own words are clear: "I want to see things, I don't trust anything else. I want to see and that's why I draw. I can see an image only if I draw it."[2] His craftsmen remember that he would design six or seven solutions on paper very quickly, then put them away "to season" while he explored others, gradually developing a pile of alternative drawings until the final choice began to appear "as a necessity." These drawings are also a by-product of Scarpa's own love of craft. Full of information, they are at the same time deliberately exquisite.

One of the most interesting aspects of Scarpa's drawings is his preference for working in orthographic projection. The integration of plan, section, and elevation in this tripartite system coded all objects and buildings so that they could be measured immediately and transformed into material reality. The didactic precision of the engineering drawing was combined with shading, shadow, and the human figure (providing scale) in order to produce a drawing of extraordinary legibility without sacrificing overt sensuality and atmosphere. The use of orthographic projection was essential to Scarpa's architecture, in which every surface was worked out with details and joinery that wrapped from walls to floor to ceiling, allowing each design iteration to be followed through all necessary planes.

Often these drawings were the very documents used for construction, as they also contained dimensions and notes to the artisans. The scale of the drawing was frequently pushed toward full size, enhancing Scarpa's ability to delve more fully into material, joinery, and surface treatment. His drawing exemplifies the idea of representation as inquiry. In the drawing for the canopy of the water pavilion at the Brion tomb, for example, Scarpa designed the wood cover, cor-ten steel supports, and concrete footings with intricate detail and a heightened sense of construction and craft. The pattern of fasteners in the wood was studied along with the complex joinery of the split cor-ten steel legs.

The struggle for clarity of thought through drawing was explored with great rigor, yet with a desire to make the drawing a pure expression of thought and feeling: pattern, texture, weight, and color were represented in real terms but also with their metaphysical and lyrical characteristics. Scarpa thus allowed the drawing to become the external manifestation of his internal process – rich, varied, sometimes moving between several ideas, but at all times precise. In each drawing the didactic information is overtaken by the poetry and emotional quality of the sketch. This mix of illustrative and expressive information was achieved not only by the addition of color, but with the incorporation of figures and vegetation and by a looseness of technique not usually seen in mechanical drawings. The margins around the orthographic drawing are sometimes filled with sketches and studies visualizing the perspectival aspects of a particular area or detail. In the plan drawings of the Brion tomb, for example, the buildings and elements are organized on the site with surrounding sketches that illustrate the forms in their three-dimensional reality. In some cases drawings were so thoroughly worked over that white paint was needed to obscure their earlier states. These densely drawn sheets are constructions in themselves. They resemble shop drawings made for construction purposes, and at the same time are detailed maps of a mental process and objects of great force and sensibility.

The artisans responded to the logic and lucidity of the drawings, replicating Scarpa's effort in their own work in a true collaboration of passion, talent, and conviction. Scarpa, a craftsman of the highest order, saw himself as one of the artisans. For this reason his work could develop and evolve through a primary dialogue between like-minded creators, clearly and loudly reasserting that the medium of architecture involves design and building as a single, indivisible act.

The pages that follow present an analysis of the strategies and techniques of Scarpa's craft and construction in eight critical mature works. The initial group of works begins with the installation of the Galleria nazionale della Sicilia within the late medieval fabric of Palermo's Palazzo Abatellis. In a selection of drawings for the Palazzo the growing precision of Scarpa's strategy of intervention may be seen: the process of reduction and refinement that came to mark his work within history; the creation of large-scale spatial relationships through the placement of small discrete objects; the establishment of a narrative scheme; and the delicate experiments in craft and construction that characterize his attention to window, stair, and support. A portfolio of drawings reveals Scarpa's approach to the dramatic installation of the fresco *The Triumph of Death*, a single work which, like the statue of Cangrande at Castelvecchio, serves as the hinge for the design scheme and its inner narrative.

Two even more radical approaches to the housing and installation of works of art follow. In the intensely simple forms of the Canova plaster cast gallery at Possagno, Scarpa linked the process of designing with objects to the composition of void and light. Few drawings survive for this project, but photographs of the lost designs and the analytical models constructed for the exhibition that is the occasion for this book reveal important points of comparison with both the contemporaneous but more Wrightian Veritti house and the last work in this group, the Museo di Castelvecchio in Verona. This most elaborate of Scarpa's dialogues with the past is analyzed through a selection from the wealth of drawings in the museum's archives and through an analytical model and a portfolio of drawings that describe Scarpa's decisive intervention between the medieval "Reggia" and the Napoleonic barracks – the critical incision within which the statue of Cangrande was finally installed.

Four interventions in the historic fabric of the city follow. The complex, highly wrought forms of the Veritti house, a villa in Udine, extends the lessons Scarpa learned from Wright. It also serves as a laboratory for the subtler formal strategies of the work done for the Fondazione Querini Stampalia, the Museo di Castelvecchio gardens, and the Brion tomb. The Olivetti showroom and the galleries of the Fondazione Querini Stampalia deal with the problem of inserting open space and incident within highly restricted existing envelopes, and with reconfiguring the relationship of the buildings to their adjacent squares. Here, in collaboration with his craftsmen, Scarpa tested radical experiments in artisanry and the construction of detail. An analytic model unfolds the complexity and transparency of the Palazzo Querini Stampalia as it cannot be seen from the ground. Two comparative projects from the 1960s – the Gavina showroom in Bologna and the renovation of the apartment of Loredana Balboni on the Grand Canal in Venice – extend the experiment at Olivetti by boldly reviving the idea of the articulated urban facade. Taken together with the late work for the Banca Popolare di Verona, in which the idea of the facade is most fully developed, these projects show Scarpa weaving independent new forms into the existing urban fabric and experimenting with radical ideas in composition, palette, construction, and materials. A portfolio of drawings in which ideas for these urban walls is encountered follows.

The sequence concludes with a detailed analysis of the design, construction, and crafting of the Brion family tomb, Scarpa's late masterpiece and a work that integrates all the concerns of the projects that preceded it. Brion establishes a new landscape within an old one, constructs a complex narrative out of newly made forms, makes space – inside and out – from the juxtaposition of independent objects, reconciles the Wrightian language of the Veritti house with the simpler vocabulary of light and water of the Canova gallery, and develops the notion of narrative into a transcendent allegory. At the same time, the project explores radical design and construction techniques and devotes intense attention to the character, pattern, and fabrication of texture, surface, connection, and joint. Two final portfolios of drawings show how Scarpa evolved the designs of two critical elements in the project: the water pavilion and the chapel.

GR

PALAZZO ABATELLIS

I HAVE A GREAT PASSION FOR WORKS OF ART, AS YOU KNOW. I HAVE ALWAYS TAKEN THE TROUBLE TO LEARN, TO KNOW, TO UNDERSTAND, AND, IT SEEMS TO ME, TO HAVE A REAL CRITICAL AWARENESS. I WOULD NOT BE ABLE TO WRITE, TO PRODUCE A CRITICAL ARTICLE; BUT I HAVE A LIVELY SENSE OF CRITICAL VALUES, AND THEY MOVE ME. INDEED, I WOULD RATHER, ON THE WHOLE, BUILD MUSEUMS THAN SKYSCRAPERS – THOUGH LOGIC MIGHT SAY OTHERWISE, SINCE THE FORMER MAY PERHAPS BE CREATIVE, WHILE THE LATTER REQUIRES ONE TO ADAPT AND SUBORDINATE ONESELF TO THINGS AS THEY ARE. ONE MIGHT ALSO SAY THAT THERE IS A CERTAIN MIMICRY INVOLVED, NOT OF A FORMAL KIND, NOT OF EQUIVALENCE, BUT RATHER IN AN ATTEMPT AT INTERPRETATION. IT CAN BE VERY IMPORTANT FOR THE PRESENTER OF WORKS OF ART TO HAVE A CRITICAL APPRECIATION OF THEM, BECAUSE PRESENTATION CAN BE A FORM OF INTERPRETATION, OF DRAWING ATTENTION TO COLLOCATION – TO THE ADVANTAGE OF THE WORKS, NATURALLY, NOT TO THE ADVANTAGE OF THE PRESENTATION ITSELF. A WORK THAT IS NOT, UNFORTUNATELY, VERY EXCEPTIONAL ALWAYS HAS SOMETHING THAT CAN BE BROUGHT OUT IN A GROUP. THE WORK NEED NOT BE NOTEWORTHY IN ANY ABSOLUTE SENSE. AND THERE ARE RARELY WORKS OF GREAT QUALITY TO WORK WITH.[3]

CARLO SCARPA, 1978

Restoration and reorganization of the Palazzo Abatellis as the Galleria nazionale della Sicilia
Palermo, 1953–54

Client: Sopraintendenza ai monumenti, Palermo
Restoration architects: Mario Guiotto and Armando Dillon
Collaborator: Roberto Calandra

Between 1490 and 1495, the architect Matteo Carnelivari supervised the construction of a palace for Francesco de Abatellis, count of Camarrata, great seneschal of Ferdinand II of Spain, "Maestro Portulano" of the kingdom of Sicily, and thrice Praetor of Palermo. In 1526, after the death of the count's second wife and following the terms of his will, the palace was turned over to Dominican monks who transformed it into a monastery, around 1535–41 constructing a large chapel as an annex to the palace.

The allied bombing suffered by the port of Palermo between January and July 1943 severely damaged what remained of the original palace, which had been considerably transformed during the preceding four centuries. In the decade that followed, the architects Mario Guiotto and Armando Dillon, working for the local Superintendent of Monuments, undertook the restoration of the Palazzo Abatellis, with plans to return it to its fifteenth-century form. In 1953, with their work nearing completion, Giorgio Vigni, Superintendent of the Galleries of Sicily, asked Carlo Scarpa to adapt the palace for the display of the medieval and modern art collections of the Galleria nazionale della Sicilia, until then housed in the national museum. Vigni had first collaborated with Scarpa in 1952, when the architect designed the installation of the exhibition *Antonello da Messina and the Quattrocento in Sicily*, which opened in the town hall of Messina in 1953. Scarpa worked at great speed, collaborating with local craftsmen and laying out some critical elements on-site. In addition, correspondence with Vigni shows him participating decisively in the selection and disposition of works and in the interior fabric of the building. Budget and time constraints limited some of Scarpa's more ambitious proposals. The Galleria nazionale (now regionale) della Sicilia at Palazzo Abatellis was inaugurated on 23 June 1954, although work continued through to December of that year. On 27 March 1963 Scarpa won the IN/ARCH national prize for the preservation and valorization of Italian heritage for his work at the palace.
J-F B

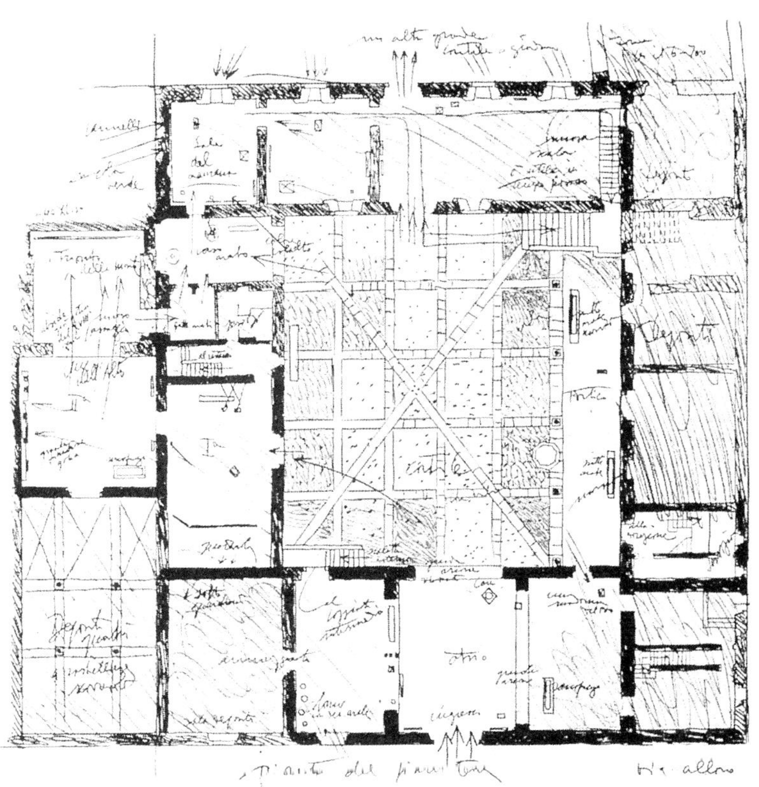

Ground-floor plan. From *L'Architettura, cronache e storia* 3 (1955), p. 65.

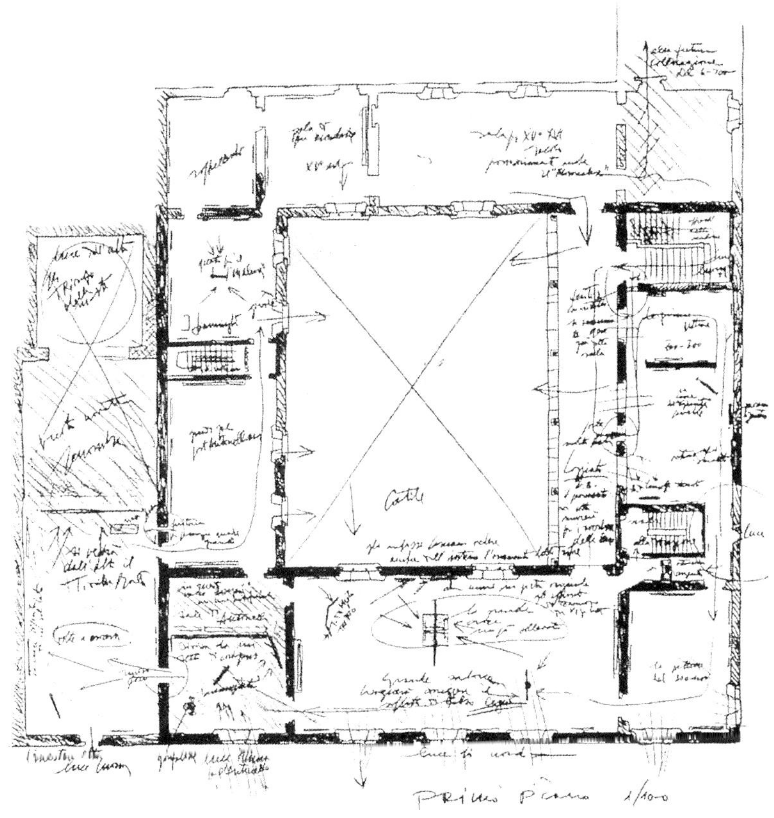

Second-floor plan. From *L'Architettura, cronache e storia* 3 (1955), p. 65.

THE PALAZZO ABATELLIS EXTENDED a dialogue with historic structures, begun at Ca' Foscari in the 1930s, that would continue throughout Scarpa's career. His patient, almost archival attention to the historic fabric of the existing structure shows remarkable judgment. With almost surgical accuracy, he moved from space to space restoring some elements and adding new ones, integrating the two in a fusion so seamless that the observer is hard pressed to find the juncture between them.

While there is some dispute about the extent of Scarpa's contribution to the fabric of the building as a whole, especially as regards the exterior and the courtyard, the drawings in the Palazzo Abatellis archive document most of what Scarpa worked on in exacting detail. Among them are studies for the new window frames suspended behind the Gothic tracery. Early designs show the lozenge-shaped frames arranged horizontally behind the vertical columns, which were changed to a more vertical arrangement set symmetrically into the orthogonal geometry of the opening. These frames established a theme – the simultaneity of old and new – that would be applied later to the windows at Castelvecchio with a largely asymmetrical result.

Despite their often small scale, these interventions dramatically transformed the physical sense of the building. One of the most beautiful elements is a stairway that appears to float in its dense masonry setting. Connecting the ground-floor gallery to the *piano nobile*, it consists of a series of separate stone steps, hexagonal in section, balanced on steel supports. In the sculpture galleries on the ground floor, Scarpa positioned richly colored plaster panels, of dark green, dark blue, and black, in front of the old walls to offset the works. Within the fields of color, strips of wood from which steel supports emerge delicately hold a carved head or bust. This investigation into exhibition method was an inventive way to bring freestanding design elements and the objects themselves into dialogue with the building. Scarpa developed a series of attached, semi-attached, and freestanding pedestals that were dispersed throughout the Palazzo Abatellis. While each support was designed to enhance its interaction with an object, together they establish an architectural presence of their own and effectively reorder the fixed proportions of the palace.

Such interventions are felt most powerfully in the room that contains the paintings of Antonello da Messina and in Scarpa's installation of the anonymous *Triumph of Death*. Scarpa substantially altered the geometry of the Antonello room without changing the masonry enclosure of the space by installing a series of wood panels, designed to hold paintings and set some distance away from the rear wall. This strategy reduces the area of the space and focuses attention on Antonello's great *Annunciation*, which stands near the center of the room, set at an angle on a Scarpa-designed easel with an ancient fabric covering. Due to its positioning, the little painting acquires the status of a wall.

The Triumph of Death can be seen from two vantages: first on the ground floor and then from a more dramatic perspective, as the itinerary of Renaissance and medieval art on the *piano nobile* is completed. Scarpa located the painting at the rear wall of the room and embedded small circular lenses into the membrane of the domed ceiling to provide the wash of light that illuminates it. He also opened a section of the building so that the painting can be re-experienced from the second-floor balcony, where there is no railing. The floor simply, breathtakingly, ends. His use of sequence, section, and light dramatically reorders the space and focuses the eye on the art within.

GR

Elevation of second-floor arcade in the courtyard, 1953–54. Graphite on tracing paper, 39.9 x 74.9 cm. Coll. GRS

Perspective and details of stairway showing hexagonal steps and glass door, 1953–54. Graphite and colored pencil on paper, 35 x 70.3 cm. Coll. GRS

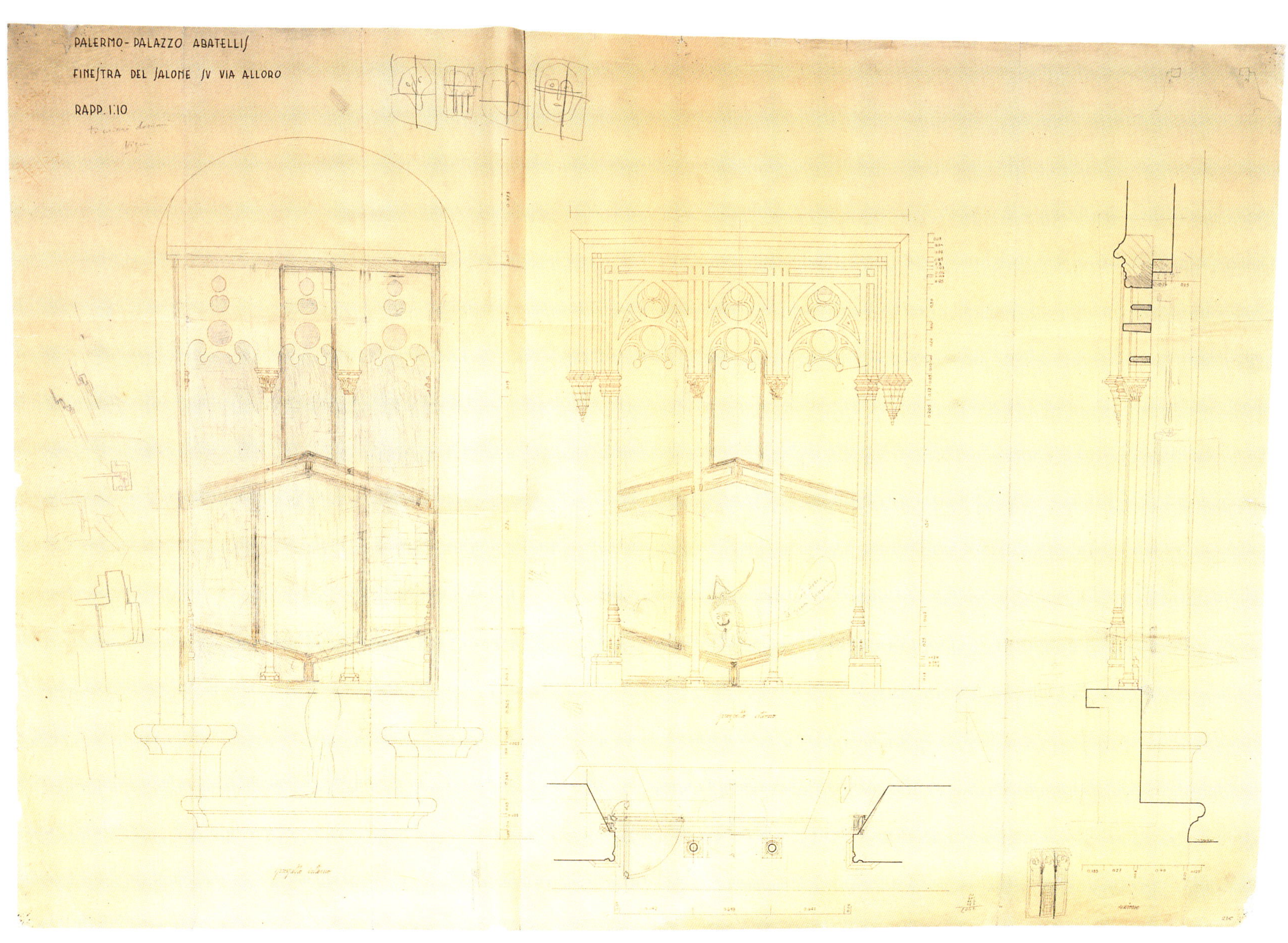

Plan, elevations, and section of window frames, 1953–54.
Colored pencil on reprographic print, 73.5 x 107.6 cm. Coll. GRS

Perspective of Sala Antonello da Messina, 1953–54.
Graphite on cardboard, 32 x 44.6 cm. Coll. GRS

Perspective and elevation of Sala dei crucifice with ceiling detail,
1953–54. Graphite on cardboard, 64.2 x 44 cm. Coll. GRS

THE TRIUMPH OF DEATH

The mid-fifteenth-century fresco *The Triumph of Death*, painted by an unknown artist for Palermo's municipal hospital at Palazzo Sclafani, is the largest and most powerful work displayed in the Palazzo Abatellis. The painting, which Scarpa placed in the apse of the former chapel added to the palace in the sixteenth century, plays a crucial role in the architect's daring installation strategy. Scarpa stages the fresco as a connector between the two floors of the converted palace, an idea which the architect later explored with great effect in his dramatic presentation of the statue of Cangrande at the Museo di Castelvecchio in Verona.

In a series of six drawings, the architect explores three distinct aspects of the installation of *The Triumph of Death*: the adjustment of the width of the end wall of the apse to fit the dimensions of the fresco; the geometry of the shading device necessary to modify the light; and the ornamentation of the pendentives of the existing dome cover. Only the first of these schemes was realized. The plan of the modified apse, the longitudinal and transverse sections through it, and, perhaps more clearly, the perspective of the corner on the right-hand side show how Scarpa chose to carve into the side walls of the apse to accommodate the excessive width of the fresco. This was necessary in order to allow the placement of the fresco at the end of the axis of the former chapel. Scarpa articulates this carving into a shallow niche, an illusion emphasized by the darker coloring of the plaster surrounding the fresco.

The shading screen or velarium situated below the skylight goes through a variety of geometric shapes, from a lozenge to a square frame draped with cloth. When Scarpa disposes this screen immediately above the fresco, he fills the upper zone of the apse with a dark material. Scarpa's favored solution for the velarium consists of two interlocking rectangular planes. Slightly protruding beyond the pointed arch that marks the edge of the apse, the frame forms in plan a ziggurat-like shape. In both solutions, Scarpa divides the velarium into crosses, Latin and Greek, emphasizing the eschatological dimensions of the fresco. For the pendentives of the apse's dome, unadorned today, Scarpa had considered a variety of ornaments, from concentric triangles to discrete, stepped-up planes, both of which recall the formal vocabulary of Frank Lloyd Wright.

J-F B

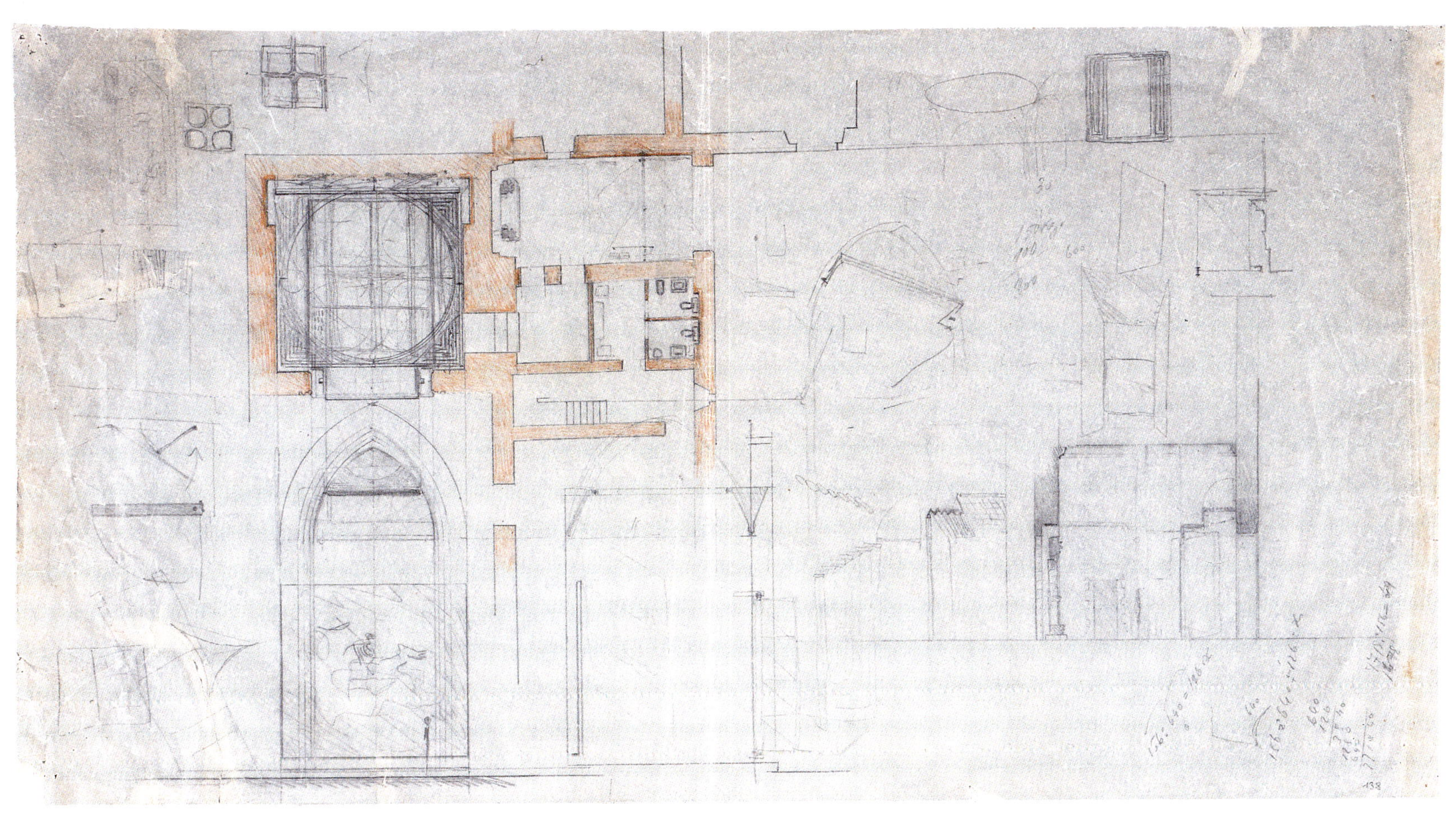

Plan and sections of *Triumph of Death* gallery, 1953–54.
Graphite and colored pencil on tracing paper, 26.6 x 49.7 cm.
Coll. GRS

Sections and reflected ceiling plan of *Triumph of Death* gallery, 1953–54. Graphite and colored pencil on tracing paper, 28.8 x 26.2 cm. Coll. GRS

Perspectives of *Triumph of Death* gallery, 1953–54.
Graphite on cardboard, 44 x 64.2 cm. Coll. GRS

Studies for northeast wall of courtyard and perspective of *Triumph of Death* gallery, 1953–54. Graphite on cardboard, 44 x 64.2 cm. Coll. GRS

Studies for pendentives of *Triumph of Death* gallery, 1953–54.
Graphite on cardboard, 64.2 x 44 cm. Coll. GRS

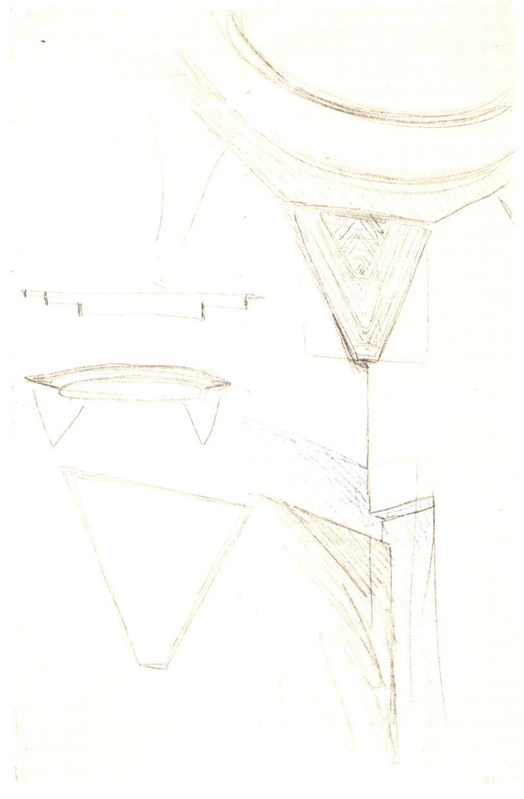

Studies for pendentives of *Triumph of Death* gallery, 1953–54.
Graphite and colored pencil on paper, 30.1 x 20.1 cm. Coll. GRS

CANOVA PLASTER CAST GALLERY

IN THE LARGE EXHIBITION HALL I ENVISIONED LIGHT FALLING FROM ABOVE, BUT NOT FROM THE USUAL OPENINGS, WHICH ARE GENERALLY UNSATISFACTORY SINCE THEY READ AS NEGATIVE SPACES ... TO THE EYE. AND SO I DEVISED THIS WINDOW-TYPE THAT PROJECTS INWARD, IN ORDER TO AVOID EXTERNAL GLAZING. RATHER THAN BUILD FOUR SYMMETRICAL ONES (I DID NOT HAVE EQUAL HEIGHTS TO WORK WITH HERE), I PLANNED THAT ARRANGEMENT UP THERE, ON HIGH, WHICH SEEMED TO ME TO BE RATHER EVOCATIVE. THE DAY OF THE OFFICIAL OPENING, THERE WAS A VERY FINE BLUE SKY; AND SINCE THE GLAZING WAS WELL POLISHED AND VERY TRANSPARENT, THE SKY LOOKED AS THOUGH IT HAD BEEN SLICED INTO BLOCKS. AND NATURALLY WE INSTALLED IT WITH SOME CARE, AND DID SOME WORK ON PERSPECTIVE, SO THE ENSEMBLE COULD BE TAKEN IN AT A GLANCE. THERE ARE TERRACOTTA MODELLI IN THOSE LITTLE DISPLAY CASES, VERY LOVELY. IT SEEMED TO ME LOGICAL TO MARRY THE NEW BUILDING TO THE OLD ONE, TO BRING THEM TOGETHER. YOU UNDERSTAND THAT BEFORE CONSTRUCTION BEGAN, THIS BUILDING WAS ISOLATED FROM THE OTHER ONE, THAT THE OLD HALL WAS BIGGER THAN THIS ONE IS NOW, WAS ALREADY ATTACHED AT THIS POINT – SO WE SPOILED NOTHING, THOUGH THIS BUILDING IS NOT HISTORICALLY FAULTLESS AND UNTOUCHABLE. THERE ARE INCONGRUITIES HERE – THE DOWNSPOUTS FOR EXAMPLE. IT WOULD HAVE BEEN BETTER TO MASK THEM, BUT I DID NOT WANT TO TAKE ANY RESPONSIBILITY FOR MEDDLING WITH THE PAST.[4]

CARLO SCARPA, 1978

Extension of the Canova plaster cast gallery (Gipsoteca)
Possagno, 1955–57

Client: Sopraintendenza alle belle arti di Venezia
Collaborator: Valeriano Pastor

In 1955, in preparation for the commemoration of the two-hundredth anniversary of the birth of the sculptor Antonio Canova (1757–1822), the Superintendent of Fine Arts of Venice decided to enlarge the plaster cast gallery built next to Canova's house in Possagno, northwest of Treviso. The basilica-like exhibition hall was built between 1831 and 1836 by Giuseppe Segusini to house plaster models and terracotta *bozzetti* brought back from Rome by a relative of the sculptor, monsignor Giovanni Sartori Canova, after the artist's death.

Scarpa's addition occupies a narrow strip of land along one side of the original building. It is articulated into three distinct volumes. A tall, cubic room lit by four corner skylights was originally destined to house a large statue then in the collection of the Accademia di Belle Arti in Venice. A second wedgelike gallery is pulled away from the existing plaster cast gallery, ending in a large window overlooking a reflecting pool. At the juncture between the two, Scarpa inserted a medium-sized volume lit by four clerestory windows.

J-F B

Rear facade, 1957. Coll. ACS

SITUATED ON THE EDGE OF A DENSE mountain village, Scarpa's additions at Possagno created a series of exceptional new relationships between the complex of existing museum buildings and the adjoining streets. Scarpa had carte blanche: nothing had to be preserved. But he revolutionized the space, as he proudly pointed out, without destroying any of the original structure. The addition – a long, horizontal arrangement of volumes seemingly pinned at the lobby and splaying out toward the narrow end of the site – links Giuseppe Segusini's basilica-plan building with the house and courtyard, while allowing the basilica to remain the dominant figural element in the composition. The volumes echo the terrain as it tumbles down toward the open countryside, with the interior spaces following the same descending path. Scarpa placed the larger volume directly off the entrance foyer, with its corner windows poetically admitting light from above. Looking down the gallery to the left, it is possible to see the small passage against the existing building filled with reflected light, the angled windows at the first ceiling interval, and a glass wall at the garden end. The garden is enclosed with a low wall that forms a pond, its water reflecting a dappled light.

In addition to the careful design of the volumes, each window and aperture was thoughtfully placed in the blocks of stucco. The most powerful of these elements are the four corner windows of the main gallery. Two matching pairs of windows sit at opposite ends of the room. The frames of the two longer windows project into the space and, although made of iron, appear to float on a thin element of white plaster. Seen from the exterior, these windows help to vary the large scale of the stucco block, through their size and through the presence of small downspouts. Opposite them are two higher cubic windows whose only visible frame is near the vertical edge. Only a small, triangular plate at the corner fastens top to sides, with the result that no visible edge exists on either side, bringing an unexpected presence of blue sky into the gallery.

The placement of the windows in the long gallery is equally potent. The simple glass and wood-frame wall on the basilica side sits under the steel structure supporting the addition. This wood frame extends into the masonry wall of the main gallery, which is filled with small translucent cubic openings. In the ceiling, four large openings of frosted glass – part window, part skylight – drape over each stepped section. These voids, which appear as if cut out of the plaster as compositional motifs, also serve to clarify changes in the ceiling height and give the room a different sense of scale.

At the narrow end of the gallery, clear lapped glass, designed with only vertical supports, affords an unobstructed view of the water directly outside and the landscape beyond. The presence or absence of the frame in each void was a significant design decision, each frame elucidating a specific relationship between wall and void.

Though elemental, the details of the gallery have an extraordinary impact on the space and the artifacts. Scarpa's decision to use white cement plaster behind white artifacts, which occurred to him "as if by intuition," was the generative idea for the whole project. Now commonplace in museum practice, this monochromatic approach was extremely provocative at the time. The black metal baseboard makes a sharp joint at the floor. There is also a small reveal between the ceiling and walls in the high room, which gives the illusion that the ceiling is suspended above the walls. The apparent difference between this reveal and the thickness of the masonry heightens the effect. The stairs leading down to the gallery are set into the floor, with two marble slabs held up by barely visible supports; the routed reveal reduces the apparent thickness of each step. To the side is the window wall between the two buildings. Although Scarpa often used exposed structural I-beams as columns, here the beam is painted white, carefully reducing its materiality. The exterior wall is stucco over masonry, but the slab lines of the roof and window openings are finished in rough concrete. This play of contrasting textures makes the elevation change scale as the eye moves between the massive wall surface and the intimate detail of its edge.

The supports for the plaster casts vary greatly in design. Scarpa used black iron wall brackets for most busts, heads, and small statues. In the main gallery, some of the bases are masonry, with reveals to mitigate the effect of what would otherwise be a cumbersome block. Small black iron leg supports, almost like

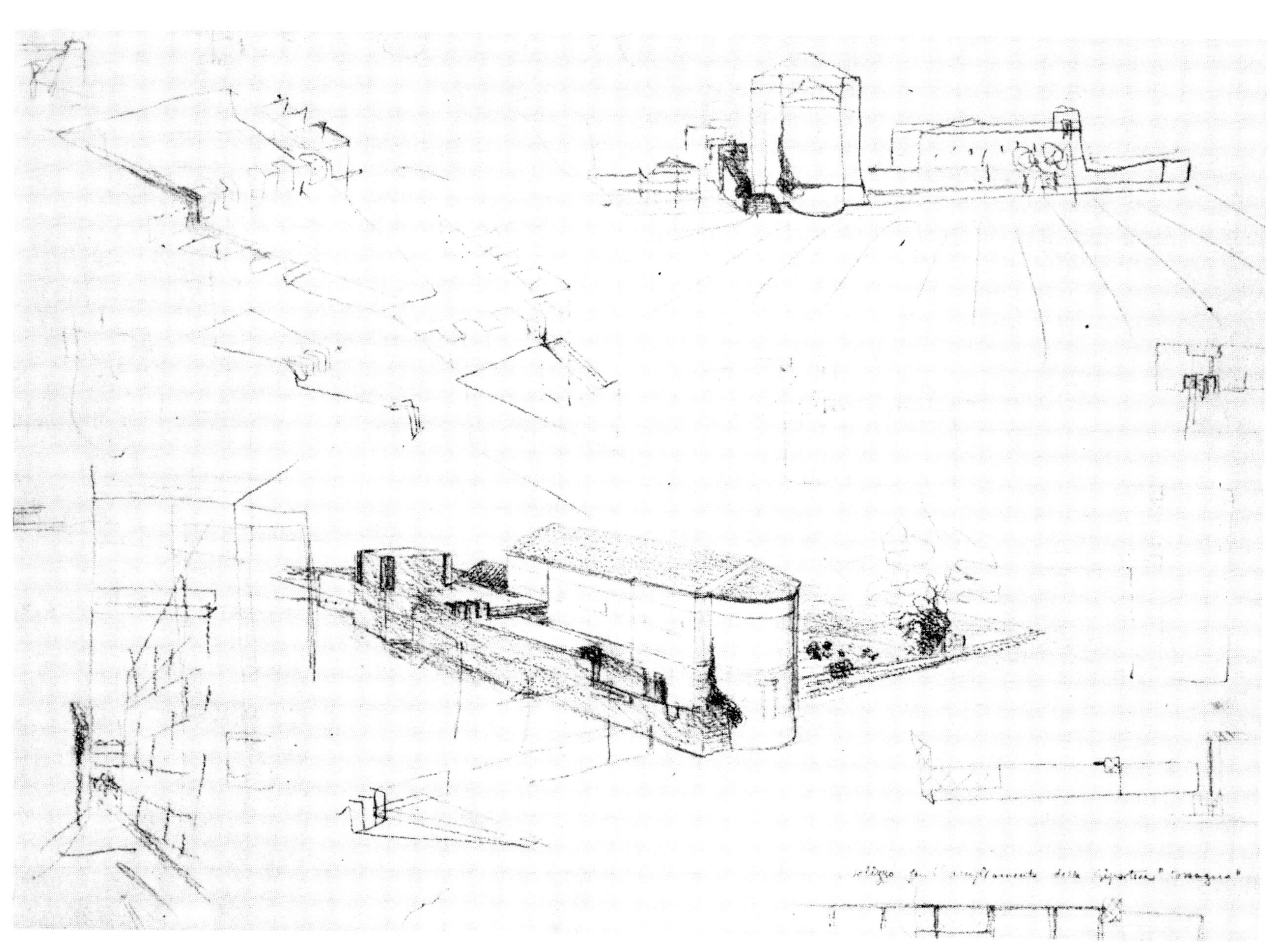

Contextual studies and roofline analysis, 1955–57.
Photograph of lost original. Coll. ACS

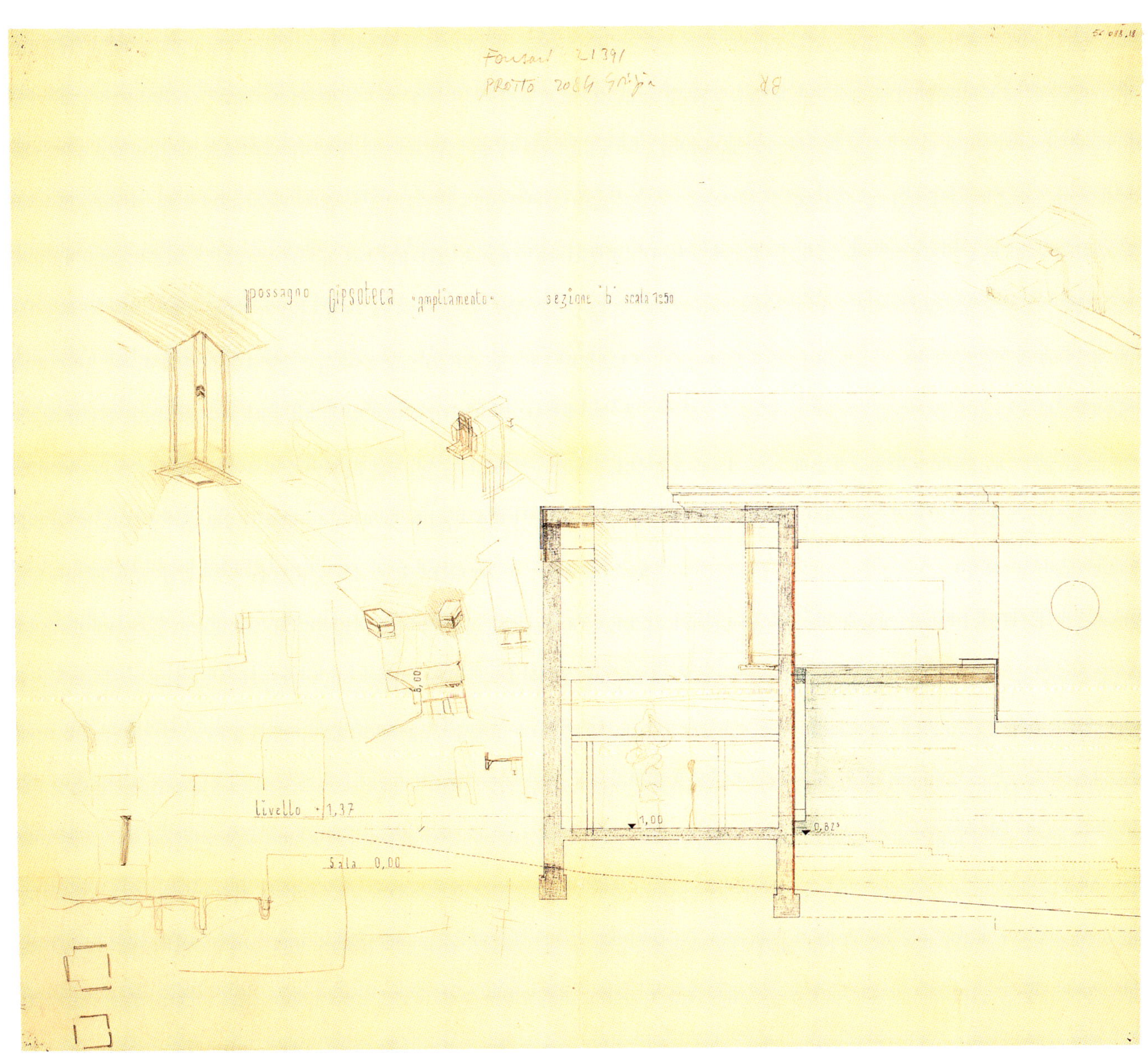

Carlo Scarpa, designer and draftsman; Luciano Zinato, draftsman. Transverse section of south gallery with studies for windows and other elements, 1955–57. Graphite and colored pencil on reprographic print, 54.3 x 61.3 cm. Coll. ACS

divans, are used for the reclining sculptures, keeping the pieces close to the floor.

It is, however, the glass and iron vitrines holding Canova's small clay models that command the most attention. As a set of repetitive sentinels, these vitrines seem to hover above the floor on three-pronged, black iron bases with a single vertical support. Scarpa explained that he was trying to achieve a kind of absolute "transparency" in which glass would appear to float on nothing, only to find that reflections made the idea of a pure transparency impossible to realize. Indeed, the vitrines appear to be a microcosm of the building's relationship to light and its determination to conceal supports. Scarpa's ability to orchestrate movement, from the overall design to the most intimate of details, provides a compelling display of how to unify and simplify a complex project.

GR

Corner window on street facade, 1957. Coll. ACS

Corner window on museum-side facade, 1957. Coll. ACS

THE ANALYTIC MODEL DESIGNED and fabricated for the exhibition clearly demonstrates Scarpa's extraordinary urban intervention in the small town of Possagno. Viewing the model from above and at the end of the town street permits the observer to see the complex situation of the existing buildings and note the delicate way Scarpa wove his addition into the fabric of the town plan while providing a new wall facing onto the street. The existing building is extremely large in scale; the model illustrates the small area of the new exhibit space added to the larger basilica-type exhibit hall on the right. Scarpa designed a seamless addition of interior space and exterior form to the Canova complex which is evident in this view of the model. The model cuts through the center of many of the existing buildings to enhance the associative relationship between these buildings and the density and weight of the new addition. The model was rendered in wood to focus the viewer onto the issues of form and detail that Scarpa introduced in this project at the urban, building, interior, and design levels – issues profoundly resolved in construction. Most clear in this view is the cascading of building form down the town street, culminating in a garden wall connecting the new wing to the basilica and projecting the end of the Scarpa project into the countryside beyond.

GR

Firm of George Ranalli, Detail of site model, 1998.
Basswood, plywood, and Plexiglas, 50.8 x 139.7 x 81.2 cm.
Coll. CCA

MUSEO DI CASTELVECCHIO

AT CASTELVECCHIO THE BUILDERS OF OLDEN TIMES HAD TACKLED THE PROBLEM OF THE FORMAL IDENTITY OF A SERIES OF DWELLINGS AND THEIR CONNECTION. THE ROOMS WERE LAID OUT IN ROWS, BETWEEN TWO WALLS DISTANT AND DISTINCT FROM EACH OTHER. THEY WERE THE TWO FACADES OF THE CASTLE. THE MORE ANCIENT OF THE TWO WALLS IS SOLID, ALMOST WITHOUT APERTURES. IT OPENED TOWARDS THE RIVER, ON THE OUTSIDE. THE OTHER, MORE RECENT ONE WAS LESS MASSIVE AND OPENED ONTO THE GARDEN. YOU SEE HOW THE BUILDING RETAINS ITS IDENTITY IN TIME: IT'S A BASIC PRINCIPLE.... I WANTED TO PRESERVE THE ORIGINALITY, THE CHARACTER OF EVERY ROOM, BUT I DIDN'T WANT TO USE THE WOODEN BEAMS OF THE EARLIER RESTORATION. SINCE THE ROOMS WERE SQUARE, I SET A PAIRED STEEL BEAM TO SUPPORT THE POINT WHERE THE TWO REINFORCED CONCRETE BEAMS CROSSED, SO INDICATING THE MAIN LINES OF THE BUILDING'S FORMAL STRUCTURE. WHERE THEY CROSSED THE IMPORTANCE OF THAT SQUARE WAS EMPHASIZED BECAUSE THE CROSSING OF THE TWO BEAMS IN THE CENTER IMPLIES THE PILLAR WHICH HELPS TO DEFINE THE SQUARE.

THIS IS THE VISUAL LOGIC I WANTED TO USE AS A FRAME OF REFERENCE. THE WAY THE BEAMS WERE MADE ALSO BRINGS OUT THE VISUAL LOGIC, BUT ONLY IN THE DETAILS. I COULD HAVE USED THE STEEL PROFILES ALREADY ON THE MARKET, BUT IT WOULD HAVE BEEN AN ENGINEERING SOLUTION WITHOUT ANY VISUAL EMPHASIS. I THOUGHT IT WOULD BE MORE INTERESTING TO TAKE THE PROFILES AND MAKE A COMPOSITION OUT OF THEM. THE NEW JOINTS REVEAL THE STRUCTURE OF THE ELEMENT AND THE NEW FUNCTIONS.[5]

CARLO SCARPA, 1978

Restoration and reorganization of the Museo di Castelvecchio
Verona, 1956–73

Client: Comune di Verona
Collaborators: Carlo Maschietto, Arrigo Rudi, Angelo Rudella

The Castelvecchio, a fourteenth-century fortified castle, was transformed into a military barracks during Napoleon's occupation of Verona, and between 1924 and 1926 was converted into a museum. Following the stylistic principles of restoration prevalent at the time, Antonio Avena, then director of the museums of Verona, and the architect Ferdinando Forlati attempted to give the utilitarian structure a period aspect. They inserted Gothic doorways and window surrounds into the courtyard facade of the turn-of-the-nineteenth-century barracks and decorated the interiors in the manner of an early Renaissance palace. The appointment in 1956 of Licisco Magagnato as museum director marked the beginning of a complete reassessment of the building's restoration and of the display of its collections. Working in close collaboration, Scarpa and Magagnato radically transformed the Castelvecchio over the next twenty years. Their work can be divided roughly into three phases.

In 1958, for the exhibition *From Altichiero to Pisanello,* Scarpa refurbished the "Reggia" or residence in the castle's west wing and reopened the Porta del Morbio, a gate (closed off in the eighteenth century) that was part of a wall dating from the time of the Comune, Verona's period as a free city republic in the twelfth century. To provide access to the Reggia from the gallery wing, he also built a new staircase in the Torre del Mastio (the tower of the *mastio* or keep) and a bridge between the tower and the Reggia.

Scarpa's most important transformations took place during the second phase. In 1959 he reinstalled the sculpture gallery situated on the ground floor of the gallery wing and moved the museum's entrance to the northeast corner of the courtyard. He began the complete transformation of the gallery wing in 1962 with the excavation of the moat of the Comune wall and

Carlo Scarpa, designer and draftsman; unknown photographer. Courtyard facade of gallery wing with first proposal for placement of Cangrande statue, 1956–60. Photocollage, 43.8 x 65.5 cm. Coll. MDC

the subsequent demolition of the last bay of the gallery wing and the Napoleonic grand staircase. It is at this important juncture in the building's and the city's history that Scarpa decided to exhibit one of Verona's most famous works of art, the statue of Cangrande della Scala. Between 1963 and 1964, Scarpa rebuilt the floor of the painting galleries, designed a new exit staircase, remodeled the courtyard into a garden, and modified the east wing to house new museum offices.

During the third and last phase of work, two years after the official reopening of the museum on 19 December 1964, Scarpa designed the library, for which he boldly cut into the Napoleonic river wall at its juncture with the medieval northeast tower. Scarpa's last intervention, in 1973, was the construction of the Sala Avena situated above the library.
J-F B

Second floor

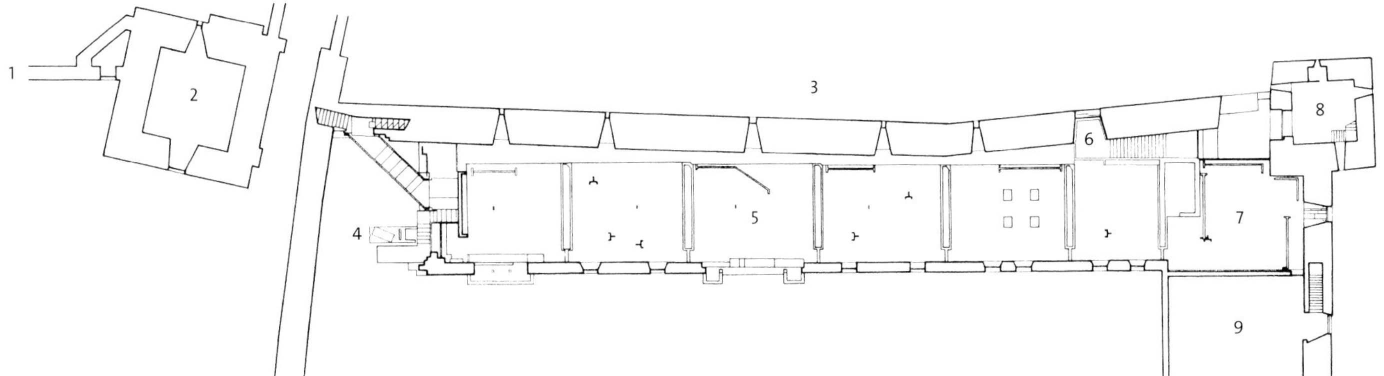

Ground floor

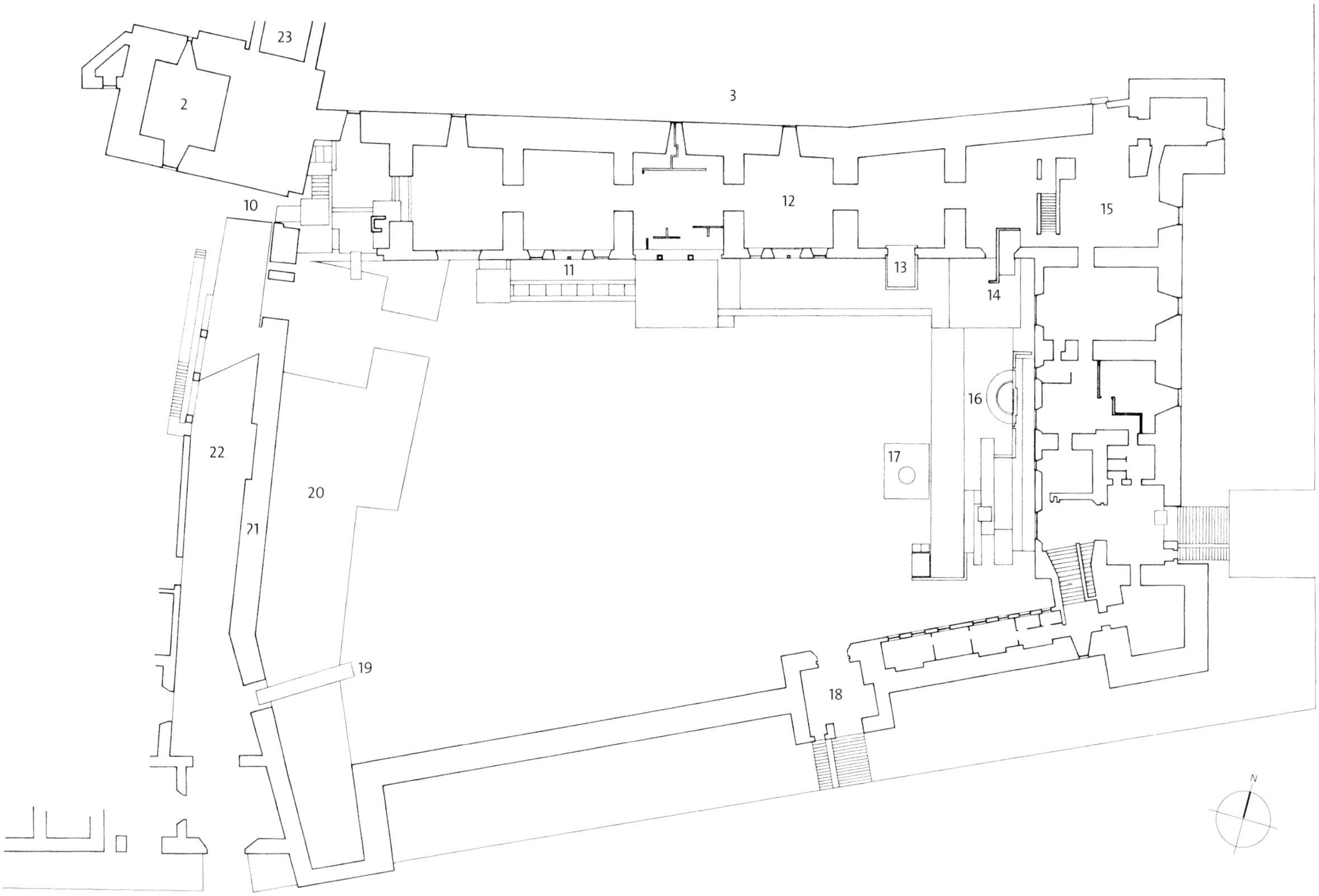

Firm of George Ranall, 1999

1 Passage to Reggia wing
2 Torre del Mastio
3 River Adige
4 Cangrande della Scala
5 Gallery (Napoleonic) wing: paintings
6 Exit stair
7 Sala Avena
8 Northeast tower
9 Sala Boggian
10 Porta del Morbio
11 Old entrance
12 Gallery (Napoleonic) wing: sculptures
13 Sacello
14 New entrance
15 Library
16 Fountain
17 Pond
18 Main entrance
19 Bridge over moat
20 Moat
21 Comune wall
22 Road to Scaligeri bridge
23 Scaligeri bridge

Unlike the Canova Gallery at Possagno, which was basically an insertion into an existing complex, the Museo di Castelvecchio was a dramatic intervention within a set of buildings that had accumulated over the centuries. Rather than viewing restoration as the opposite of renovation, Scarpa embarked on an intriguing strategy of demolition, change, and modification. He layered history, allowing each historical moment to come alive and take its place next to the others. Essentially functioning as a curator in deciding how to treat each fragment of the existing structure, he removed some elements, restored others, and interspersed new ones. He was able to achieve this while setting up a dialogue between old and new, provoking the older elements into conversation with wholly invented new forms, surfaces, textures, and motifs.

Scarpa transformed the design of the gallery spaces with an astonishing level of finish. Each room was imbued with a quality of light, surface, color, and texture that was specific both to the art within and to the character of the building itself. This subtle reworking of the original building extended to the outside. While the main courtyard remained largely unchanged, Scarpa introduced shallow pools of water containing historical artifacts displayed on cast-concrete supports. These pools form a path to the entrance, in which Scarpa inserted new doors and a large, freestanding wall. Unlike the less vigorous window treatment of the Palazzo Abatellis, each Gothic opening was filled with a contradictory Scarpa window. Framed in iron and wood, these windows explore the relationship between the apparent symmetry of the Gothic tracery and the asymmetry of the works exhibited within. "I decided," explained Scarpa, "to adopt certain vertical values, to break up the unnatural symmetry: the Gothic ... especially Venetian Gothic, isn't very symmetrical."[6] Developed through many drawings, the design for the windows expresses the interplay between the original opening and the new frame. An elevation of the entire courtyard facade shows Scarpa trying to extend this play, proposing a more extensive intervention into the old wall than finally he could realize, with large vertical openings extending from the roofline to midway down the wall.

The most important of these moves was the separation of the 'Gothicized' Napoleonic building housing the original museum from the medieval Reggia, and the pivotal placement of the equestrian statue of Cangrande della Scala within the cut. By opening a void that reveals the archeology of the original structure and leaves many elements of the subsequent accretions raw, Scarpa's introduction of a radically different formal vocabulary makes, contradictorily, an articulate seam between many moments in time. This juncture explodes with movement, structure, and detail. Platforms are suspended over exposed moats; bridges connect galleries at several levels. All these activities place the viewer in direct contact with Cangrande at several vantages. The concrete and iron pedestal for the statue is perfectly scaled to fill the void created by Scarpa's operation. It is in this act of almost archeological separation that the present confronts antiquity. Scarpa himself acknowledged its central role: "The most challenging item was the location of Cangrande, the equestrian statue. It wasn't easy to work that one out. Even set where it is, up in the air, it's related to movement and conditions it, stressing one of the most important historical connections between the different parts of the castle. I decided to turn it slightly, to emphasize its independence from the structure supporting it: it's a part of the whole, yet it still lives its own separate life."[7]

Other powerful intersections of old and new occur on the facade of the Napoleonic barracks. Near the portal next to the old central entrance door, Scarpa added a projecting treasure chest, or *sacello*, which contains a small number of objects lit by an opening in the roof. The outside wall of this block is covered with a pattern of small, rose-colored stone squares. The alternating texture of the stone from rough to smooth helps to emphasize the positioning of the smaller *tesserae* within a field of larger ones. The interior is finished in a dark olive-green plaster. Scarpa moved the entrance to the right of the *sacello*, and here constructed a wall that projects away from the building, partially enclosing the entry space. At the center of the revival wall, the original entry was marked with three Gothic arches. In closing it off, Scarpa set a new wall back from this existing masonry skin. He split this screening wall into two planes, incising a black plaster

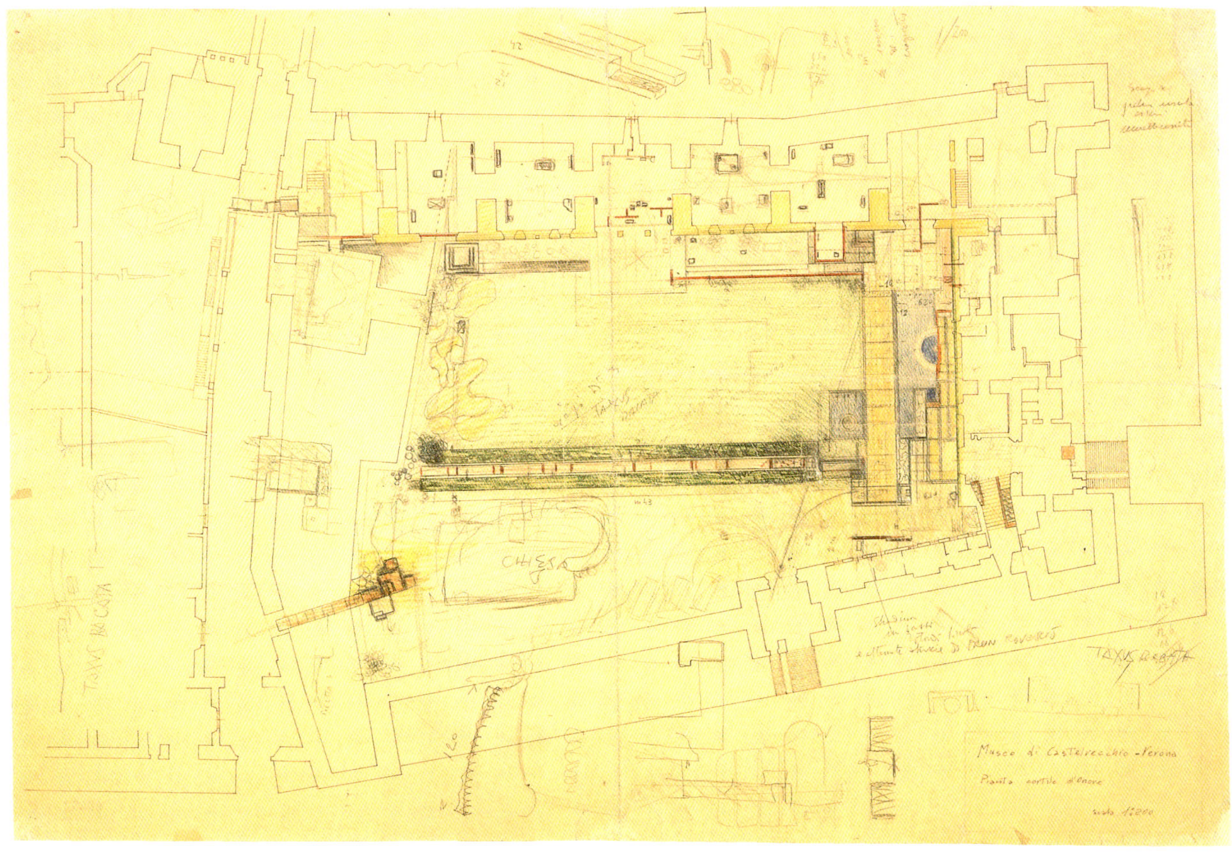

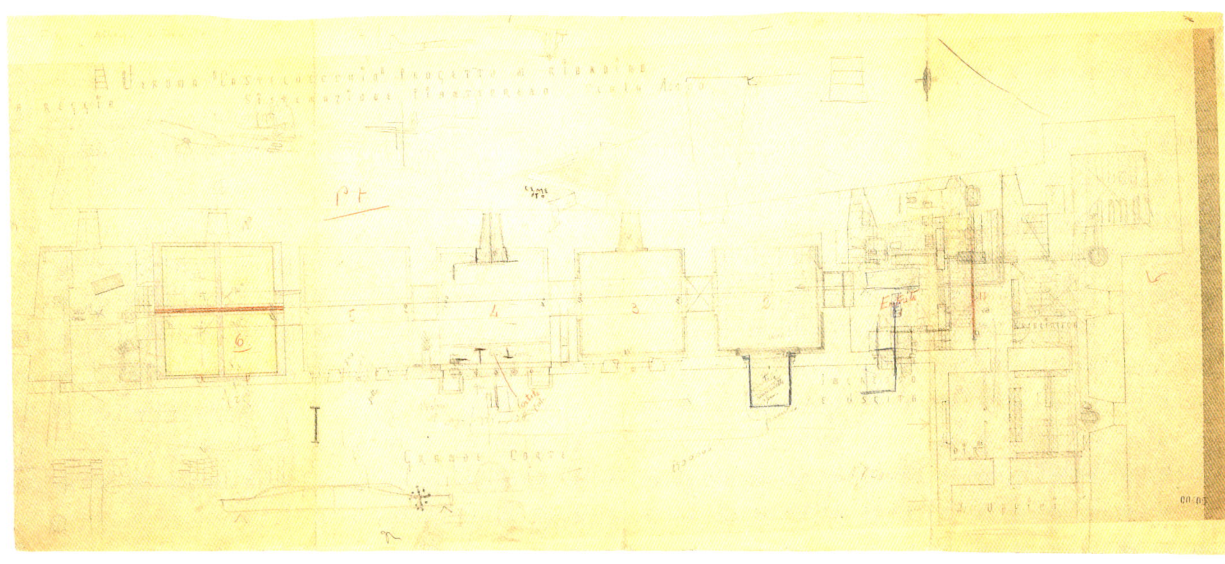

Carlo Scarpa, designer and draftsman; Angelo Rudella, draftsman. Ground-floor plan with final proposal for the garden, 1962–64. Graphite and colored pencil on reprographic print, 43.8 x 65.5 cm. Coll. MDC

Carlo Scarpa, designer and draftsman; Angelo Rudella, draftsman. Ground-floor plan of gallery wing and reflected ceiling plan of gallery 6, c. 1956–64. Graphite and colored pencil on reprographic print, 40 x 94 cm. Coll. MDC

and iron wall at the bottom and cantilevering an iron, wood, and glass wall above, which lets light into the gallery. He unified the wall through an asymmetrical composition that has, at its center, a small sculpture replicating the Gothic arches. In this way, the facade is interrupted, made asymmetrical, and yet conceived as a whole.

The interior sequence of rooms takes the viewer from the entrance to the statue of Cangrande. Scarpa noted, "The paving [is] one of the key surfaces in defining the geometry of a space. I had to solve the problem of the dihedron between the wall, which is a luminous vertical surface, and the dark, horizontal floor.... Thinking of the water flowing round the walls of the castle, I got the idea of creating a version in negative. The floor of every room is individuated, as if they were a series of platforms. By changing the material round their edge for a crowning piece in lighter-colored stone, so as to define the square more clearly, the movement is modulated.... The objects to be displayed have to be arranged accurately on the paving, to avoid any interference with the geometry of the rooms."[8]

Scarpa placed each work of art according to the fall of light. The floor on the ground level was remade in a regular geometric pattern in cast concrete with a trough around the edge to absorb the irregularities of the old walls. On this new floor he arranged a variety of sculpture pedestals. Fabricated in iron and plaster with incredible precision, they are set slightly off the floor and appear to float. Other pedestals consist of simple raw iron cubes, such as those for the crucifixes. Scarpa also designed an iron and black-plaster cross as support for the white-marble figure of Christ. In the last room of the main-floor gallery, clear glass installed in the floor opens up a view of the Roman ruins under the building. To frame the arched opening to the statue of Cangrande at the end of the long gallery sequence, Scarpa designed a simple iron, wood, and glass frame over which slides a security grill of woven flat steel.

For other floors, Scarpa invented varied designs of floor- and wall-mounted easels and pedestals. Two such easels were developed, for framed and unframed paintings. Constructed of thin strips of wood, the easel for framed paintings is held together by angled brass brackets sitting on a three-legged iron base. The second type of easel (known as *paragoni*) consists of two plates of iron with rectangular cut-outs between which the painting is sandwiched. Two thin strips of iron support these angled plates, which connect to a larger base piece and then are fastened to iron bars at the ground. This investigation into joinery in wood and metal was developed in collaboration with Anfodillo and Zanon.

Scarpa's drawings for Castelvecchio begin with a survey of existing conditions and proceed through all levels of the project, down to the pedestals and brackets. The complex restructuring of the building is seen through the details in the sections – evidence of Scarpa's concern for construction methods as well as his highly developed sense of space. The vast array of door, window, and other detail studies demonstrates his persistent search for a materially clear and measured reality. For example, a beautiful set of window drawings ranges from rough sketches showing the idea of an infill in the portal to measured drawings indicating the thicknesses of the fixed and moveable frames. All areas of design, from issues of construction to studies for the arrangement of paintings, were drawn with equal energy and passion.

GR

Studies of *sacello* including plan of paving, interior and exterior views, and display elements, c. 1956–64. Graphite and colored pencil on reprographic print, 33 x 71 cm. Coll. MDC

Interior elevation of window frame above *sacello*, c. 1956–64. Graphite on cardboard, 70 x 50 cm. Coll. MDC

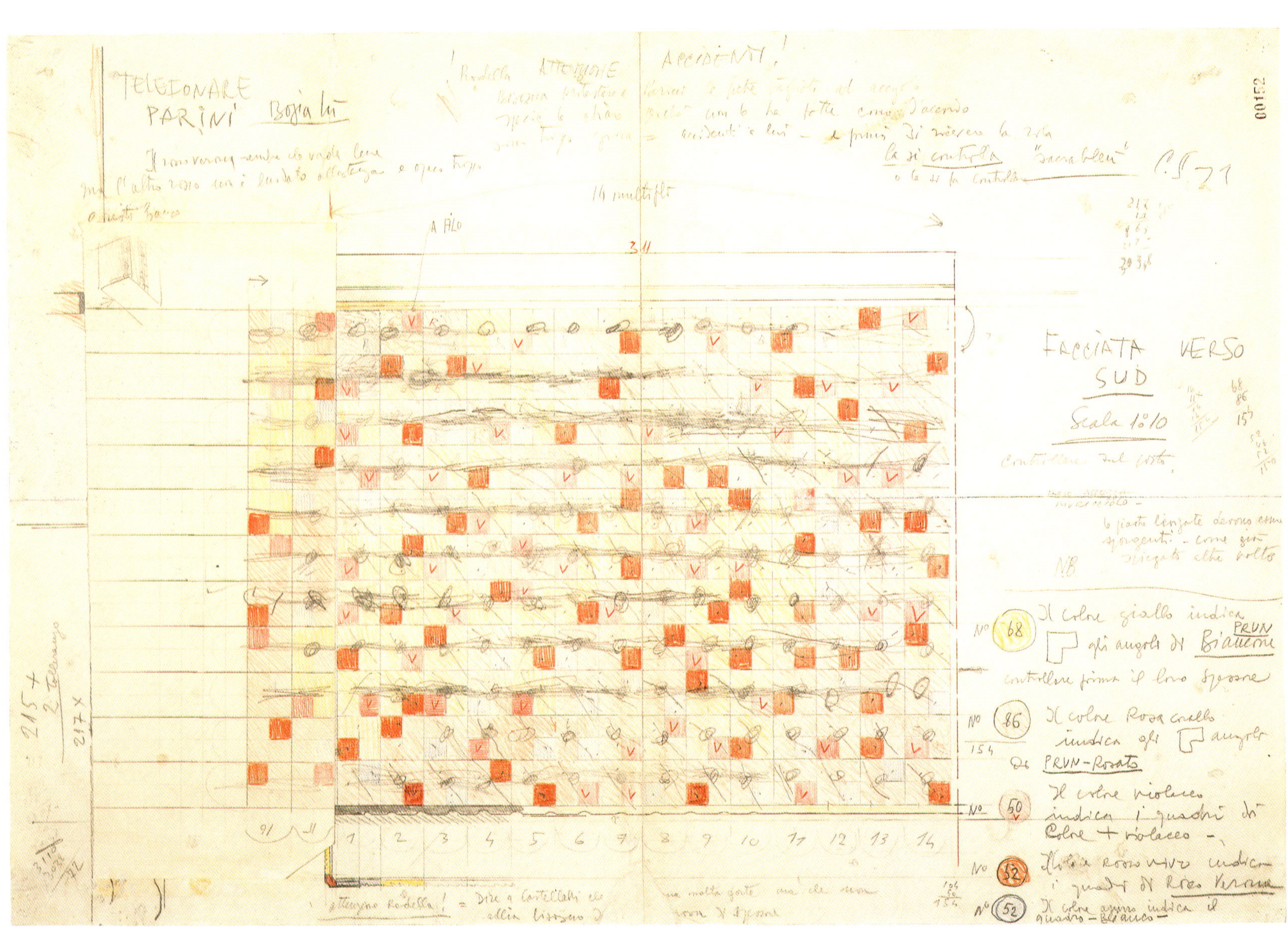

Elevation of south wall of *sacello* with specifications for paving scheme, c. 1956–64. Graphite and colored pencil on cardboard, 43.2 x 63 cm. Coll. MDC

Interior elevation of ground-floor window frames in gallery wing with sketches for display vitrines, c. 1956–64. Graphite and colored pencil on cardboard, 21 x 29 cm. Coll. MDC

Interior elevation of ground-floor window frame in gallery wing, c. 1956–64. Colored pencil on gelatin silver print, 24 x 30 cm. Coll. MDC

CANGRANDE DELLA SCALA

The statue of Cangrande della Scala, an outstanding example of Veronese fourteenth-century sculpture, commemorates one of the city's most distinguished rulers, descendants of whom constructed the Castelvecchio. Scarpa had originally considered placing the statue in the northeast corner of the main courtyard, to which he had moved the museum's main entrance in 1959. Puncturing the courtyard wall of the gallery wing and disengaging the medieval tower at the northeast, Scarpa proposed a deep entrance porch that would act as a gigantic niche for the statue. The excavation of the moat of the city wall along the western edge of the courtyard (which resulted in the demolition of the Napoleonic staircase and the last room of the gallery wing) prompted Scarpa to reconsider his initial idea. He decided to make the statue the nexus of many circulation routes. A ground-level path links the garden and the gallery wing to the Torre del Mastio and to the Reggia beyond. A diagonal bridge does the same on the second floor. Staircases branch off from the bridge and lead to the Torre del Mastio and to the battlement walk along the river. Finally, a public walkway follows along the city wall toward the Scaligeri (della Scalla) bridge.

Scarpa's carving out of the space for the statue of Cangrande is part of a larger system of perforations that the architect envisioned for the former barracks. Scarpa had originally planned to fray the facade at its juncture with the roof, thereby revealing its falseness, but finally designed asymmetrical window frames undermining the symmetrically-arranged Gothic archways and window surrounds inserted in the 1920s.

Scarpa carefully considered the shape of the support for the statue and the position of the viewer in relation to Cangrande. In early proposals (and in situ after the excavation of the Porta del Morbio and the construction of a new base, unveiled in 1964), Scarpa had preserved the sculpture's original trapezoidal stone base (actually the roof sheltering Cangrande's tomb), complementing it with another pedestal or replacing it with a new base that closely follows the shape of the original. He then considers a platform supported by clustered columns, finally favoring a folded concrete shell, shaped as a curved bracket or an upside-down L. The shape of the accompanying viewing platform varies considerably according to the orientation given to the statue. When placed diagonally facing the Comune wall, the platform reaches its maximum dimension, extending nearly to the fortification wall. Scarpa then decides to turn the statue toward the gallery wing, and the platform becomes a simple cantilevered steel bridge. The visitor can thus observe Cangrande's enigmatic smile either from the level of the painting gallery or from below.

J-F B

Carlo Scarpa, designer and draftsman; Angelo Rudella, draftsman. Elevation and axonometric of existing base of Cangrande and section-elevation of a preliminary proposal for its placement, 1958–62. Graphite and colored pencil on tracing paper, 34.3 x 56.2 cm. Coll. MDC

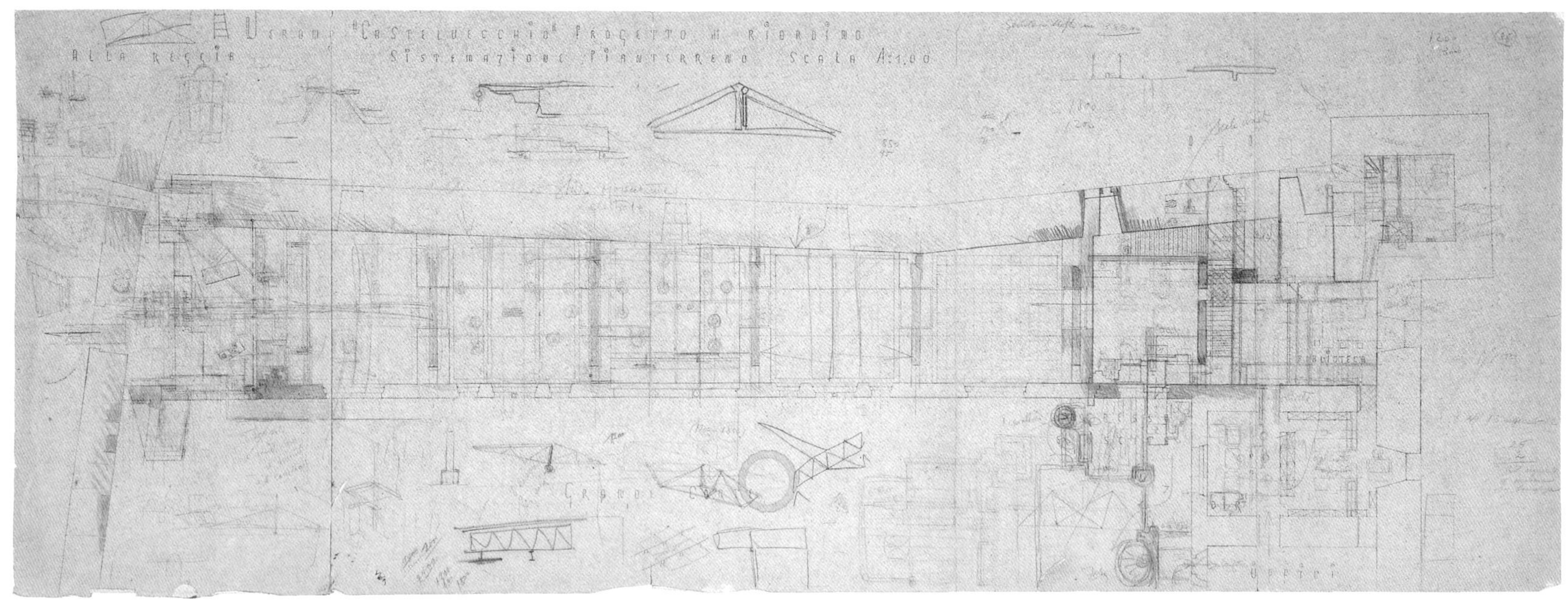

Plan of gallery wing with studies for structural details showing second proposal for installation of Cangrande, 1961–62. Graphite and colored pencil on reprographic print, 37 x 100.7 cm. Coll. MDC

Carlo Scarpa, designer and draftsman; Angelo Rudella, draftsman. Elevation of courtyard facade of gallery wing showing second proposal for installation of Cangrande, 1961–62. Graphite and colored pencil on reprographic print, 29.5 x 96.4 cm. Coll. MDC

Carlo Scarpa, designer and draftsman; Angelo Rudella, draftsman. Plan of the Cangrande cut and Torre del Mastio showing second proposal for placement of Cangrande with elevation studies for its installation, 1961–62. Graphite and colored pencil on reprographic print and tracing paper, 61 x 63.6 cm. Coll. MDC

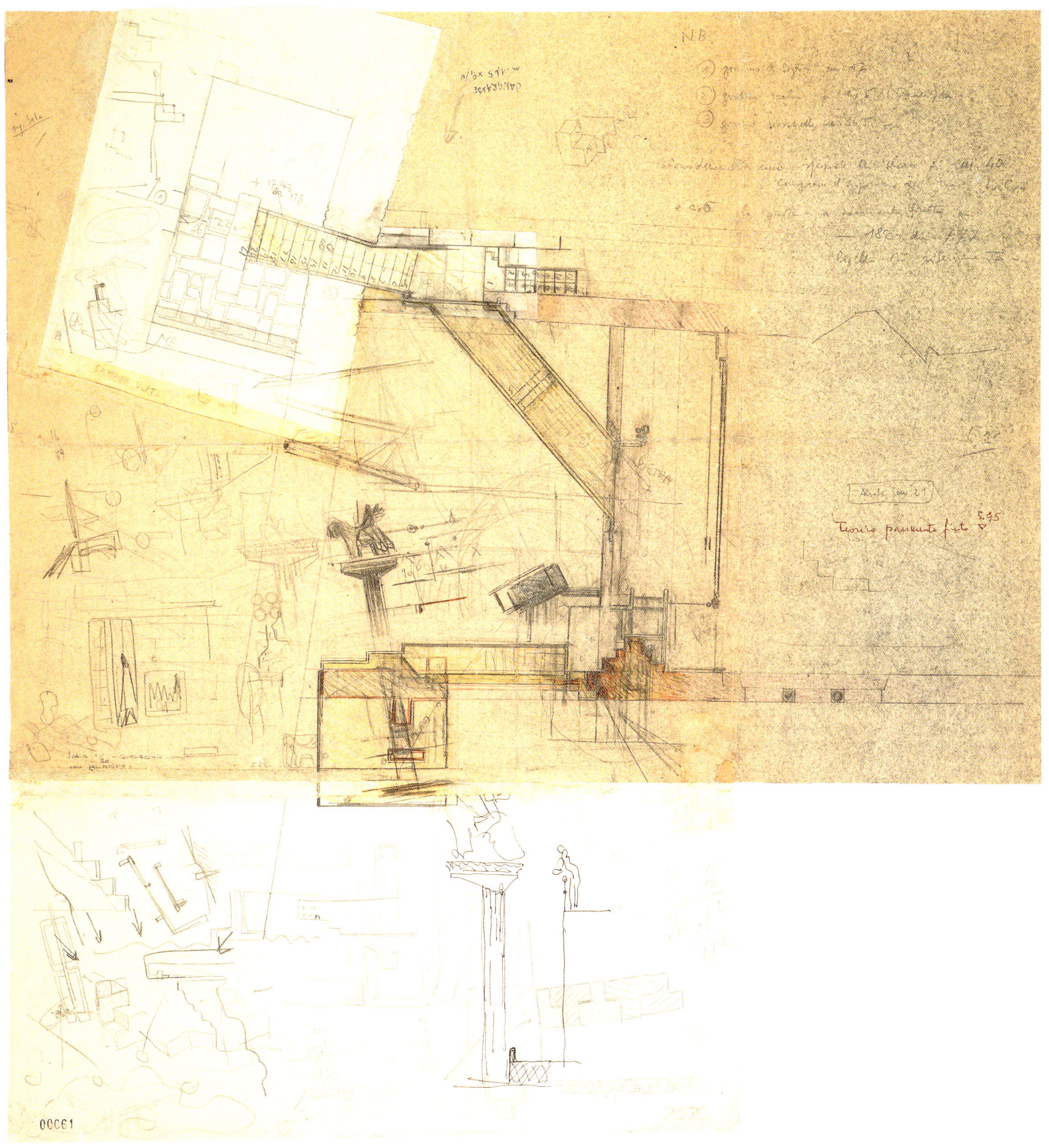
N.B.
00061

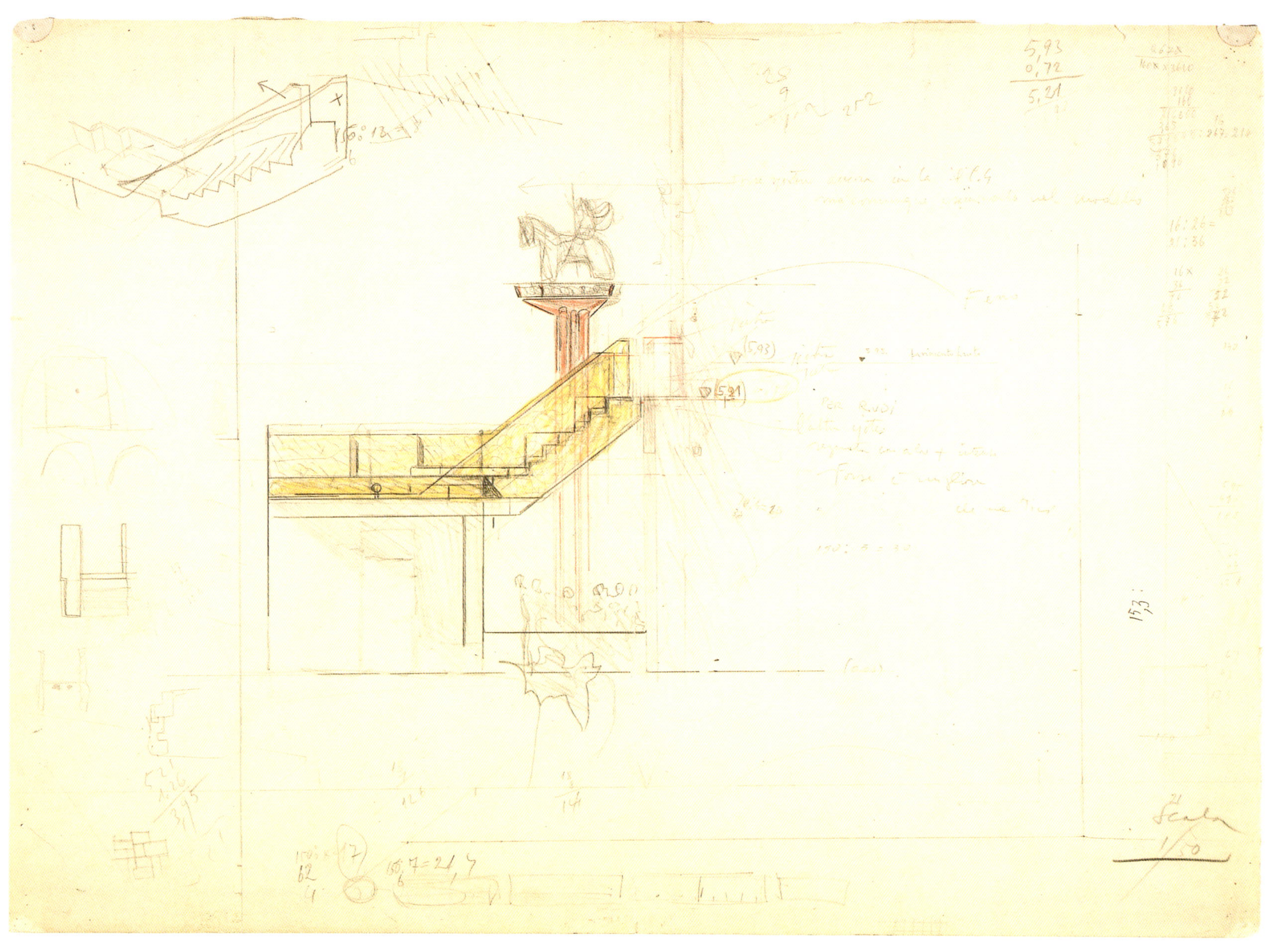

Elevation of second proposal for Cangrande installation, 1961–62. Graphite and colored pencil on cardboard, 35 x 50 cm. Coll. MDC

Section-elevation of final proposal for Cangrande installation, c. 1962–64. Graphite and colored pencil on tracing paper, 42 x 33.5 cm. Coll. MDC

Elevations and detail studies of final proposal for base of the Cangrande, c. 1962–64. Graphite and colored pencil on reprographic print, 32.8 x 56.8 cm. Coll. MDC

Section-elevations of final proposal for base of the Cangrande, c. 1962–64. Graphite and colored pencil on cardboard, 43.2 x 31.5 cm. Coll. MDC

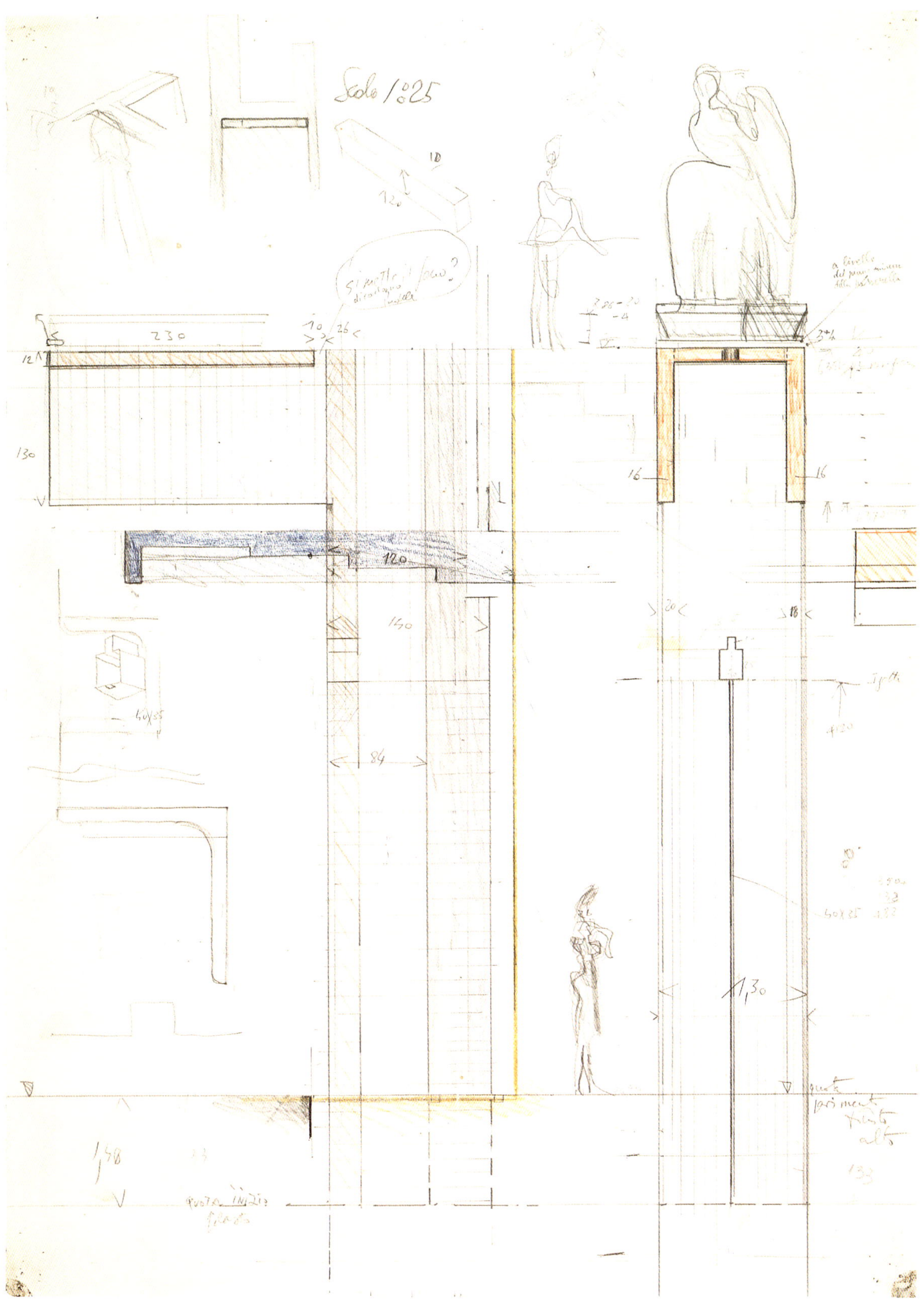

Scala 1:25
230
130
120
140
84
16
16
1,30

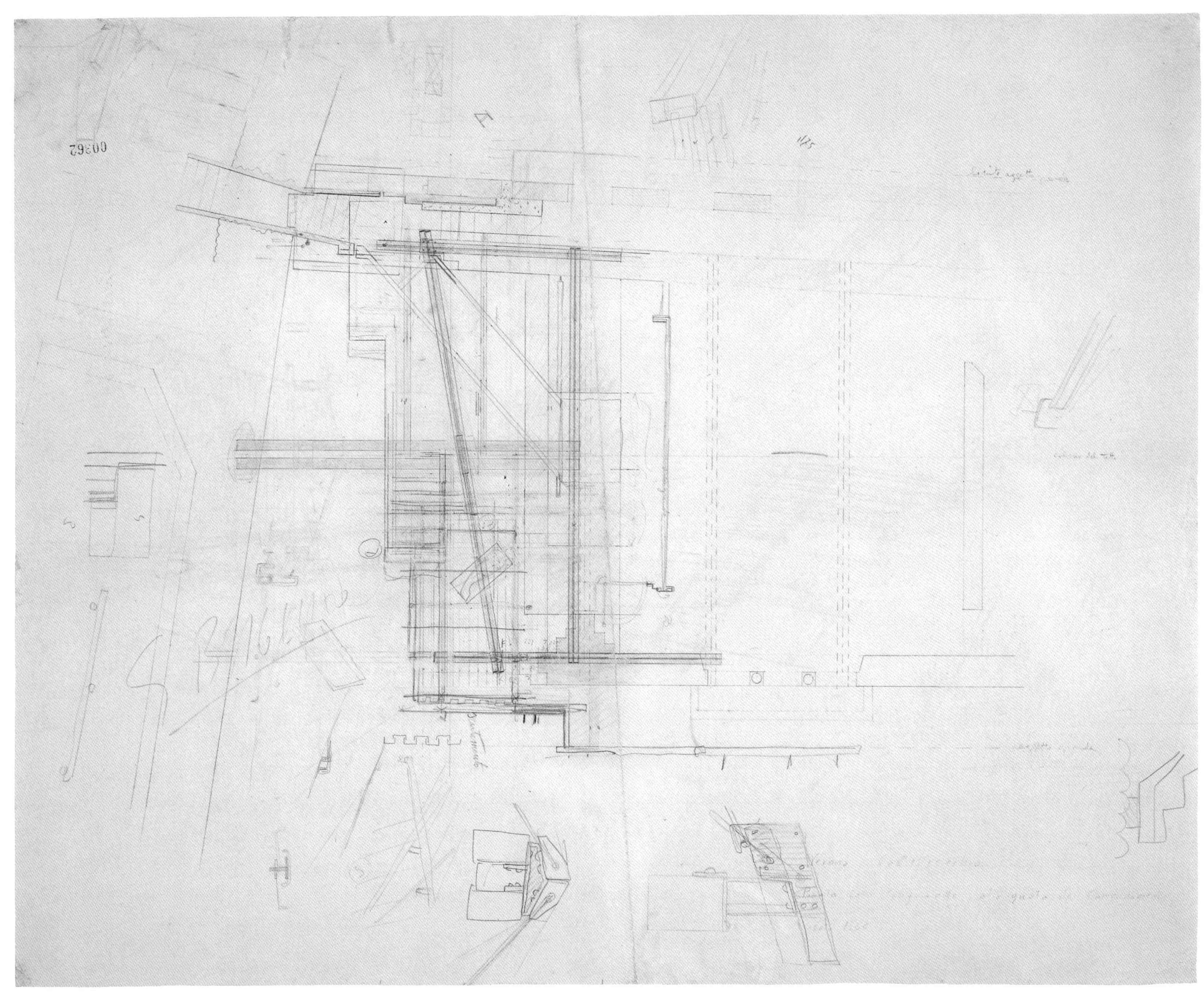

Reflected ceiling plan and studies for details of roof for final proposal of the Cangrande, c. 1962–64. Graphite and colored pencil on reprographic print, 50.5 x 64.2 cm. Coll. MDC

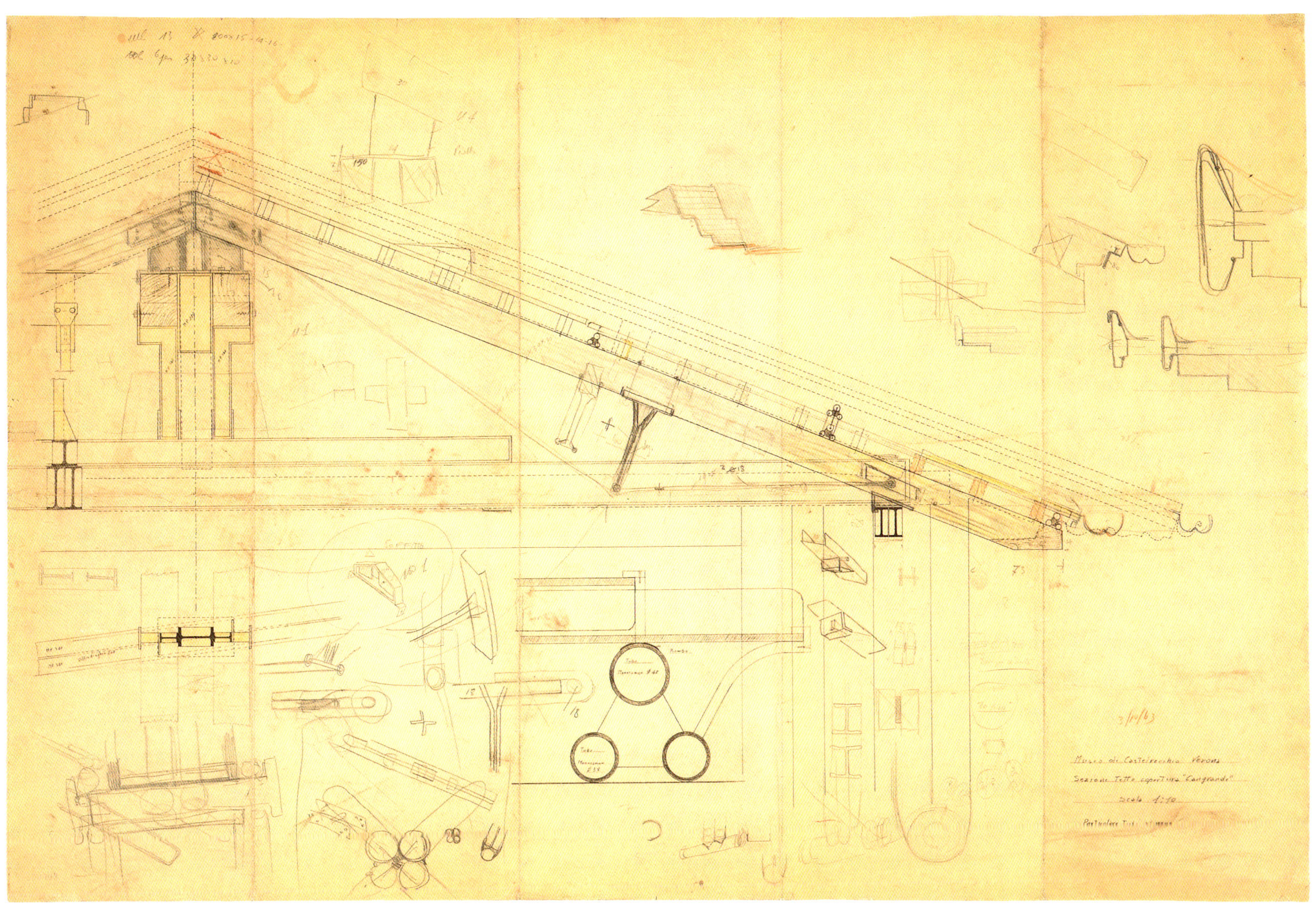

Carlo Scarpa, designer and draftsman; Angelo Rudella, draftsman. Section and details of roof for final proposal of the Cangrande, c. 1962–64. Graphite and colored pencil on reprographic print, 67.5 x 102 cm. Coll. MDC

THE ANALYTIC MODEL IS MADE at the intersection of Scarpa's most revelatory excavation into the fabric of the existing buildings. The limits of the model were set further back into the building and past the old wall of the complex. Within these parameters the model shows Scarpa's deft and extraordinary placements of new form into varying conditions of historic space. Each side of the model shows the differing conditions of Scarpa's insertions, which introduced the new architecture of the museum into the old historic building fabric. Views through the massive old wall reveal minor elements by Scarpa interwoven with the dense masonry, while the other side of the model illustrates the section through the museum building and Scarpa's almost surgical work on the structure, fenestration, and exhibit spaces of the building. It is, however, at the statue of Cangrande that the model is most revealing. As the viewer looks down into this space from above, it is possible to see the orchestrated complexity of movement, surfaces, and artifacts which reside in this space as well as the opening Scarpa effected by cutting back the existing building. The model is made as an exploratory section, sympathetic and related to the use of the section by Scarpa as a generative design tool. The model expresses the idea of the section as the outer manifestation of an inner process powerfully employed by Scarpa in the Castelvecchio renovation. The side view of the model, showing the elevation from the entry garden, illustrates the archeological excavation into the garden, with openings into the lower wall and the positioning of the Cangrande statue in the space between the medieval wall and the Gothic facade. Scarpa's intervention can be seen most dramatically in this space and in the new windows inserted into the Gothic openings. It is an orchestration of materials across time, with all elements in constant harmony and communication.

GR

Firm of George Ranalli, Model of Cangrande cut, 1998.
Plywood, basswood, and birch veneer. 52 x 46.9 x 43.1 cm.
Coll. CCA

Detail of model showing Cangrande statue

VERITTI HOUSE

IT WAS WRIGHT'S WORK THAT REALLY RAVISHED ME. I HAD NEVER HAD AN EXPERIENCE LIKE IT. IT SWEPT ME AWAY LIKE A WAVE – YOU CAN SEE THIS IN SOME OF MY DESIGNS FOR HOUSES. I WAS TOO DEEPLY IMPRESSED BY WRIGHT'S WORK. NOW I DON'T LIKE THOSE HOUSES ANY MORE, BECAUSE I DON'T THINK ONE SHOULD IMITATE SO SHAMELESSLY.[9]

CARLO SCARPA, 1978

Veritti house
Udine, 1955–61

Structural engineer: Angelo Morelli

The lawyer Luciano Veritti originally approached Scarpa to design a house on the outskirts of Udine. The location proposed by Scarpa was in a relatively undeveloped locale, but Veritti favored a site located in a more densely built-up area surrounded by freestanding houses. It is an elongated plot of land within a city block accessible only via a narrow lane, the Viale Duodo. Scarpa's first proposals for the house consisted of two low cylinders, one housing the main living quarters, the other a winter garden, linked together by a glazed passageway. In the final design, Scarpa regrouped all functions within a single, taller volume crowned by a terrace and a penthouse containing a guest apartment. A single overall circle, which determines the shape of the outside wall to the north and that of the reflecting pool to the south, unifies Scarpa's complex interplay of geometric forms.

J-F B

Site plan with sections and perspectives of first proposal, 1955–61. Photograph of lost original. Coll. ACS

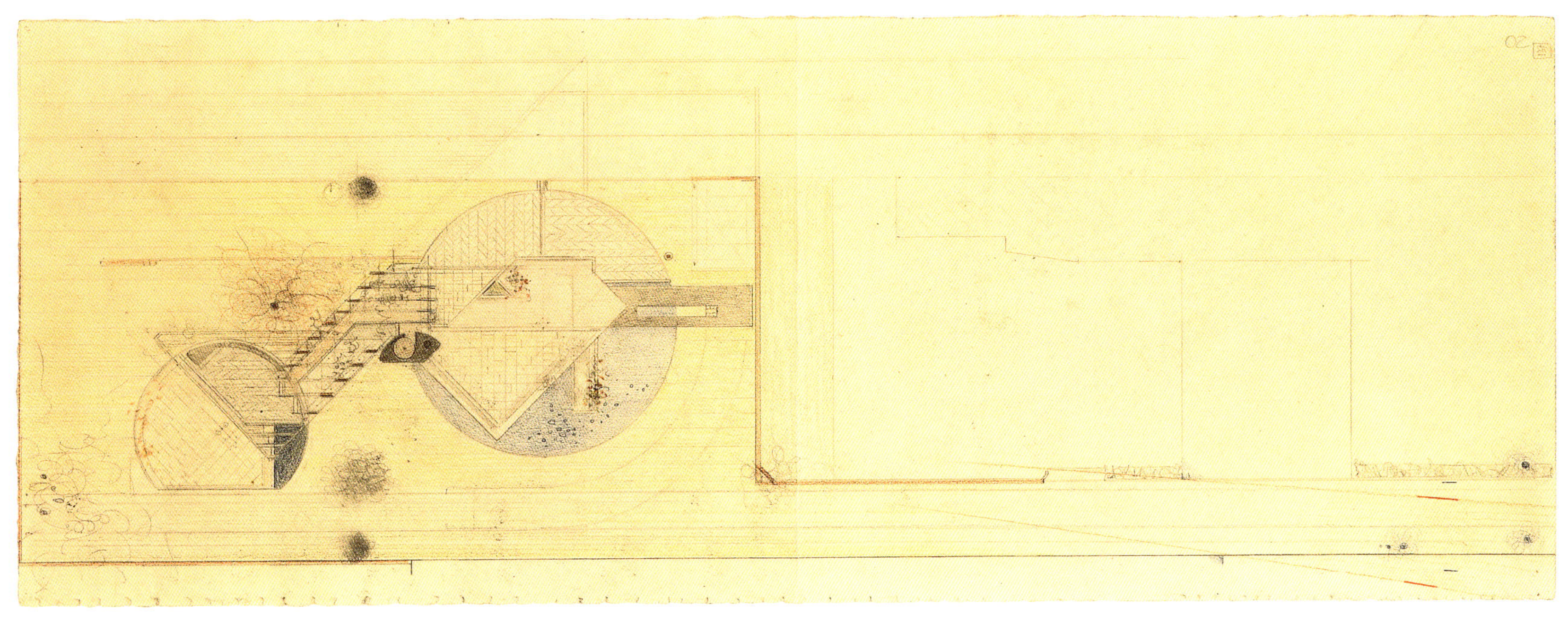

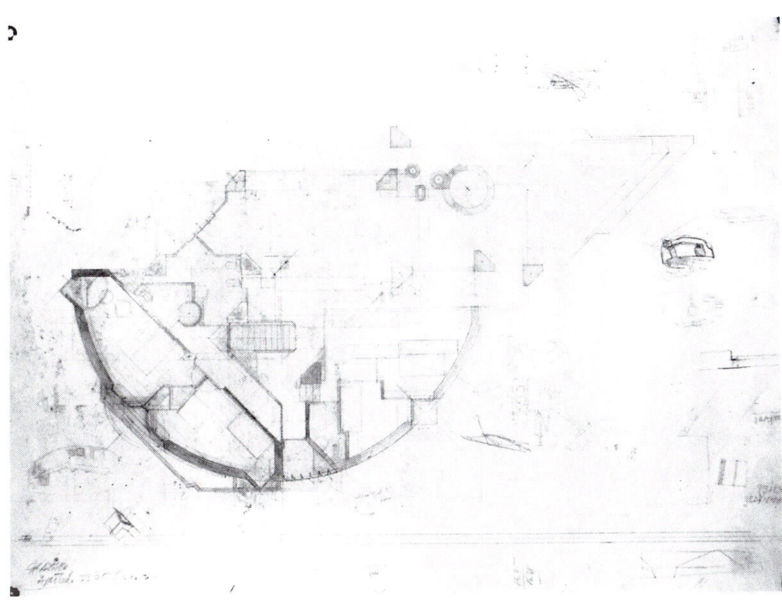

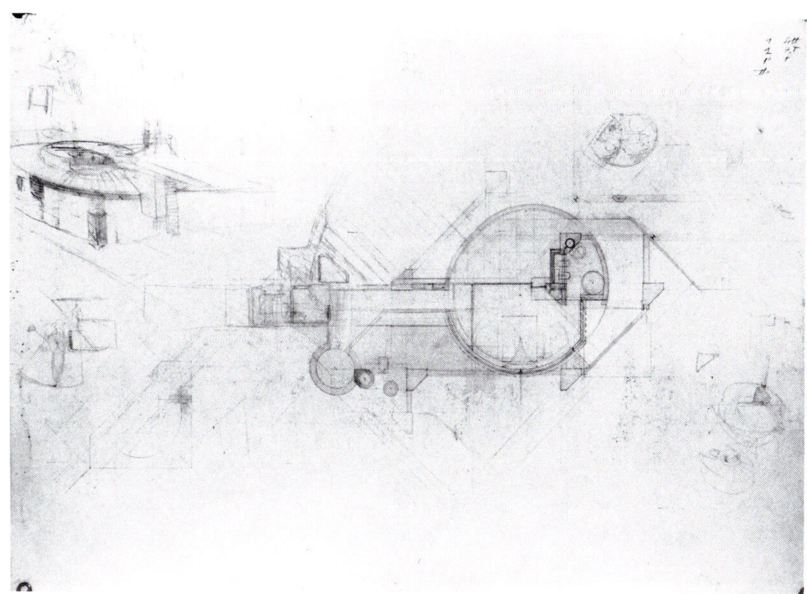

Ground-floor plan of second proposal, 1955–61. Graphite and colored pencil on cardboard, 19.5 x 52.8 cm. Coll. ACS

Second-floor plan, 1955–61. Photograph of lost original. Coll. ACS

Third-floor plan and perspective sketches, 1955–61. Photograph of lost original. Coll. ACS

THE VERITTI HOUSE IS ONE OF THE few freestanding buildings realized by Scarpa in this period. Developed over seven years, it served as a critical laboratory for new ideas and offers an extraordinary set of comparisons with the museum work – especially the Canova gallery at Possagno – that runs parallel to its long gestation. Upon first observation it appears to be influenced by, or even to imitate, Frank Lloyd Wright, but further study assigns it its own territory of spatial and material invention. The reference to Wright is immediately evident in the pre-cast elements of the pilasters, which produce a surface texture reminiscent of Wright's concrete-block houses. Here pattern enhances the vertical nature of the pilasters as they move out beyond the roof line and into the sky. Unlike Wright, however, Scarpa began to explore a language of multiple materials in the Veritti house rather than the monolithic effect of a single material. Treating the architectural elements as if they were works of art, he began to construct a kind of narrative out of them. At the same time, his use of water and circular forms and his approach to landscape signal the acquisition of a new sculptural vocabulary, working in dialogue with the terrain, that would mature in his work of the 1960s and 1970s and reach a climax in the Brion tomb. Much like the works of art at the Palazzo Abatellis and Possagno, these independent forms, both inside and out, constitute a set of discrete objects that demarcate and organize the space and engage in the same sort of conversation. By looking at the Veritti house in association with Scarpa's museum designs, the similarities in strategy between such independent work as Brion and the museum interventions and installations become apparent.

The building, placed on a long, flat, nondescript parcel of urban residential land, is incised into the ground through the use of a circular pond. Outdoor plantings, walks, concrete forms, and garden spaces assist in rooting the house to its site. This strategy of using walls, garden, and water to create a topography in sympathy with the structure (first fully explored in the Italian and Venezuelan pavilions at the *Venice Biennale*) will appear again at the Palazzo Querini Stampalia and reach an apotheosis in the Brion tomb.

Encountering water in a landlocked site is an unexpected pleasure. Its effect is heightened as one enters the building over a bridge, giving the sense of leaving the larger landscape and moving to a new, reserved place. Held in beautifully designed vessels, the water produces a quiet sound that further contains the site. The presence of water is apparent in the interior through the constantly changing reflections. This interplay of water and light reminded Scarpa of Venice, and his ability to evoke this highly personal recollection through a contemporary material idiom was one of his many startling inventions in this project.

Originally organized as two separate circular volumes, the design was gradually transformed into one large circular volume with triangular and rectangular volumes incised into and extending from it. One half of the plan's geometry was completed by the building, the other by a pond. Within the circle, many vertical spatial openings connect the three levels of the house and allow for communication between the upper and lower floors. The spatial play is rich and diverse, constantly placing the occupants in an open and free-flowing relationship to one another. Most of Scarpa's drawings for the house have been lost, but a recently discovered file of photographs of these drawings shows the intensive working-out of the design in plan and section.

The complex material choices for the Veritti house often involved using two or more substances for a single element – such as the wood and steel window wall or the wood and plaster walls of the interior. Sometimes these constructions were sent from one artisan to another to facilitate the necessary interaction and joinery. The multiple-material palette would later unfold into an even more extreme approach to surfaces and joinery as the complexity and budgets of Scarpa's projects increased.

GR

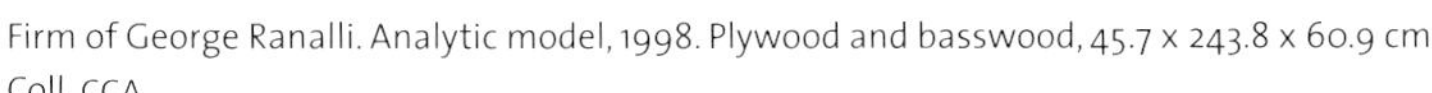

Firm of George Ranalli. Analytic model, 1998. Plywood and basswood, 45.7 x 243.8 x 60.9 cm. Coll. CCA

Rear facade

THE ANALYTIC MODEL OF THE VERITTI house reveals the totemic power of one of Scarpa's few freestanding buildings. The scale and solidity of the house becomes evident as the model is viewed in the round. Also apparent is the way the delicate use of frame and transparency opens the entrance side. The model is made with the elongated shape of the site illustrated as a block of earth upon which the house is deposited. Detail and decorative elements indicate the complexity of Scarpa's formal program and how it evolved into built form. Scarpa's power as a maker of architectural form is in clear evidence in this model, especially when the building is viewed as a unique sculptural object unattached to any existing structure.

The Veritti house model along with the three other models (all were built to the same scale) illustrate the four types of project that occupied Scarpa's imagination throughout his career. The Querini model represents the impacted type with new elements imposed within an internal world of old building fabric. Castelvecchio is the historic amalgam, altered with exquisite skill and blending techniques. The Canova gallery is the addition, as a partially visible form attached to an existing building. And the Veritti house is the embodiment of Scarpa imposing his vision of architecture in the open landscape.

The end view pictured here illustrates the density of the circular half of the private living quarters on the left and the fragile and transparent winter garden at the end of the house. Also visible in this elevation is the complexity of the massing. A bird's-eye view of the model clearly illustrates the Veritti house in relation to the elongated site plan as well as the rooting of the building into the ground through the elaborate landscape gestures of the pool, the path, and the changing terraces extending from the house.
GR

OLIVETTI SHOWROOM

I THINK THAT VENICE, MORE THAN ANY OTHER ITALIAN CITY, COULD ACCOMMODATE THE MODERN EXPRESSION OF ARCHITECTURE. BECAUSE OF CERTAIN OF ITS ASYMMETRIES – ITS VERY VARIED SKYLINE, WITH HIGH AND LOW BUILDINGS, ITS STREETS BROAD AND NARROW. AND IT HAS VERY BEAUTIFUL INTERIOR SPACES. SO IF IT WOULD BE POSSIBLE TO PRESERVE THINGS OF THIS TYPE IN THE HISTORIC FABRIC, THERE WOULD BE NO FEAR OF SPOILING THE CITY, SO LONG AS DESIGNS WERE CARRIED OUT IN A MANNER ... WORTHY OF IT.[10]

CARLO SCARPA, 1978

Olivetti showroom
Venice, 1957–58

Collaborator: Gilda D'Agaro
Structural engineer: Carlo Maschietto

Adriano Olivetti, president of the Italian office equipment firm then noted for its innovations in design, commissioned the Olivetti showroom the year after Scarpa received the Olivetti Prize for architecture. The showroom is located on the ground floor of the Procuratie Vecchie, at the intersection of a narrow service street (the Sottoportico del Cavaletto) with Venice's Piazza San Marco. The project began with the complete gutting of the shop of a household-appliance retailer and the strengthening of the building's structure. Scarpa inserted a new mezzanine to increase the available floor space and to provide access to offices located above an adjacent shop. Two principal elements structure the ground floor: a gilded bronze sculpture by Alberto Viani (*Nude*, 1955) placed in a shallow black marble pool near the entrance and Scarpa's Aurisina marble staircase (ornamented at its base with a geometric metal structure of Scarpa's own design), which takes the visitor to the mezzanine floor.
J-F B

Exterior view before intervention, c. 1957.
Photograph: Paolo Monti. Coll. ACS

Side facade with staff entrance, 1962.
Photograph: Paolo Monti. Istituto di fotografia Paolo Monti, Milan

Display windows on side facade, 1962.
Photograph: Paolo Monti. Coll. ACS

THE PIAZZA SAN MARCO, THE MOST important public space in Venice, does not accept new architectural elements easily. A heavy colonnade shields the shops and cafes from the open space of the Piazza; sheltered within it, they seem to be immutable, antique, and laden with history. Scarpa's architectural career had been marked by a series of small interventions into the Venetian fabric of streets and squares – boutiques and cafes, art galleries, shops for antiques and books. This commission from Olivetti, however, represented an extraordinary opportunity to create a showplace for contemporary design within an assertively historical environment. It began an ambitious series of architectural dialogues with Italy's historic urban fabric that culminated in the controversial late work for the Banca Popolare di Verona.

"The showroom consisted of a front section, and then, after a wall, there was another area," explained Scarpa. "You had to go to the floor above; there were spaces you couldn't change, a central pillar, two windows – where should the stairs go? I decided to put [them] wherever I could gain elbow room.... By putting them at the most difficult point I could throw something out – and I was interested in getting rid of things. In this way I could make better use of the length."[11] Scarpa placed his entrance to face the square, but within the hollow of the masonry wall set a large iron gate of woven steel. In the masonry openings he floated a new window with a strong brass frame and reinforced corner members. On the other facade he opened large display windows and a second entrance for staff beside a square of texturally varied cast concrete with the word "Olivetti" cast into its surface.

Although these facades were both startlingly new, they also resonated with the old city. Without either sacrificing his creativity or holding back on his architectural agenda, Scarpa developed a way of connecting an avant-garde design to the sensibility of the work that for centuries had been produced in this quarter. One of his strategies was to use the same artisanal techniques of construction that had formed the historic city in order to evolve new forms.

The small space of Scarpa's intervention was crowded with different materials and unfolds as a place of intense complexity, with both horizontal and vertical movement. Yet the room possesses a certain serenity, and the material and formal complexity manages to expand rather than constrict the sense of space. At the front, space moves out through the large plate-glass openings and into the arcade of the Piazza, as well as up onto the second level. The floor was designed as an integral cement and mosaic tile inlay. The imperfections of the cement tile settings and their high lustre make the floor appear to ripple and undulate like moving water. The staircase, the room's focal point, is composed of a complex arrangement of granite slabs and marble blocks that cantilever in an asymmetrical pattern right and left. This dynamic yet stable form cascades down from the mezzanine and spills out onto the showroom floor. Each slab and block rests on brass pin supports that slightly separate them, producing another range of spaces between the slabs.

At the top of the staircase, a small mezzanine that functions like a bridge wraps around three sides of the space and affords a view to the floor below. It is suspended from the ceiling by a metal tension structure and pinned to the columns laterally, with one end projecting into the entry space and overlooking the fountain and sculpture. The structure is enhanced by the lighting, hidden in vertical slots in the wall behind frosted glass. Many apertures balance natural and artificial light, making the space luminous. The most interesting openings are the oval wood screens on the mezzanine, which baffle light from the outside. The two oval shapes are filled with wood lattice and connected horizontally to the wall by wood strips that extend the oval to the corners of the room: they become stylized eyes through which to view the Piazza.

This detailed work was possible only with the close collaboration of the artisans and an intense focus on materials. The level of joinery and the interrelation of different crafts was extraordinary. Integrating the wood on the balcony with the balcony's bronze edges, for example, required that the two artisans work together so that the small tolerances demanded by Scarpa could be achieved. This dialogue was facilitated by Scarpa himself, who was constantly present in their shops and on site, modifying and pushing the limits of traditional processes.

GR

Staircase, 1962. Photograph: Paolo Monti.
Istituto di fotografia Paolo Monti, Milan

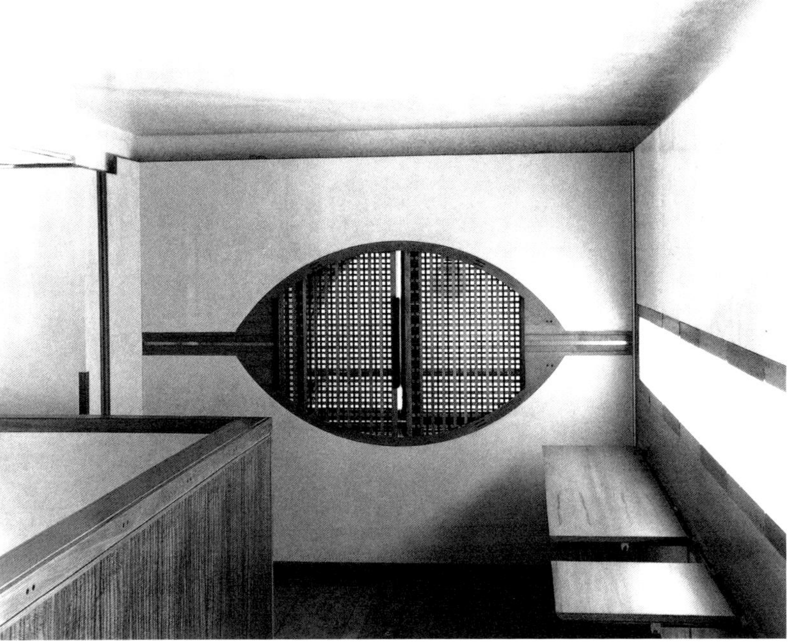

Mezzanine window, 1962. Photograph: Paolo Monti.
Istituto di fotografia Paolo Monti, Milan

PALAZZO QUERINI STAMPALIA

ONE MUST THINK OF THE GREAT SKILL WITH WHICH THE JAPANESE USE A VERY SMALL SPACE AND CREATE MAGICAL THINGS.... I HAVE HAVE REALLY AND TRULY SEEN THINGS THERE IN VERY SMALL SPACES THAT FOR SHEER INGENUITY BEGGAR DESCRIPTION.... WHERE I LIVED IN KYOTO, IN A LITTLE HOUSE, ONE COULD OPEN THE LITTLE DOOR AND SEE THREE DROPS FALLING – DRIP, DRIP, DRIP – TO BE ABSORBED IN A PATCH OF LAND LIKE THIS, THREE OR FOUR METERS LONG. AND THERE WERE THREE OR FOUR PLANTS THAT NEEDED THIS MOISTURE, AND WERE EVEN IN BLOOM, AND THE SPACE SEPARATING THE HOUSES (THE WALL BELONGED TO THE HOUSE NEXT DOOR, AND OUR ENTRANCE WAS COVERED) WAS NO BIGGER THAN THAT.... AT THE QUERINI STAMPALIA THERE IS A MODEST ATTEMPT AT THIS SORT OF THING.... THIS QUERINI GARDEN, IF YOU HAVE SEEN IT, SHOULD BE BASICALLY A TINY ONE, DELICATE, REFINED, DISTINCTIVE, AUTHENTIC, AND VERY, VERY WELL GROOMED.[12]

CARLO SCARPA, 1975

Reorganization of the ground floor and courtyard of the Palazzo Querini Stampalia
Venice, 1961–63

Client: Fondazione Querini Stampalia
Collaborators: Carlo Maschietto, Luciano Zinato

In 1949, Manlio Dazzi, director of the Fondazione Querini Stampalia, approached Scarpa to reorganize the ground floor and redesign the garden of the Fondazione, a research library and art collection housed in the early sixteenth-century Palazzo Querini (later Querini Stampalia), willed to the public by Count Giovanni Querini Stampalia, who died in 1869. Unrealized due to financial difficulties, Scarpa's project was later picked up by Dazzi's successor, Giuseppe Mazzariol, a friend and colleague of Scarpa at the faculty of architecture of the Istituto universitario di architettura di Venezia.

The renovations involved, first, the displacement of the entrance door to the palace's principal facade on Campiello S. Maria Formosa, via a new bridge and a new front door inserted into an existing window. Inside, Scarpa reclaimed the ground floor, subject to periodic flooding, by the use of elevated platforms allowing for the passage of flood waters into the entrance hall via the water gate. He also elevated one exhibition room, leaving the other at its original level. Scarpa covered the walls with plaster and travertine panels detached from the walls to enhance air circulation. These corrective measures not only improved the salubrity of the palace's exhibition spaces, they also reflect Scarpa's critical dialogue with history. Finally, Scarpa transformed the palace's courtyard into a garden with the collaboration of Mazzariol, who selected the plants, and the mosaicist Mario de Luigi. The renovated building was opened on 26 June 1963.

J-F B

View of the bridge from the Campiello, 1993.
Photograph: Maria Ida Biggi.

THE PALAZZO QUERINI STAMPALIA is located in the center of the old city, not far from the Piazza San Marco. After winding through very tight streets and alleys, one reaches a small square alongside a minor canal crossed by two bridges sitting side by side. The old bridge connects to a small alley, while the new bridge, designed by Scarpa, leads to the Palazzo's front door. The old bridge is made of a single, monolithic material, while Scarpa's wood and steel construction employs a combination of materials to express simple structural ideas. Two sheets of steel compressed into an arch span masonry supports separated by steel spacers. Wood treads sit atop the plates, whose fasteners are revealed on the surface. Vertical struts for the railings extend up from the steel plates with an elaborate system of joinery culminating in a wooden handrail with brass joints. In its clarity of construction, the bridge prefigures the interior space of the building. Clearly seen from the middle of the bridge are the two new elements that Scarpa inserted into the old facade: a gateway for boats, made of a highly textured woven iron set within the existing heavy masonry wall, and the institution's name, carved in Istrian stone. This trio of bridge, gates, and plaque announces the presence of another layer of time linked to the historic building.

Scarpa's solution to the problem of a ground floor that was periodically flooded represents the starting point for his investigation into renovation and restoration. Scarpa built a new floor above the high-water line and pulled it away from the old walls on all sides in a way that was similar to his work at the Museo di Castelvecchio, yet here the design was more vigorous. This platform, situated behind the canal gate, is reached via a set of concrete steps that climb out of the water and over the floor tray. From this vantage point, the fragments of the existing building become visible. Scarpa further elucidated them by constructing newly cast concrete walls between the fragments of old brick and resituating the old pilaster arches within them.

The floor tray connects the three interior rooms of the ground floor, forcing the visitor to step down into each new space. On one side, the tray leads to the entry at the new bridge – a foyer with a mosaic floor of orange, green, and white stones arranged in a dynamic grid, and plaster panels fixed to the masonry wall. The panel joints are accentuated with iron edges, creating a second scale in the space. On the other side, the tray descends to an irregular room whose walls are a composite of the original structure and new plaster panels edged with iron. There is a constant sense of fusion between old and new – of what Scarpa called the "visual logic"[13] of its different parts.

Centered on the main steps, the central gallery links this entry sequence to the garden behind the building. The floor of this hall-like space is made of rough-textured concrete with intermittent smooth stripes, and wraps up onto the walls as far as the high-water mark. Above that line sit sheets of travertine arranged in two rows. Between them is a horizontal strip of brass designating the position of vertical lights distributed asymmetrically across the wall. A block of irregularly carved Istrian stone housing the heating unit sits in the center at the end of the gallery. Glass at both ends allows dappled light from the water of the canal to reach the gallery, where it fuses with the green glow of light from the garden. To achieve this effect of transparency, Scarpa removed the wall at the back to fill the gallery with light and space and to leave the columns of the old building visible through glass doors from the garden.

The garden is composed of a manicured lawn with tiny interventions by Scarpa delicately placed around its periphery. A water trough runs the length of the yard. The water moves through a shallow, carved marble spillway, zigzagging around geometric carvings, pouring out into the long, thin trough, and arriving at a small metal scupper that empties into a circular basin and drain (a design similar to that of many Japanese water gardens admired by Scarpa). Here an antique stone basin is inserted into a new cast-concrete support. To protect the fragile concrete, Scarpa inlaid marble blocks at the corners of the support, in the process taking it to another level of design. Mazzariol, the sympathetic client, referred to the design as the essence of what Scarpa found so intriguing in Venice: the quality of being seen and not seen. "One could look from the campiello through openings, balustrades, screens, and discern the garden at the other side … and behold something at once a mystery and reality."[14]

GR

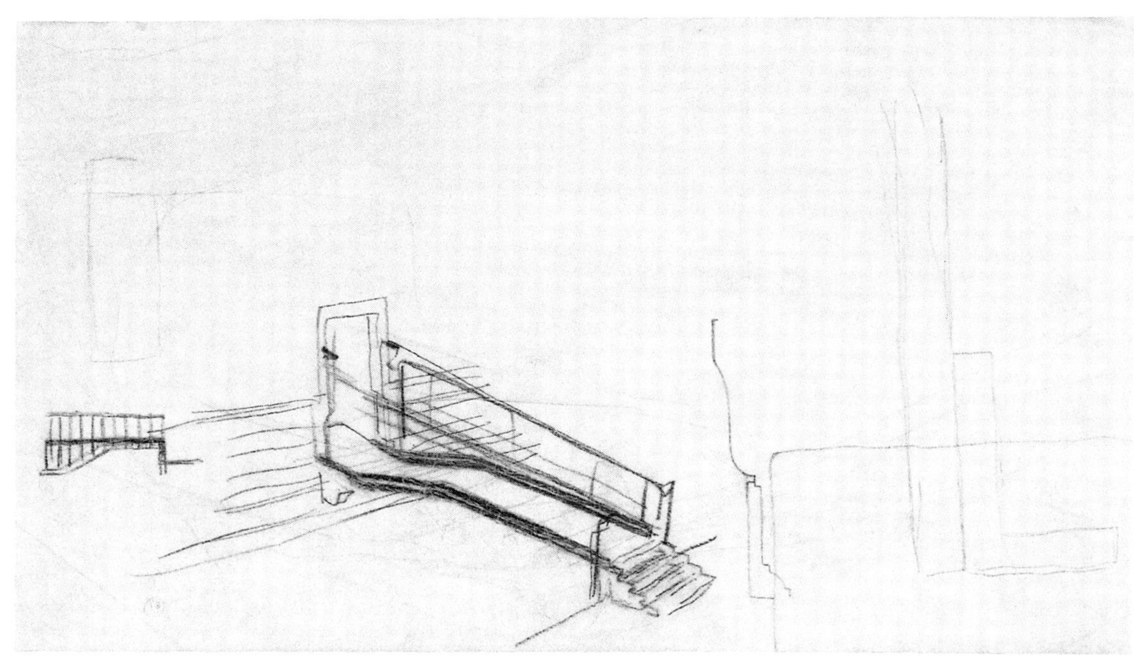

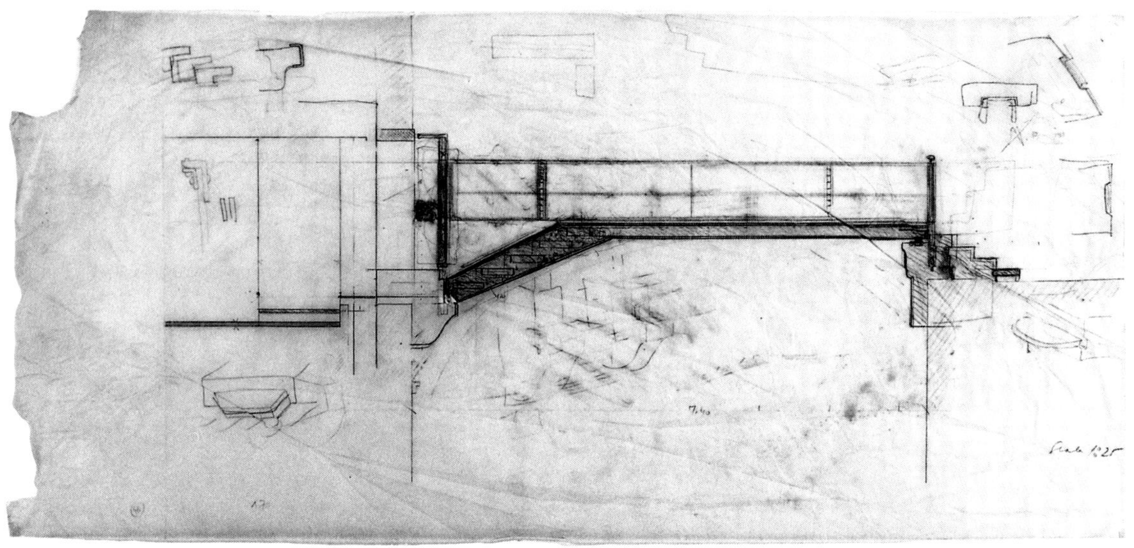

Perspective, section, and detail of preliminary proposal for the bridge, 1959–63. Graphite on tracing paper, 29.8 x 55.5 cm. Coll. FQS

Section of preliminary proposal for the bridge, 1959–63. Graphite on tracing paper, 29.6 x 65.5 cm. Coll. FQS

Sections of the bridge and section detail of handrail, 1959–63. Colored pencil and pen-and-ink on reprographic print, 37.5 x 91.5 cm. Coll. FQS

Section and details of the bridge, 1959–63. Graphite, pen-and-ink, and colored pencil on cardboard, 75.2 x 125 cm. Coll. FQS

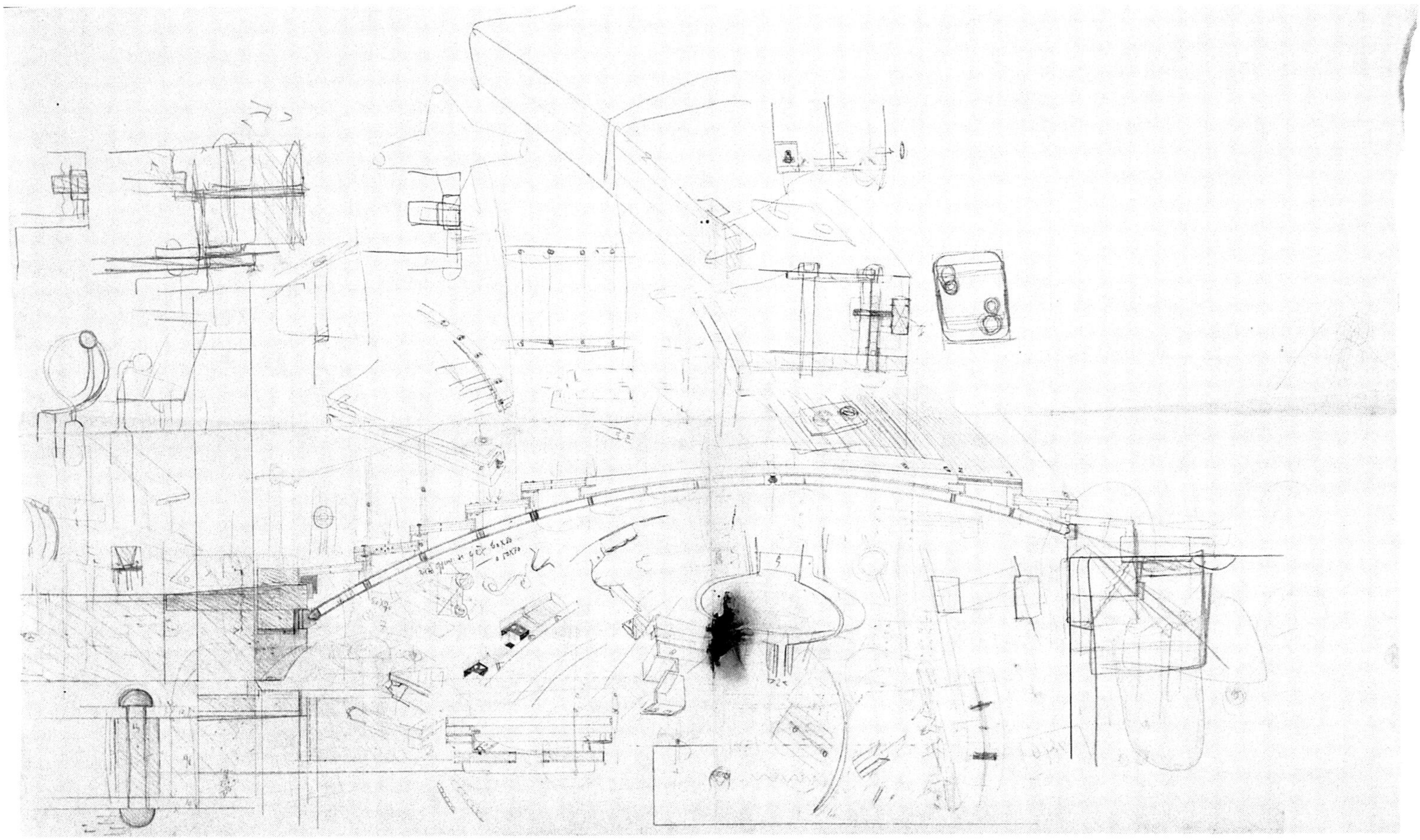

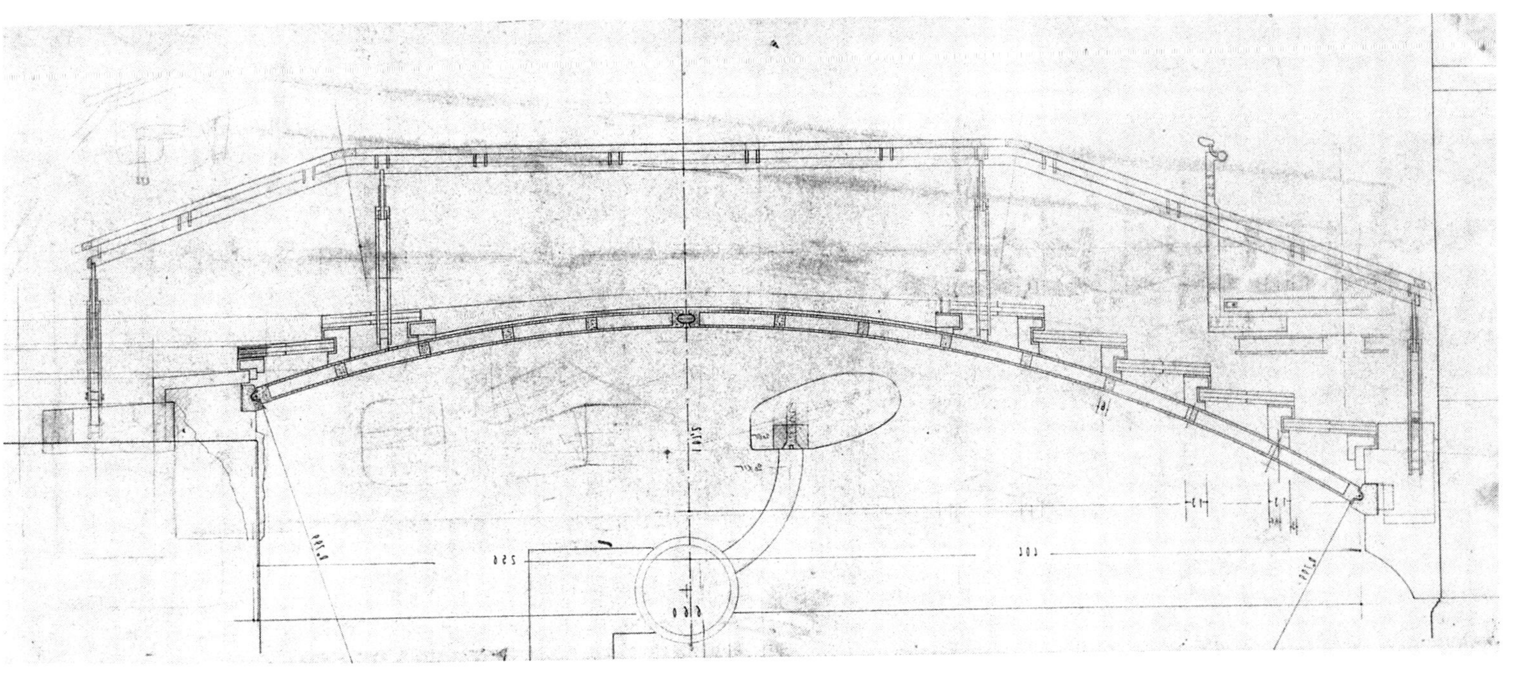

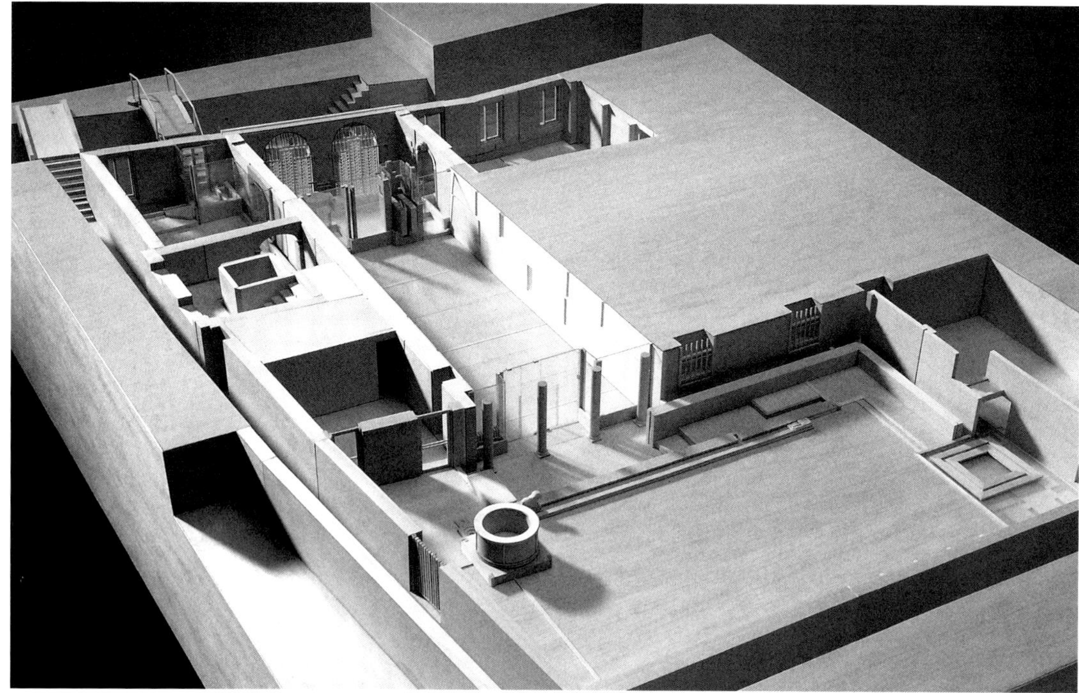

Firm of George Ranalli. Detail of model showing horizontal section of Scarpa's intervention, 1998. Plywood, basswood, birch veneer, and Plexiglas. 213.3 x 101.6 x 66 cm. Coll. CCA

Detail showing the bridge

THE ANALYTIC MODEL CLEARLY illustrates the passage of space that Scarpa incised into the city fabric, moving from the public realm through the interiors to the hidden garden. In this plan and section Scarpa understood those elements that are intrinsically Venetian and wove them into a unity of space, material, form, and structure, at the same time relating them back to the city. The two aerial views shown here demonstrate how Scarpa comprehended the solidity of the existing buildings and renovated them in such a way as to reveal their true nature. Both the application of material to the existing walls through revealed joinery and the troughs separating the floor from the walls set this work into a precise urban location. The model views show the passage of space from city to garden providing an understanding that cannot be had by actual experience of the building. The existing buildings are rendered in solid wood to highlight with great clarity Scarpa's incision into this built landscape. Clearly visible are the bridge and the iron gates, which represent a rethinking of the capacity of modern design to connect with historical architectural form. The two views also show the highly differentiated rooms, the design elements in them, and their relationship to the garden beyond, all connected in a synchrony of movement.

GR

Guido Guidi. Garden, 1997. Chromogenic color print,
19.5 x 24.6 cm. Coll. CCA

BANCA POPOLARE DI VERONA

BEHIND THE VERONA ARENA THERE ARE TWO SQUARES: .... IN ONE SQUARE THERE'S A RUN-OF-THE-MILL CHURCH, IN THE MIDDLE THERE IS A BUILDING DIVIDING UP THE TWO SQUARES, AND ON THE CORNER A BANK, AN EIGHTEENTH-CENTURY BUILDING. WHEN I WAS GIVEN THE COMMISSION TO DESIGN THE NEW BANK, THE ADJOINING LOT HAD BEEN BOUGHT TO ENLARGE THE PREMISES. THE FIRST THING I SAID WAS THAT MORE LAND HAD TO BE PURCHASED, BECAUSE THAT WAS THE ONLY WAY THE BANK FACADE COULD EXTEND BEYOND THE BUILDING DIVIDING THE TWO SQUARES. THE NEW FACADE WOULD HELP UNIFY THE TWO SPACES, ESTABLISHING AND EMBODYING THE CONTINUITY. IT WAS NEITHER NECESSARY NOR POSSIBLE TO KNOCK DOWN THE BUILDING BETWEEN THE TWO SQUARES – IT WAS ENOUGH TO SHOW THE SPACE WAS CONTINUOUS. THIS IS THE FACADE'S ROLE.

THE NEW BUILDING IS AN EXTENSION OF THE OLD ONE, BUT THE ADDITIONS ARE BIGGER THAN THE EXISTING BUILDING. YOU COULDN'T JUST COPY THE ORIGINAL ARCHITECTURE, BUT YOU DO HAVE TO UNDERSTAND IT. THE OLD BUILDER KNEW THERE WERE CRITICAL POINTS, WHICH HAVE TO BE WORKED ON MORE THAN OTHERS.... THE CORNICE, WINDOW, PLINTH, STEPS (A DOMINANT ELEMENT OF THE INTERIOR): THE SAME PLACES AS ALWAYS CONCERNED BUILDERS IN THE PAST. THE PROBLEMS INVOLVED ARE THE SAME AS EVER; ONLY THE ANSWER CHANGES.[15]

CARLO SCARPA, 1978

Extension and reorganization of the Banca Popolare di Verona head office
Verona, 1973–81

Client: Banca Popolare di Verona
Architects: Carlo Scarpa with Arrigo Rudi
Collaborators (studio Scarpa):
Bianca Albertini, Maristella Ronin
Collaborators (studio Rudi): Valter Rossetto, Franco de Franchi, Roberto Ulisse, Giovanni Federici
Structural engineer: Renato Scarazzai
Mechanical engineer: Francesco Zanini
HVAC: Giuseppe Anini
Electrical engineer: Dino Boni
Acoustical engineer: Nello Moresi

Banca Poplare di Verona, courtyard facade under construction, 1979.
Photograph: Dario Busato. Coll. Dario Busato

In the fall of 1973, the Banca Popolare di Verona (then the Banca Mutua Popolare di Verona) called upon Carlo Scarpa to revise a project for the extension and reorganization of its head office in the historic center of Verona. The bank intended to expand onto an adjacent site on Piazza Nogara and Via Conventino, then occupied by two buildings: an extension for the bank's credit services and an apartment house, both twentieth-century Neoclassical pastiches. Scarpa's project was presented for municipal approval in January 1974; a construction permit was granted on 25 February. Scarpa proposed an entirely new building for offices distributed on five floors, including mezzanines: two devoted to customer services, two to the offices of the direction and general administration. The architect developed new facades, one facing the Piazza Nogara, the other the courtyard, at one edge of which Scarpa sank a semicircular garden which provides natural light to the semi-basement floor.

By 1976, important modifications were made to this first project, notably the addition of an elevated circulation tunnel connecting the new building to existing ones across a courtyard and the transformation of the shape of windows in the main facade. The building was completed in 1981, after Scarpa's death, under the supervision of the architect Arrigo Rudi.
J-F B

Guido Guidi. Banca Poplare di Verona, detail of main facade, 1997.
Chromogenic color print, 19.5 x 24.6 cm. Coll. CCA

The Head Office of the Banca Popolare di Verona demonstrated a major development in the way new buildings might intervene in a historic center. This discourse had been opened up by Scarpa's work for Olivetti and was extended in two lesser works prior to the Banca Popolare: the Gavina showroom in Bologna (1961–63) and the Balboni house in Venice (1964–74).

The Gavina (now Simon) showroom on Via Altabella in the historic center of Bologna was built for the manufacturer Dino Gavina, sponsor of most of the great names in post-war Italian furniture design. After his firm's buy-out by Knoll in 1968, Gavina continued his involvement in the design industry by founding the firm Simon International with Maria Simoncini. For that company Scarpa designed numerous pieces of furniture, including the "Doge" (1968) and the "Valmarana" (1972) dining tables and the "Cornaro" sofa (1973). As in the Olivetti showroom, Scarpa attempted to free himself from the constraints imposed by the existing store. He removed existing load-bearing walls and hid the necessary structural supports within large pilasters, each surfaced in a different finish. The plasticity of the new space is accentuated by the receding arrangement of these bold chromatic elements.

The showroom is located in the city center, in an old building on a small street that is without Bologna's typical arcades. The facade, a plane of cast concrete horizontally formed with wooden boards, has three major punctures: a double oval on the left and a single circle on the right, with the entry between them. Large recessed lines set in the concrete and filled with gold leaf anchor the composition of these openings. Scarpa positioned iron elements at the corners of the entry, which changed the perception of scale. He filled the circle openings with iron-framed glass secured with brass clips. Elaborate mosaics and polished wood surfaces were made for an interior with a high sense of color and luxe. While the Olivetti showroom was delicately woven into the existing fabric of the facade, the Gavina intervention was more radical, and it anticipated the sense of a new urban wall realized in the Banca Popolare.

Begun in 1964, the Balboni house is located on the ground and second floors of the northern half of Casa Marioni (later Mainella), a palace built by Lodovico Cadorin in 1858 on the Grand Canal at the intersection of the Rio di San Trovaso. In this apartment Scarpa made several decisive interventions (the project was completed by others). Inside he elaborated on his experiments with light, space, and surface in the Olivetti showroom to construct a serene, sensual, magical set of plaster rooms. The central focus of the apartment is a mathematically complex spiral staircase that occupies the middle of the plan and rises with ease and grace from the lower floor to the upper mezzanine, where two ovoid light wells open to the floor below. The polished marble of the stairway ascends as if it were weightless. The union of stair, circle, oval, and bridge – four of Scarpa's fascinations – into one sculptural form is astonishing. While the interiors of the Olivetti and Gavina showrooms are marked with a Byzantine palette of mixed materials, high color, and gilding, the Balboni house (where the client overruled Scarpa's plans for a polychrome staircase) instead plays with the virtuoso effects of a single material. In a neutral tone, the marble stair is molded from floor to ceiling into a single form, like the lustrous interior of a convoluted seashell. Scarpa's facade studies for the canal side of the house continue the design ideas developed at Gavina, using semicircular openings in large planes of concrete. Again, Scarpa proposes the notion of a thoroughly articulated urban wall that was boldly realized in his last urban project, the Banca Popolare di Verona.

Gavina showroom, entrance hall, c. 1963.
Photograph: Paolo Monti. Istituto di fotografia Paolo Monti, Milan

Guido Guidi. Balboni house, light wells on second floor, 1997.
Chromogenic color print, 19.5 x 24.6 cm. Coll. CCA

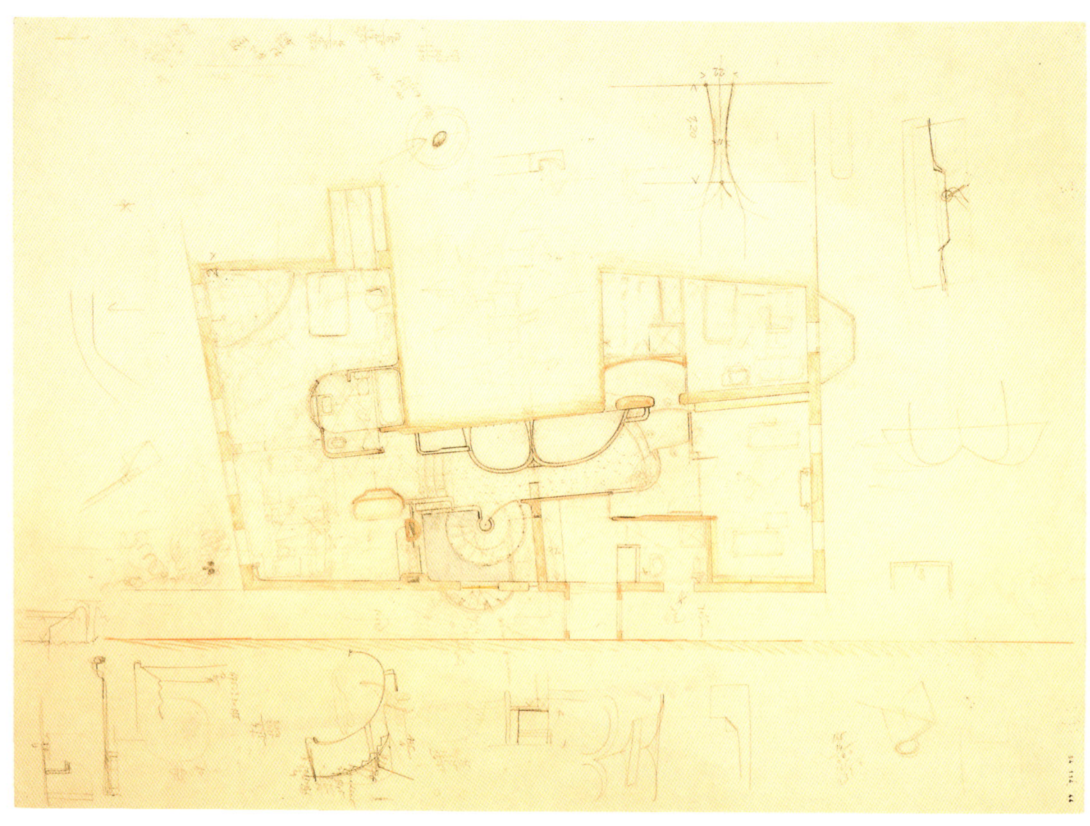

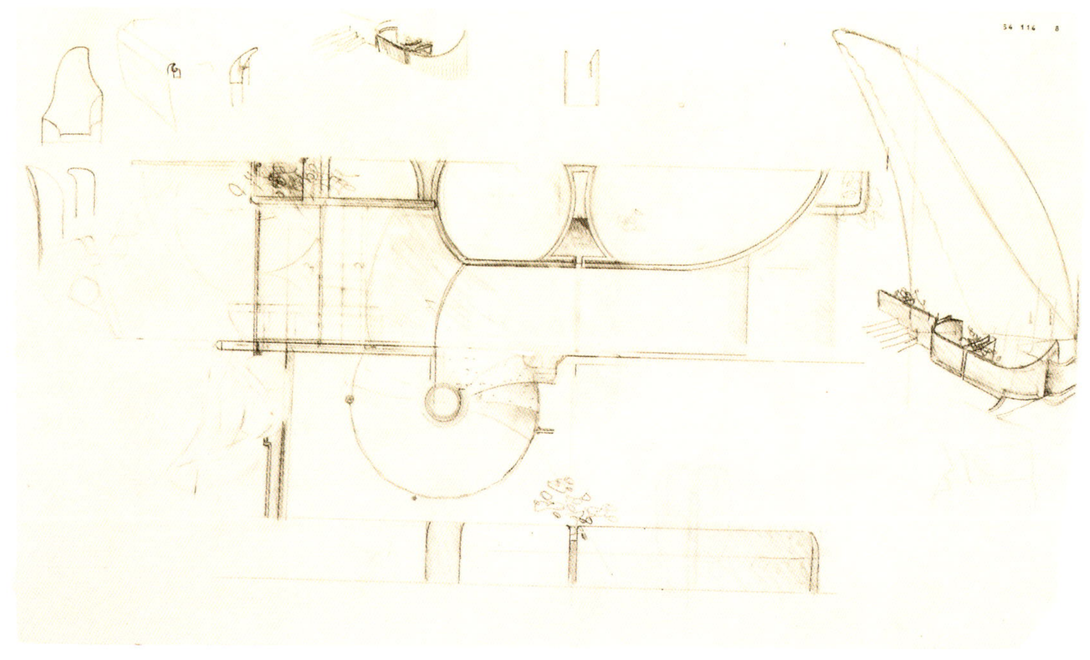

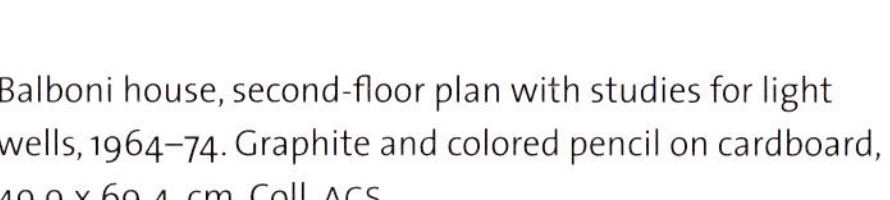

Balboni house, second-floor plan with studies for light wells, 1964–74. Graphite and colored pencil on cardboard, 49.9 x 69.4 cm. Coll. ACS

Balboni house, second-floor plan showing staircase and light wells with studies for light wells, 1964–74. Graphite on tracing paper, 32.9 x 57 cm. Coll. ACS

The scale of the Banca Popolare head office as well as its location near the Roman arena and other Veronese landmarks made it a critical work. The Museo di Castelvecchio had been conceived as a dialogue with its setting, no matter how well evolved and powerful the design became. In the Palazzo Querini Stampalia and the Olivetti showroom, even in the Gavina showroom, Scarpa had modified rather than recast the public facades. The Banca Popolare, however, demanded a new structure within the old center with no existing historical constraints. Scarpa proposed a thin building stretched across a garden with one facade on the Piazza Nogara and another on an interior courtyard. Building on his Gavina experiments, Scarpa did not simply extrude the plan, as was the prevailing norm, but chose instead to explore the meaning of the building's vertical surface by incorporating diverse ideas about the role of the public wall. The Banca Popolare project echoed a traditional aspiration for the facade expressed as an artistic artifact, developed through the building's construction system and reinforced by secondary details.

The Piazza Nogara facade is an exquisite work both in its use of projecting apertures on the surface of the wall and in the tripartite transformation of the wall section from base to middle to top. The bottom of the masonry wall indicates a heavy, thick building. On the next floor, the wall is expressed as a thin screen with various circular openings cut into it. Wood and glass fenestration is set back into the voids, and a small strip extends down from the circular cut-outs holding the run-off drain, which culminates in a small spout. The top floor is a layer of paired steel columns that sit on the masonry. Behind them floats a frame and glass surface more in keeping with an accepted modern vocabulary, and just above the paired columns is a white marble cornice with the same ziggurat motif Scarpa developed for the Brion tomb. Scarpa called it "a line of geometric character, realized with industrial techniques, that lightens the crown of the building." But the facade is more than a composition; its materiality is critical. In its effect, the wall is a layering of multiple materials, rich with shadows cast on varying surfaces. "The sense of space," said Scarpa, "is not communicated by a pictorial order but always by physical phenomena, that is by matter, by the sense of mass, the weight of the wall. This is why I assert that it is the apertures, openings, and orifices that create spatial relationships. Modern architecture, abstractly stereometric, destroys all sensitivity to framework and de-composition."[16]

Other elements accentuate the design of the facade. Some articulate interior space or indicate linkages to the existing building; others are simply decorative. The large void at the right end exposes the stairway connecting the second and third floors. A carved marble ziggurat molding extends horizontally across the length of the facade, moving up and down as it defines the edges of openings. In the thin, middle layer above, Scarpa projected solid stone and glass blocks, volumes that are reminiscent of the vitrines and windows at Possagno. These are linked by vertical stems of the marble ziggurat molding to the horizontal molding below, which terminates at the large bronze entry door. This molding, also used as a bracket under the upper two vitrine windows, serves to organize all the diverse elements on the facade into one composition.

The drawings for the bank clearly explain the journey Scarpa took. Plans illustrate the tension between the building's envelope and the volumetric insertions of the elevator and stair as they were counterposed against the column grid. Early facade studies explore conventional fenestration systems, but as the drawings develop, different iterations of the circle begin to appear, first constant, then in the variable diameters of the final scheme. One composite drawing contains a plan, elevation, and section of the paired columns accompanied by all the necessary details: stone base, beams with brass joints, steel-plate fastener with bolts, and carved stone cornice. The three views communicate clearly the design, spatial position, and joinery of this complex formal strategy as well as its material representation.

The same tripartite strategy was used for the base, middle, and top of the courtyard facade. At the right end, however, the wall contains a massive void, with the glazed drum of the stair situated behind it. At the left end, a bronze tube spans the court, connecting the new structure to an existing building. Both the front and the courtyard facades are of a composite of ground marble dust and cement that produces a dense, rose-colored surface similar to the stucco facades on some of the surrounding buildings. Like the front facade, the upper part of the courtyard wall was designed in structural steel with multiple columns connecting to the masonry wall and bronze elements holding the columns together. A mosaic pattern of small tiles was inlaid into the flange of the beam at the top of the columns. Steel beams on top were joined with plates bolted in intricate patterns. Together, the courtyard and piazza facades allow Scarpa to make a link with the past and create a window to the future.

GR

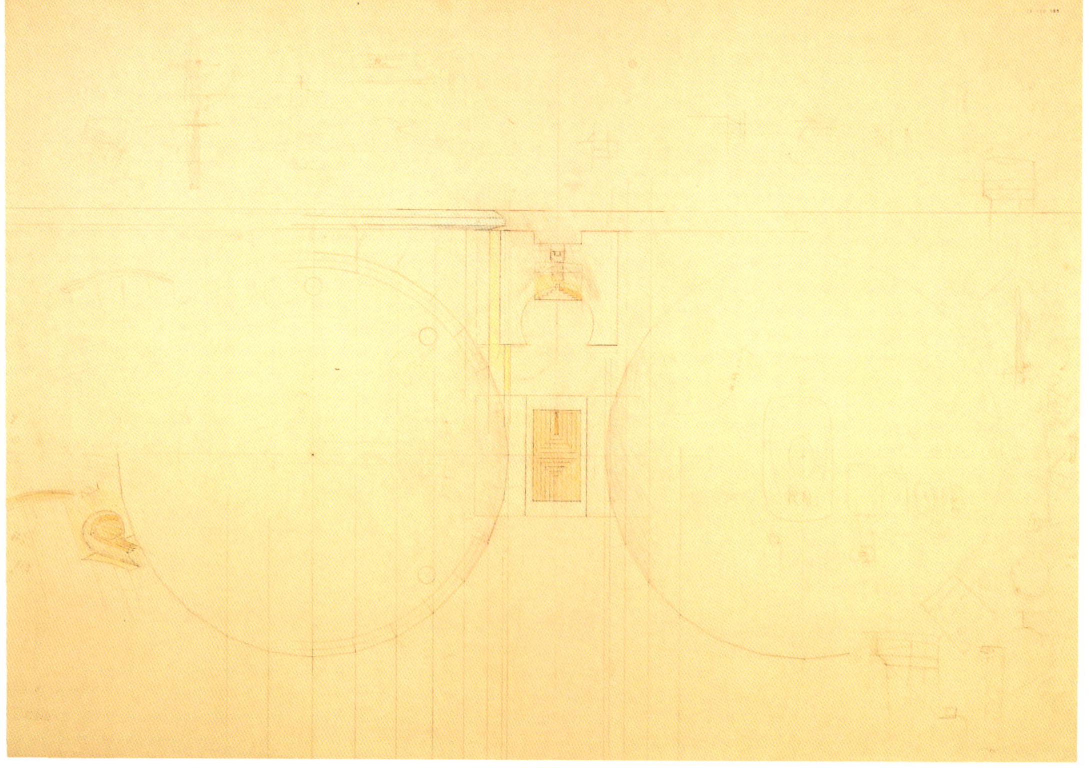

Banca Popolare di Verona, plan and elevation of interior paired columns showing metal fastener, 1973–78. Graphite and colored pencil on cardboard, 69.8 x 100 cm. Coll. ACS

Banca Popolare di Verona, perspective of fastener between interior paired columns, 1973–78. Graphite and colored pencil on cardboard, 49.9 x 70 cm. Coll. ACS

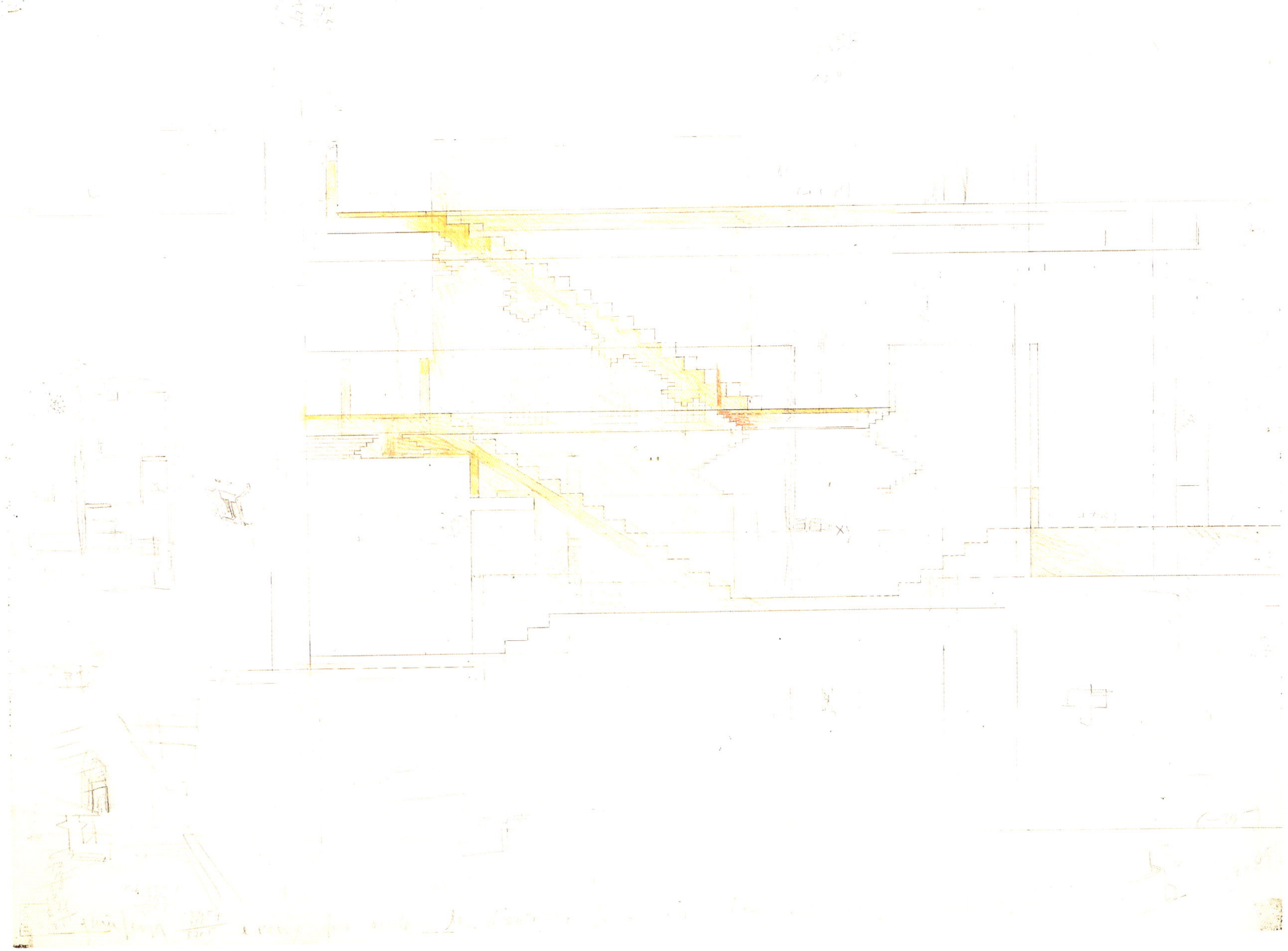

Banca Popolare di Verona, section of main entrance and staircase, 1973–78. Graphite and colored pencil on cardboard, 48.1 x 65.9 cm. Coll. ACS

Although conceived for three very different projects, the facade designs for the Gavina showroom, the renovation of the Balboni house, and the extension of the Banca Popolare share many common characteristics. All include variations on the theme of the circular opening, an important element in Scarpa's formal vocabulary. But in all three projects, faced with the problem of inserting a radically modern form within an existing building and urban context, Scarpa resorts to the same design strategy: the thin appliquéd facade.

The facade of the Gavina showroom is a large slab of textured concrete stretching along the entire facade of the furniture shop, superimposed upon the exterior wall of the existing building. Scarpa punctures this abstract field with three openings bearing little relation to the rest of the building. Scarpa details the steel window frames to minimize their presence. In the manner of a painterly composition, the openings are linked to each other with gilded bands recessed into the surface of the concrete.

In an unrealized design for the entrance facade of the Balboni house, Scarpa develops the facade in two distinct planes, each with its own geometry: the orthogonal order of the window openings and their frames and the skinlike outside surface, into which Scarpa carves half-circular openings responding to the rectangular windows.

The concept of the double wall recurs in Scarpa's most important experiment in the design of an urban wall: the front facade of the Banca Popolare di Verona. Scarpa intended to regroup the services of the bank into a single volume. That intention is made apparent by a unified facade that reinterprets the tripartite division (base/wall/cornice) of the facade of the existing head office and bridges the two parts of the public square it faces. Yet Scarpa's nod to the compositional order of classical architecture is undermined by his expression of the facade as a thin membrane. As in the Balboni design, Scarpa recesses the orthogonal window frames behind the facade wall into which the architect punctures circular openings; alternatively, he designs windows that are glass boxes attached to the wall surface. Scarpa terminates the facade with a clerestory of windows punctuated by double steel columns and an ornamented stone cornice.

J-F B

Gavina showroom, facade elevation, 1961–63. Graphite and colored pencil on paper, 49.8 x 69.9 cm. Coll. ACS

Balboni house, elevation of garden facade, 1964–74. Graphite and colored pencil on cardboard, 35.1 x 70.2 cm. Coll. ACS

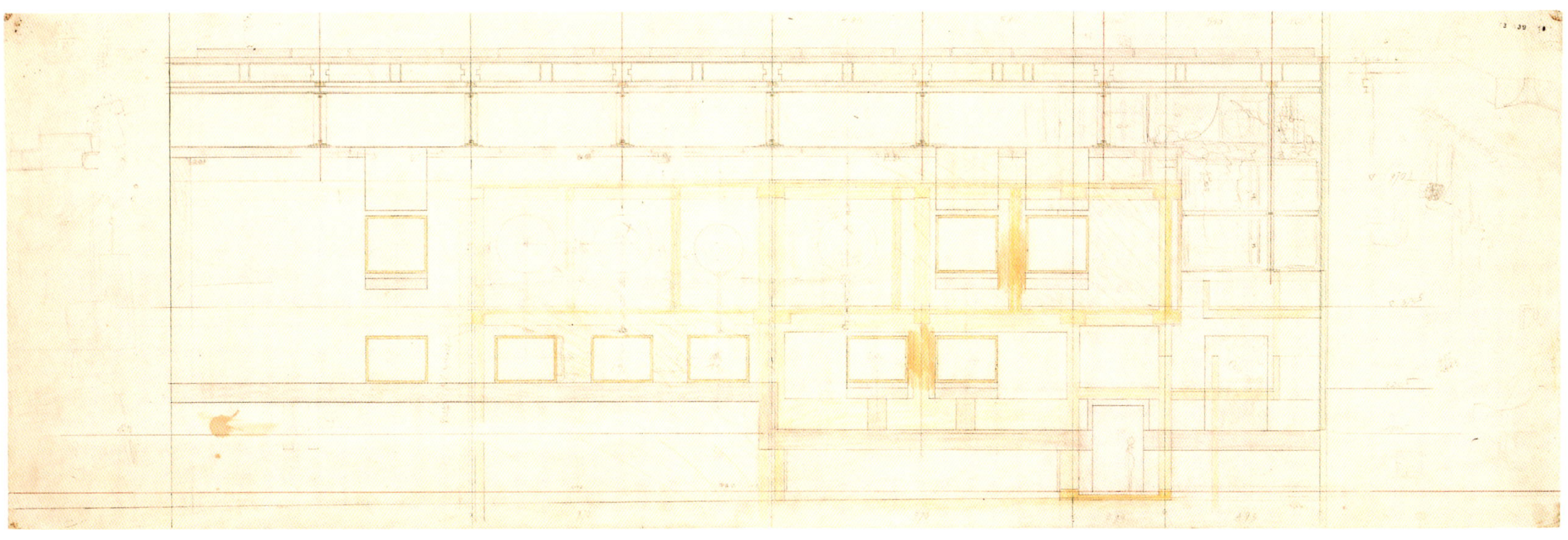

Banca Popolare di Verona, preliminary elevation of main facade, 1973–78. Graphite on tracing paper, 32.3 x 99.8 cm. Coll. ACS

Banca Popolare di Verona, elevation of main facade, 1973–78. Graphite and colored pencil on cardboard, 32.4 x 100.4 cm. Coll. ACS

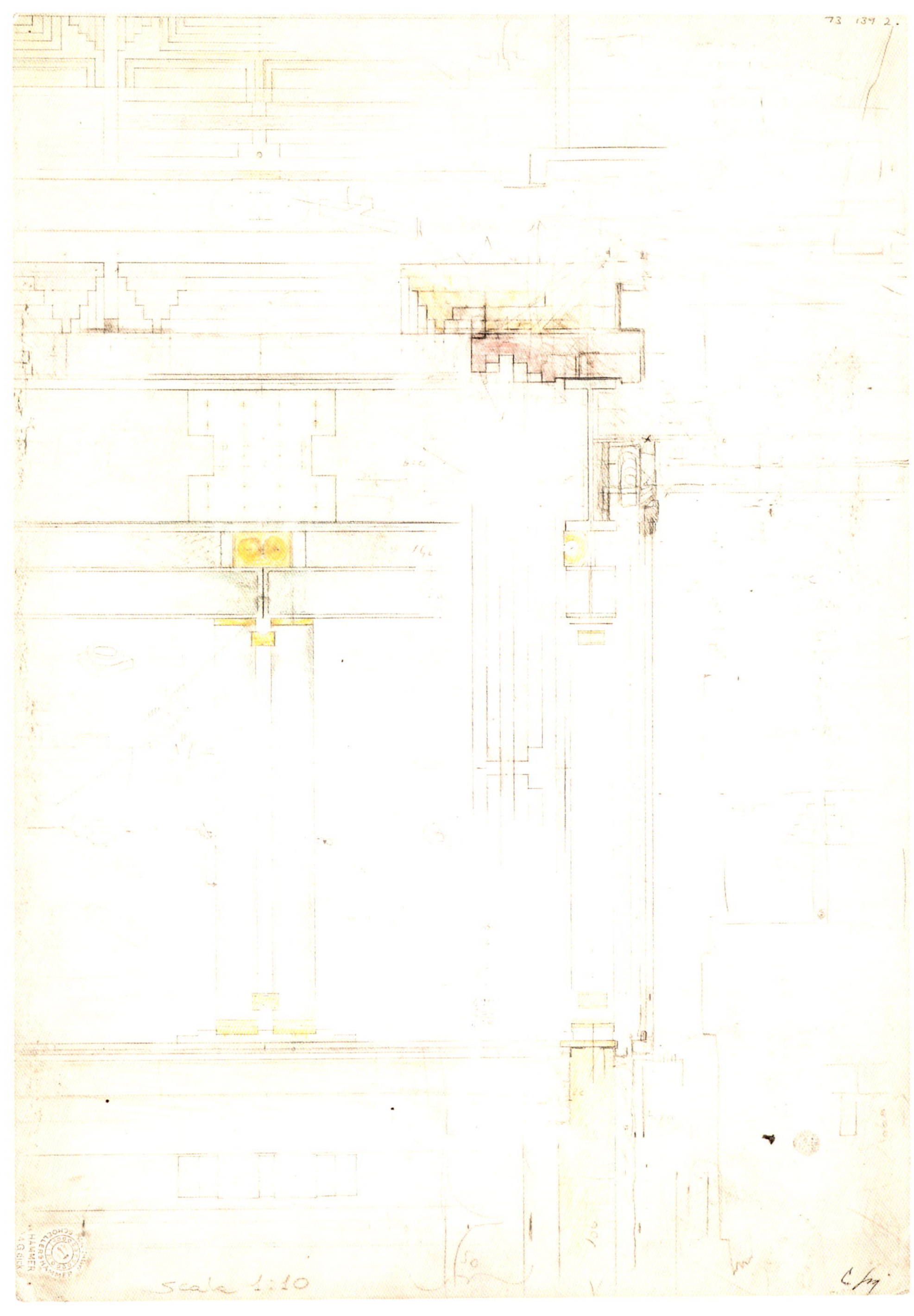

Banca Popolare di Verona, elevation, section, plans, and details of paired columns, 1973–78. Graphite and colored pencil on cardboard, 50.8 x 36.4 cm. Coll. ACS

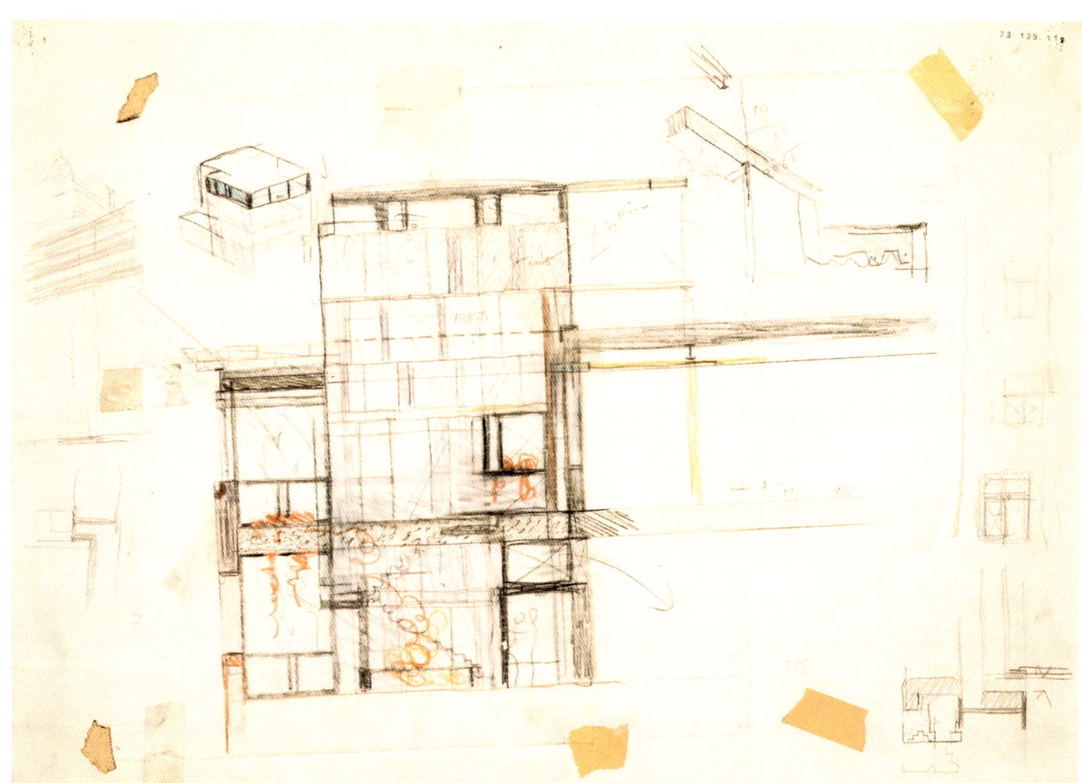

Banca Popolare di Verona, preliminary elevation of courtyard facade, 1973–78. Graphite and colored pencil on tracing paper, 29.9 x 61 cm. Coll. ACS

Banca Popolare di Verona, section-elevation and axonometric of elevator and staircase tower, 1973–78. Graphite and colored pencil on tracing paper, 34.9 x 49.9 cm. Coll. ACS

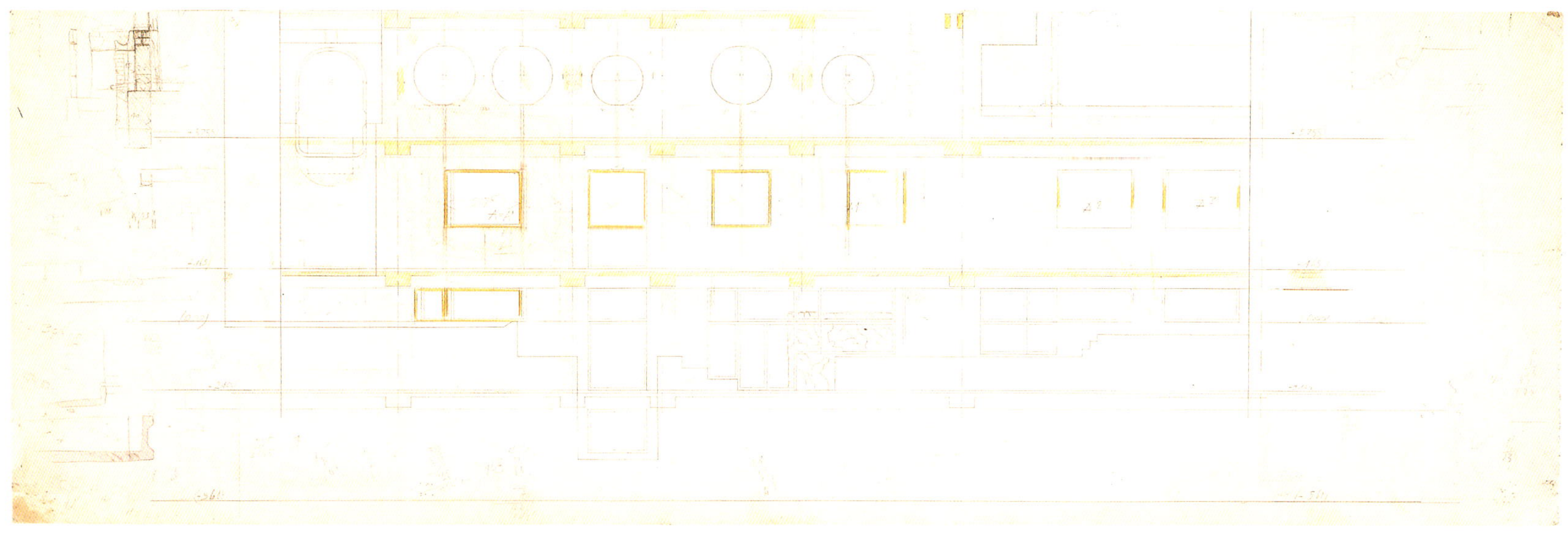

Banca Popolare di Verona, partial elevation of courtyard facade showing elevator and staircase tower, 1973–78. Graphite and colored pencil on cardboard, 35.1 x 49.8 cm. Coll. ACS

Banca Popolare di Verona, partial elevation of courtyard facade, 1973–78. Graphite and colored pencil on cardboard, 32.3 x 99.8 cm. Coll. ACS

BRION FAMILY TOMB

I CONSIDER THIS WORK, IF YOU PERMIT ME, TO BE RATHER GOOD AND [SOMETHING] WHICH WILL EVEN GET BETTER OVER TIME. I HAVE TRIED TO PUT SOME POETIC IMAGINATION INTO IT, THOUGH NOT IN ORDER TO CREATE POETIC ARCHITECTURE BUT TO MAKE A CERTAIN KIND OF ARCHITECTURE THAT COULD EMANATE A SENSE OF FORMAL POETRY. I MEAN AN EXPRESSED FORM THAT CAN BECOME POETRY, THOUGH, AS I SAID BEFORE, YOU CANNOT INTENTIONALLY MAKE POETRY.

THE DECEASED HAD ASKED TO BE CLOSE TO [THE] EARTH SINCE HE WAS BORN IN THIS VILLAGE – SO I DECIDED TO BUILD A SMALL ARCH, WHICH I WILL CALL ARCOSOLIUM. (ARCOSOLIUM IS A LATIN TERM FROM THE TIME OF THE EARLY CHRISTIANS IN THE CATACOMBS. IMPORTANT PERSONS OR MARTYRS WERE BURIED IN THEM.) I USED A MORE COSTLY VERSION.... I THOUGHT IT [WAS] A GOOD IDEA FOR TWO PEOPLE WHO HAD LOVED EACH OTHER TO BE PUT IN SUCH A WAY AS TO BE ABLE TO GREET ONE ANOTHER, AFTER DEATH. SOLDIERS STAND ERECT, MOVEMENTS ARE HUMAN. THE ARCOSOLIUM BECAME AN ARCH, A BRIDGE SPAN, AN ARCH OF REINFORCED CONCRETE AND WOULD STILL HAVE LOOKED LIKE A BRIDGE IF I HADN'T HAD IT ILLUSTRATED, I MEAN DECORATED. BUT INSTEAD OF PAINTING WE USED MOSAICS, A VENETIAN TRADITION THAT I INTERPRETED IN A DIFFERENT WAY.[17]

CARLO SCARPA, 1976

Brion family tomb
San Vito d'Altivole (Treviso)
1969–78

Client: Onorina Brion
Landscape architect: Pietro Porcinai
Collaborators: Guido Pietropoli, Carlo Maschietto
Contractor: Ditta Prati

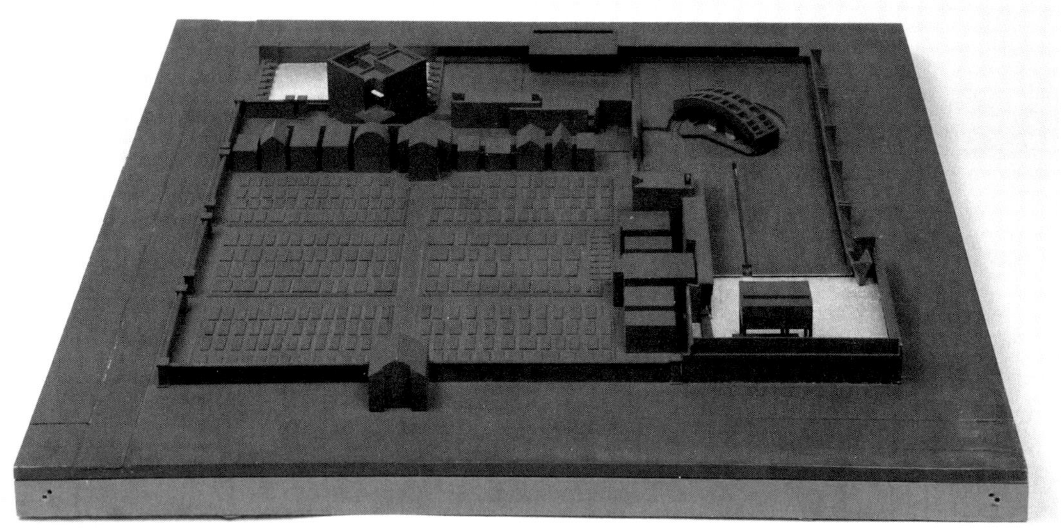

Carlo Scarpa, designer; unknown modelmaker. Site model, 1971. Painted and gilded wood, 60.5 x 60.5 x 13.2 cm. Coll. British Architectural Library, RIBA, London

Shortly after her husband's death in September 1968, Onorina Brion (née Tomasin), co-founder with Giuseppe Brion of the innovative electronics firm Brion-Vega, called upon Carlo Scarpa to design a tomb for her late husband, herself, and their family in the municipal cemetery of San Vito d'Altivole northwest of Treviso. The family already owned a rectangular site and a funerary chapel in the northeast corner of the cemetery in Giuseppe Brion's place of birth. Scarpa's earliest designs were conceived for this site and followed a program limited to tombs for the Brion couple and their family. In these schemes, altogether different from the final project, Scarpa generates the key elements that will remain until the end: the "arcosolium" sheltering the sarcophagi of the Brion couple (so named by Scarpa following the burial arches of early Christians) and the pavilion surrounded by water that, in this early stage, served to protect the tombs of the Brion relatives.

In May 1969 the family purchased an L-shaped plot of land along the northern and eastern edges of the cemetery. By March 1970, at the time of the municipal review and approval of the construction documents, the funerary complex approached its final form. Three principal elements, each situated in a corner of the site, structure Scarpa's plan. The arcosolium is moved to the northeastern area to benefit, in Scarpa's own words, from the best view and the sunniest exposure. Situated in the corner of the L, it acts as a planimetric and visual hinge between the northern and eastern portions of the plot. Scarpa completely reconfigures the family graves and places them under a pitched canopy in the center of the north perimeter wall. He nevertheless retains the idea of a pavilion in a pond, this time without tombs, at the southern end of the site. Finally, in the western end, Scarpa designs a square chapel which he connects to the country road through a cypress grove doubling as a burial ground for the local priests. A second access, enclosed by an aediculum (which Scarpa called a "propylaeum"), links the Brion site to the existing cemetery at the point where the original Brion funerary chapel had stood.

J-F B

1 Propylaeum
2 Water pavilion
3 Pool
4 Arcosolium
5 Scarpa's grave
6 Family tomb
7 Sacristy
8 Chapel
9 Pond
10 Cypress grove
11 Lych gate
12 Perimeter wall

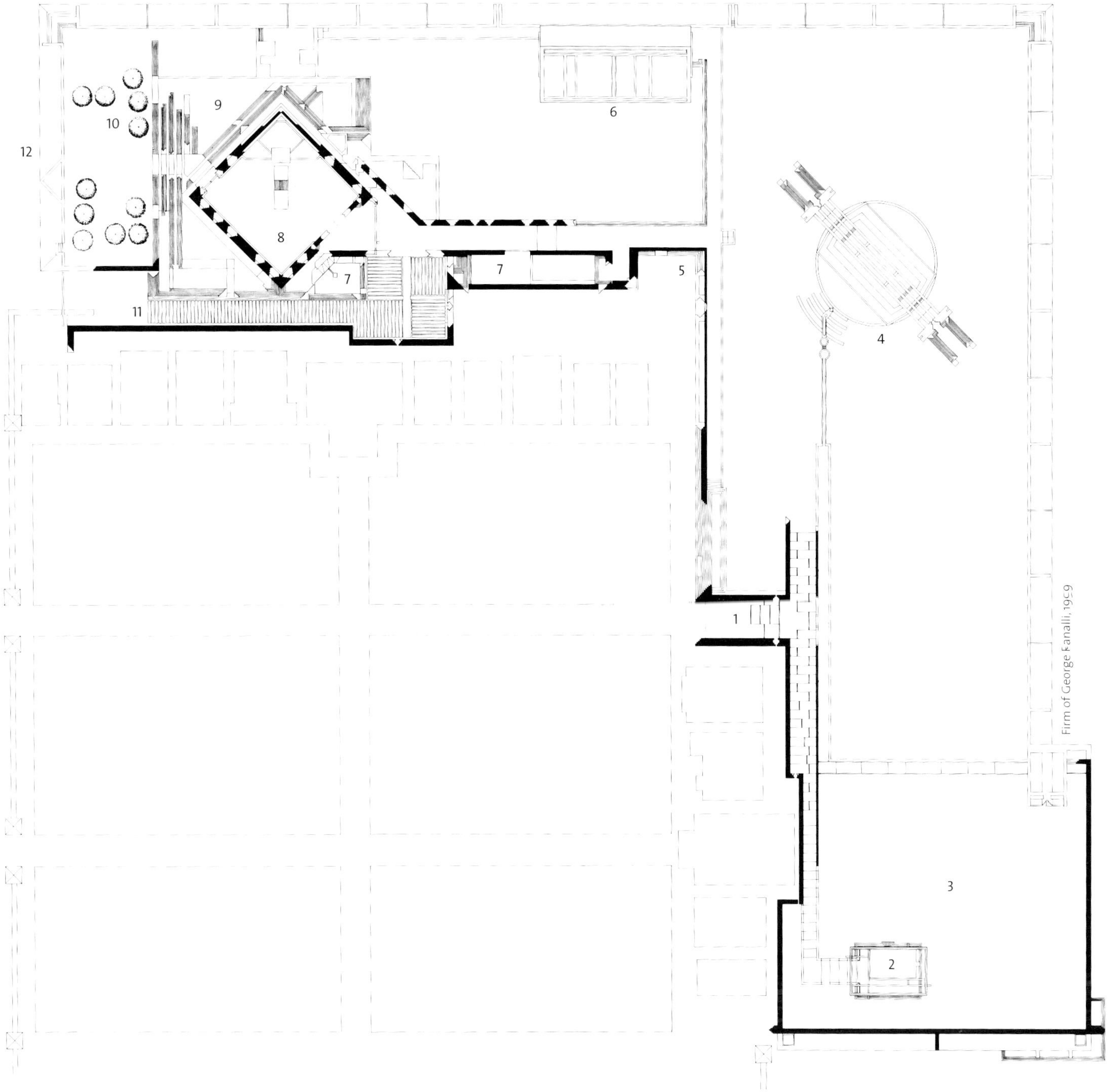

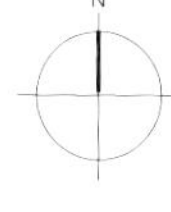

Firm of George Ranalli, 1989

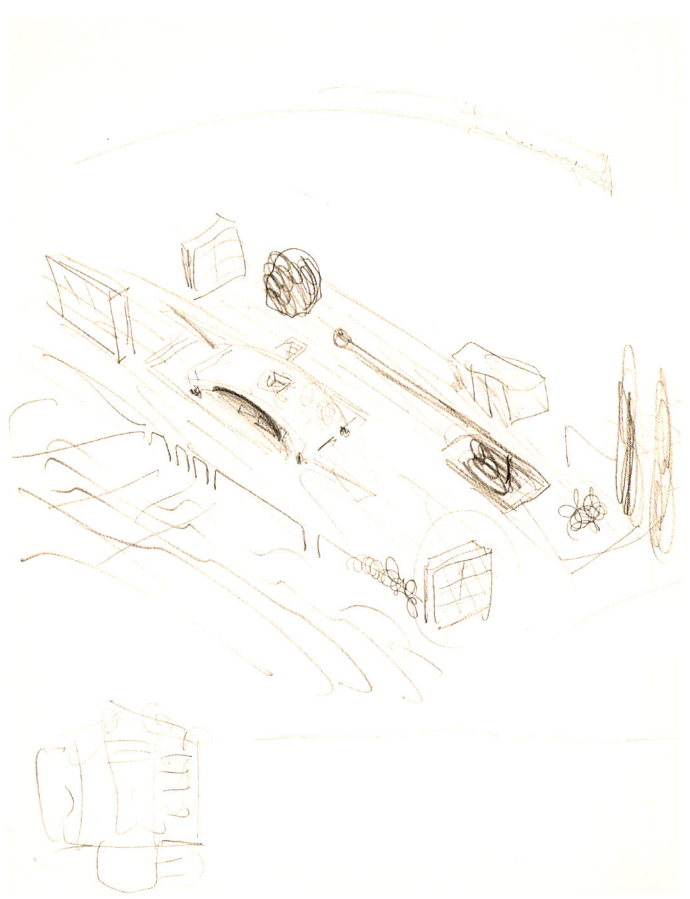

Bird's-eye perspective and studies for rectangular site, 1969. Graphite on wove paper in notebook, 34.5 x 28 cm. Coll. ACS

Bird's-eye perspective for L-shaped site showing walls of existing cemetery with sketch elevation for water pavilion, 1969. Pen-and-ink on vellum in notebook, 28 x 34.5 cm. Coll. ACS

THE BRION TOMB IS THE TRIUMPHANT masterwork of Scarpa's final years, raising his material, formal, and symbolic inquiry to a poetic level unparalleled in its time. Although the Brion family spent most of their lives in Milan, they wished to be buried in San Vito d'Altivole, their town of origin. The cemetery, a grid of monuments and mausoleums in the traditional image of a city of the dead, was located in a field on the town's outskirts. Scarpa's construction was both a private family tomb and an extension of the existing public cemetery. What it provided, essentially, was a public open space for the little town. The notion that monuments to the dead can embody social ideas about life and death, and serve as a collective expression, is an old one. In Aldo Rossi's design for the Cemetery of San Cataldo, Modena (1971–78), which was contemporary with the Brion tomb, the ossuary and the empty house were both used to revive the notion of a collective. Scarpa too saw his cemetery as civic in nature, as a place for picnics and play as well as for meditation on the great questions of life, death, nature, and society. Working within the terms of the existing walled *camposanto*, he enfolded the new plot – an L-shaped piece of land bordering the cemetery on two of its three sides – with a new wall. Upon it he composed an open lawn, a lily pond, a meditation space, the tomb for the Brions, a space to contain the family headstones, and a chapel.

Instead of using the structures as the dominant elements, as Rossi had done at Modena, Scarpa suppressed the forms and increased the open space. Visitors are free to wander in this space, to decipher the meanings implied in the architecture or, as Scarpa suggested, to invent their own, as if in an allegorical garden. Although Rossi and Scarpa began with different approaches and intentions, the two projects deal with very similar issues. The Modena cemetery was a public project; the Brion tomb was a private burial ground made public by Scarpa. While it would seem that Scarpa was concerned with the architecture of the garden rather than with the city, Brion viewed from the adjacent fields becomes a walled city waiting to be entered and experienced. The extraordinary impact of Rossi's cemetery was made with strong elemental forms; Scarpa took very simple forms and elaborated them through juxtaposition, detail, and design. But the strength of both schemes is in their public character. "Almost all cemeteries look like boxes, ... I wanted to show some ways in which you could approach death in a social and civic way; and further [to express] what meaning there was in death, in the ephemerality of life – other than ... shoe-boxes."[18]

Flat stone grave markers line the path as one enters the old cemetery gates; mausoleums define the back edge. In a corner of the public cemetery, a simple gravestone marks the secluded, but appropriate, location of Carlo Scarpa's interment in this, his final work. At the end of the axis is the entrance building, or propylaeum, of the new complex. From a distance, the great doorway looks like the entrance to another mausoleum, but closer inspection reveals a weeping larch carefully draped across, acting as a protecting door, yet allowing a view of the interior space. The left wall opens onto a view of the garden space and of the shell covering the two tombs in the distance. On the walls of the interior hall are white cement shapes with brass coins set into the concrete, meant to recall the markers used in Roman catacombs and in wall tombs. Cor-ten steel is embedded in the concrete of the ceiling and floor. In front, two intertwined steel circles inlaid with glass tiles on the edge of the frame are cut into the concrete wall and allow another view into the garden. The circles may well represent the lives of the two people the monument commemorates as well as the indivisibility of life and death.

To the right the space narrows and the cor-ten steel in the floor refocuses the path, indicating spatial change. At the narrowing point a glass and steel door opens onto a platform that appears to float on top of the water. It leads to the meditation platform, which turns the visitor around and focuses the visitor's vision directly on the tomb at the other end of the line of sight. This meditation space sits in a large pool of water, and the platform is detailed in such a way that the supports going into the water are not visible. Covered by a wooden canopy held up with four legs of cor-ten steel cut, shifted, and reconnected by brass joints, the platform, although physically fixed, appears to entertain the possibility of motion.

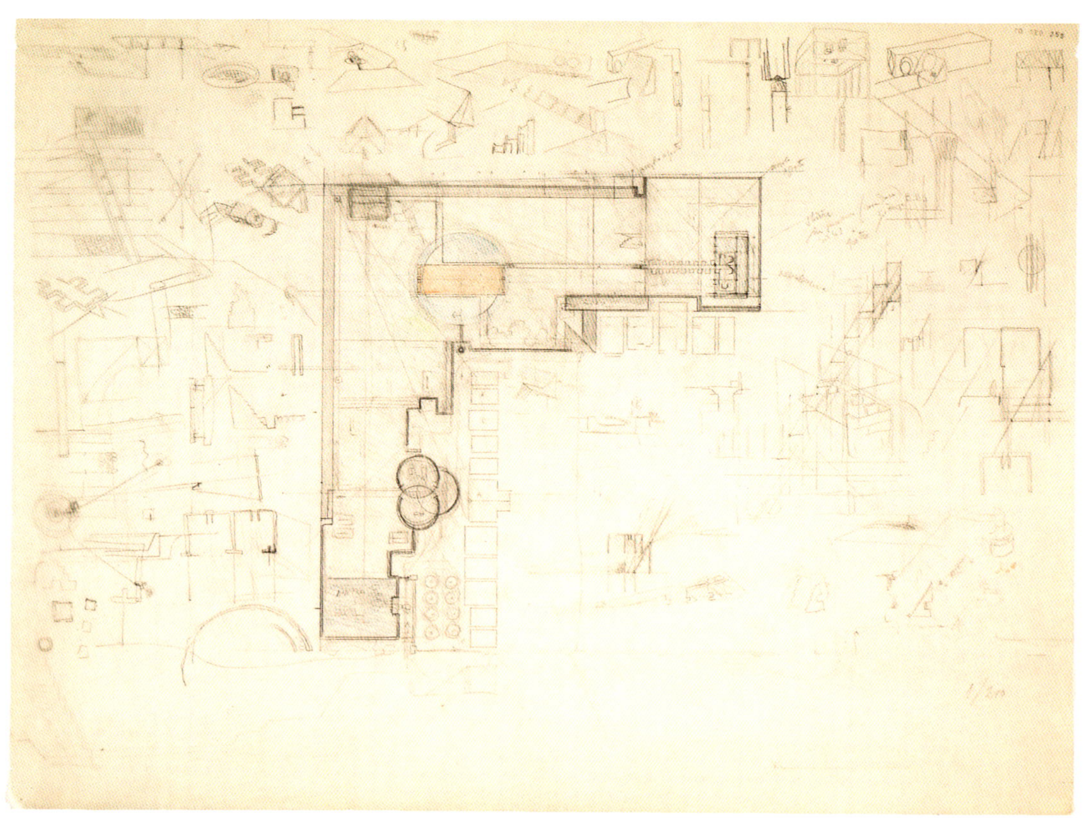

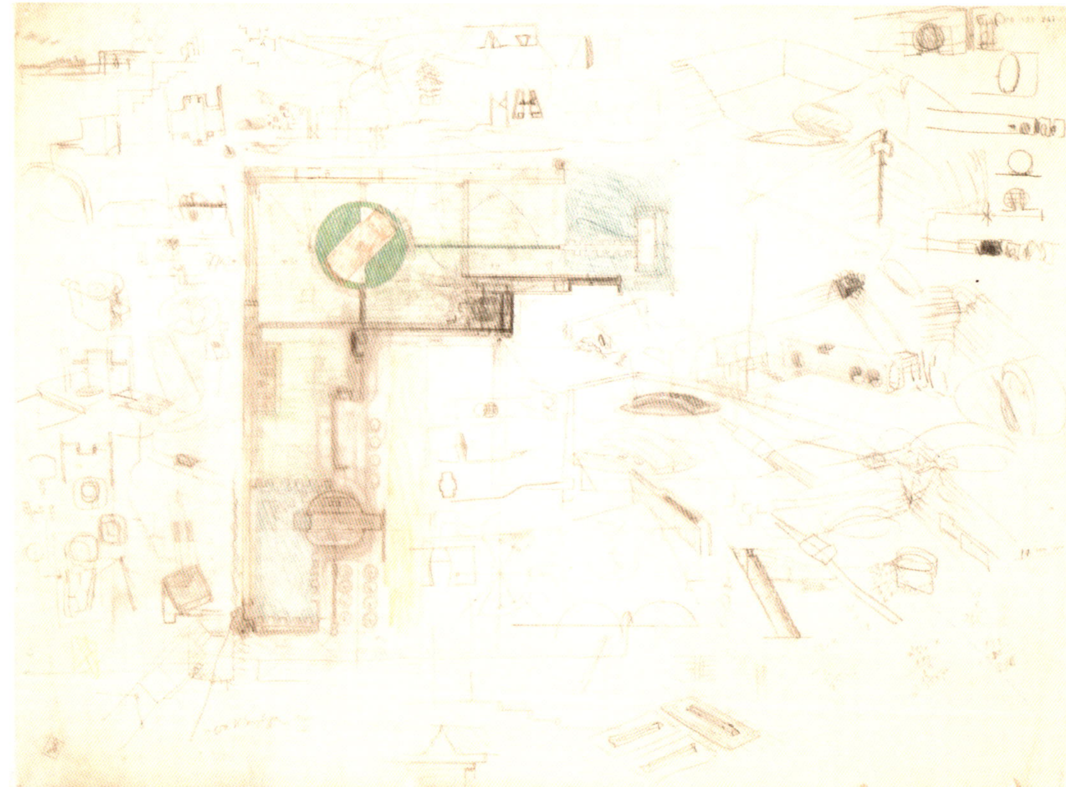

Preliminary overall plan with studies for perimeter wall, propylaeum, pool, and water pavilion, c. 1969–70. Graphite and colored pencil on tracing paper, 45 x 62.5 cm. Coll. ACS

Preliminary overall plan with studies for perimeter wall, propylaeum, pool, and water pavilion, c. 1969–70. Colored electrostatic print and blue ink on drafting film, 44.7 x 62.2 cm. Coll. ACS

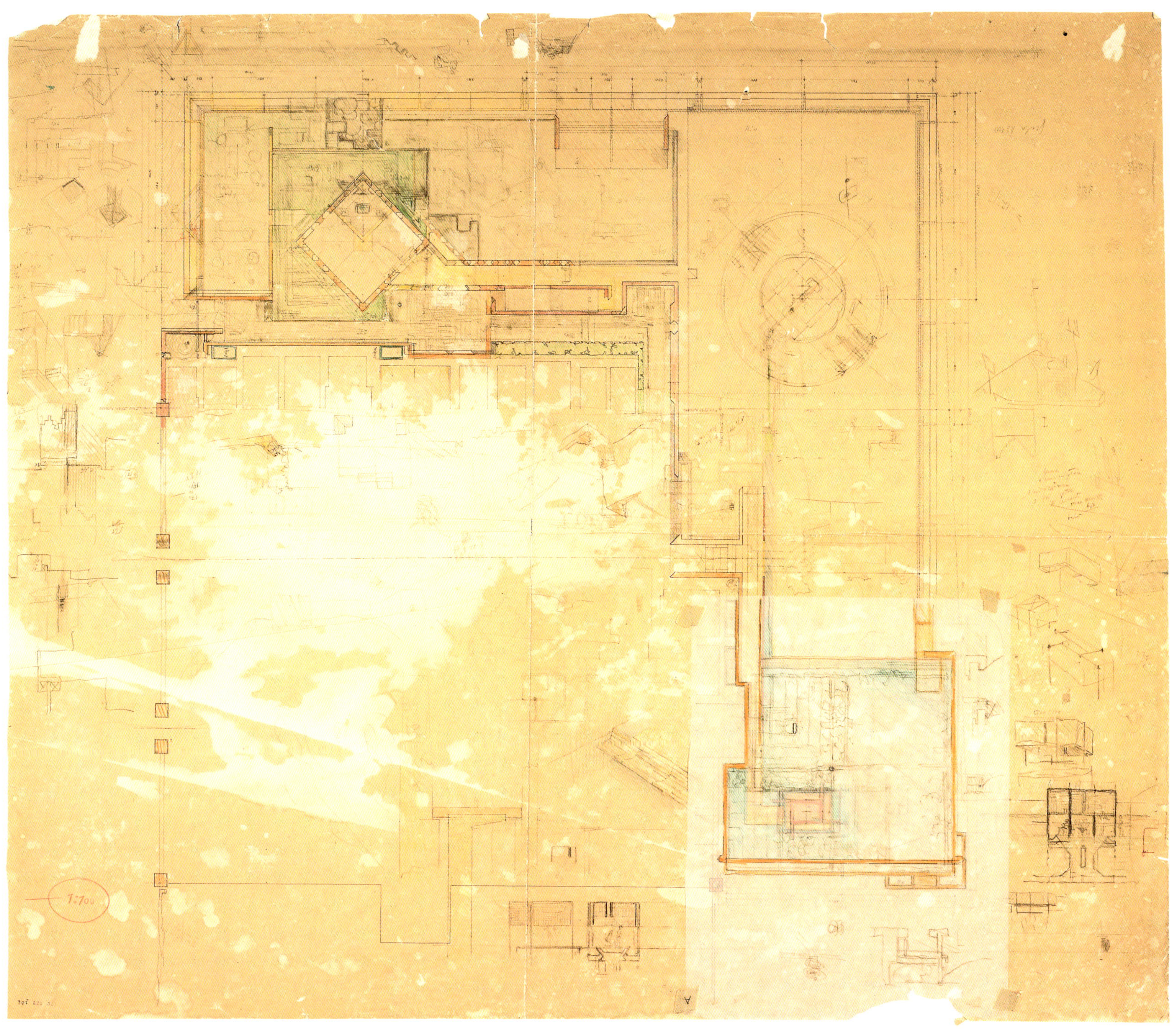

Overall plan with studies for water pavilion (lower right) and other elements, c. 1970–74. Reprographic print with colored pencil on drafting film overlay, 82.5 x 98.3 cm. Coll. ACS

Perspective studies of propylaeum entrance, c. 1970–74.
Graphite on cardboard, 18.8 x 69.8 cm. Coll. ACS

Perspective of east facade of propylaeum with pool, c. 1970–74.
Graphite on tracing paper, 28.2 x 49 cm. Coll. ACS

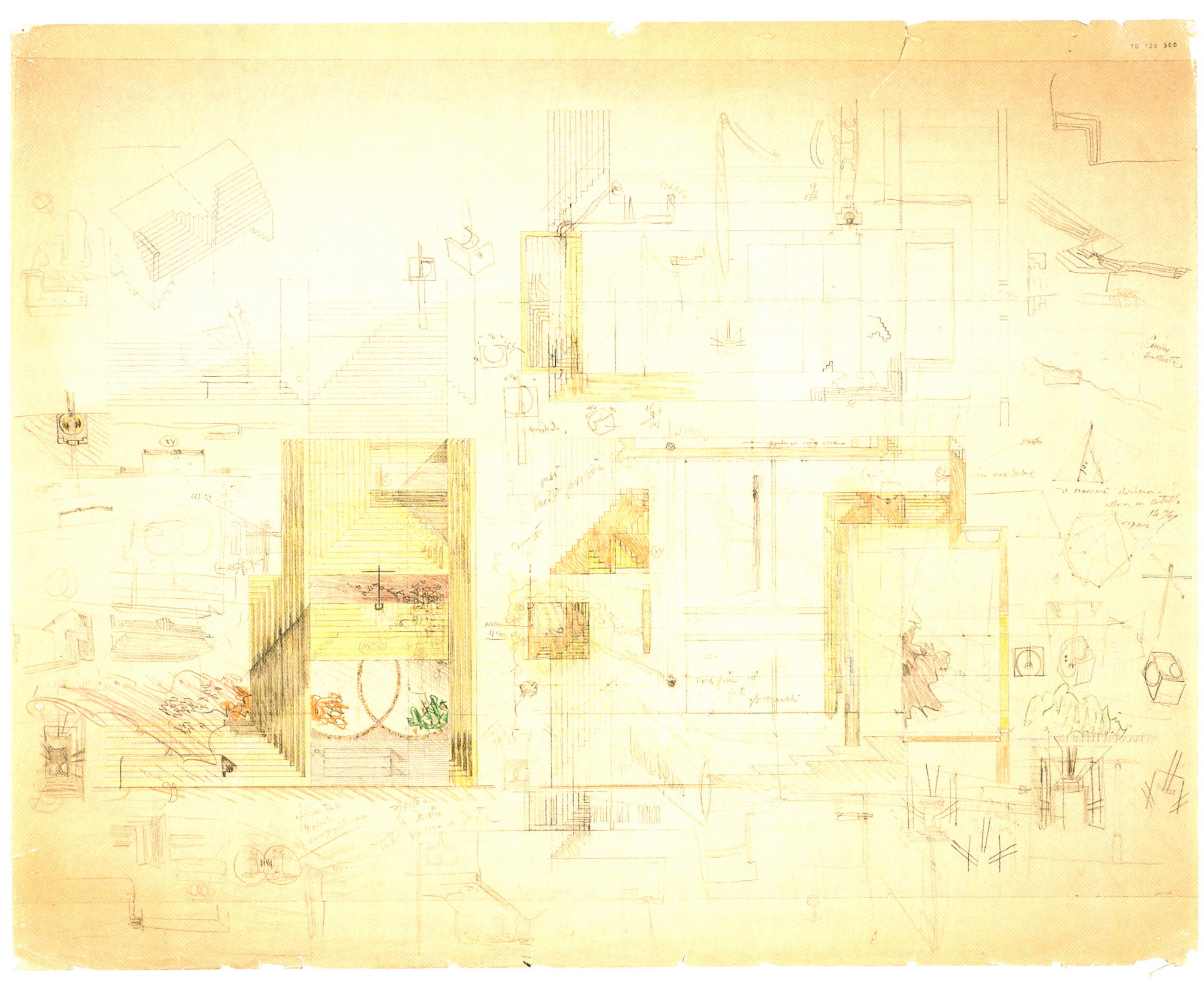

Elevation, plan, and horizontal section of propylaeum entrance with detail studies, c. 1970–74. Graphite and colored pencil on reprographic print, 60.5 x 77.5 cm. Coll. ACS

The plan of the area holding the tombs acts as a hinge, the connecting element of the entire L-shaped composition. While everything else is orthogonal, this sector is curved in plan and in elevation. Small steps cut into the earth lead down to the tombs themselves. They rest on a pad under the low curved arcosolium, which is anchored to the earth by two massive concrete retainers. These forms are molded and shaped with a continuous stepping that reaches out and back onto the lawn – restraining the physical and visual thrust of the arch and repeating the pyramidal theme found in the chapel and the boundary walls. Massive arched concrete beams run across the center, springing from buttressed ends. The canopy is like a thin stretched membrane that becomes more attenuated as it moves away from the beam. The concrete seems to be applied in four stepped layers. The surface is smooth at the edges, but the rest of it is scratched to reveal the aggregate. The underside of the arch hangs very low. Embedded in its surface are green, blue, and gold glass tiles; highly reflective, they fill the space with an extraordinary green glow.

The pair of freestanding sarcophagi are curved at their bases and lean in toward one another, as if about to touch. White marble at the base with a black stone top, each box holds a slatted ebony nameplate, inlaid with ivory letters. The meticulous carving and the color of these objects make them a formidable part of the garden. Over time, the lush vegetation growing over the canopy has given the tomb the appearance of a grotto and sets it apart from the other objects and buildings in the complex. One can look back from under the canopy and survey the garden as if from some hidden place.

One of the elements visible from this vantage point is the roof over the headstones of the family tomb. This form is both part of the outer wall of the complex and an extraordinarily powerful object in itself. The roof supports consist of two large blocks of concrete whose sloped, hooded cover looks as if it has been pushed back. Although the space is voluminous, a slit along the top of the form allows light to filter through and play against the wall. Under this canopy are the various grave markers for the other family members, which were designed to recall the products made by Brion-Vega. Cast on the ground almost randomly, these assertive objects in black and white stone resemble adding machines or computers. They all carry cuts, indents, or gouges, as if they had been subjected to some violent act. The roof of the family tomb, leaning on the wall of the compound, resonates magically against the mountains in the distance, recalling their profile in concrete.

The chapel (rotated forty-five degrees to the geometry of the garden) and its attendant outdoor spaces lie at the opposite end of the L-shaped plot from the meditation platform. Approached from the tomb, the structure develops the connection between the new complex and the old cemetery and functions as a chapel for both the family and the village. A second entrance connects to the old cemetery, along a processional path that opens directly onto the street and accommodates the movement of caskets to the chapel. A large gate in the wall of the compound announces the beginning of the funerary route, a path lined with concrete strips spaced to allow grass to grow between them. Over time, the cortege wagon wheels have worn down the grass, leaving tracks that provide a visible communal memory of the passage of the dead.

Square in plan, the chapel appears different in section and elevation. One quarter of the plan becomes a pyramidal volume that rises over the altar and gives vertical form to the elevation. Scarpa accentuated this by redirecting the boards forming the concrete from vertical to horizontal. The entrance to the chapel is through one large pivoting door sized to accommodate a coffin and made of a deep section of cor-ten steel and white cement plaster. A second ebony door contained within it allows for individual passage. Once inside, one moves from a vestibule through a large circular opening, reminiscent of the circles in the propylaeum, into the chapel itself, an open space paved with small granite blocks. In the corner of the room over the altar the concrete ceiling begins a ziggurat figure, changing to wood at midpoint and culminating in a square skylight. Behind the sheet-brass altar are two small doors that open to admit reflected light from a pool around the chapel, dappling the walls and ceiling. Another pair of plaster and cor-ten steel doors lead out across concrete stepping stones to an enclosure between the water and the cemetery wall. Protected by cypress trees, this

Bird's-eye perspective of the arcosolium with studies of the exterior curve of the arch and the mosaic decoration, c. 1970–74. Graphite and colored pencil on paper, 22 x 28 cm. Coll. ACS

Perspective, plan, and sections of the arcosolium, c. 1970–74. Graphite and colored pencil on cardboard, 16 x 20.5 cm. Coll. ACS

space is accessible only from the chapel. The stepping stones lie barely above water and continue below its surface in ziggurat lines of concrete connected to the wall of the chapel itself. Each elevation of the chapel is treated with unique compositional dexterity, clarity, and invention.

Scarpa cants the wall around the entire complex, conveying the impression of a walled city or fortification. Spaced intervals reveal structural buttresses, and where the wall turns corners a lattice opening of formed concrete appears. Ivy and local growth now cover the wall and have transformed the strict geometric forms of the original construction into an earthen shape that merges into the landscape, blurring the distinction between built and natural elements. Nevertheless, the scale, size, and density of the complex give it a distinct presence.

Scarpa's drawings of the Brion tomb are exceptional. Each full study is a rigorous orthographic working of the plan, section, and elevation that organizes the complicated ziggurat concrete forms in three dimensions with exacting measure. These didactic drawings were then lushly colored to convey their poetry. Surrounding the orthographic drawings are dozens of sketches revealing the true complexity of the three-dimensional shapes. From these drawings it is clear that Scarpa's working method and his constructional certainty were fused in this, his most powerful work.

GR

Plan of the water-pavilion roof with plan and perspective studies of the arcosolium, c. 1970–74. Graphite and colored pencil on paper, 21.8 x 27.9 cm. Coll. ACS

THE WATER PAVILION

Originally designed as a burial structure for the Brion relatives, the water pavilion takes on, in its final form, a secular, meditative function. The site plans show that Scarpa had originally linked the pavilion to the lawn (*prato* or *gazon* in Scarpa's annotations) and to the arcosolium beyond it via a serrated path. In its final form, it retains only its visual alignment to the center of the circumference of the arcosolium. Scarpa erected several barriers between the pavilion and the remaining portions of the funerary complex. These include the expanse of the pool, a surface left unbroken when Scarpa shifted the path leading to the pavilion to its side; a cluster of steel cables (*tirante*) stretched across the lawn; and finally the sliding glass door that closes the corridor leading to the pool. As these barriers intimate, the pavilion is conceived by Scarpa as the only truly "private" portion of the Brion tomb, with chapel, lawn, and tombs belonging to the public domain.

Scarpa's complex design for the tomb-pavilion was greatly simplified when it was moved to its current location. Although Scarpa starts with the simple theme of a box resting on four stilts, he nevertheless achieves a high degree of proportional and rhythmical complexity. He places the columns in a pinwheel pattern, each located away from the corners, before enriching their expression by doubling the steel sections and splicing the columns. The simple volume of the pavilion's roof hides a complex section where solids and voids are arranged to generate precise light effects. Traces of Scarpa's metrical studies are preserved in the exterior surface of the pavilion, where they determine the disposition of the rough-cut spruce planks and that of the rivets of the skirt-like metallic lower portion.

In later drawings, the pavilion's function as viewing apparatus oriented towards the arcosolium becomes clear. In many sections and elevations, Scarpa positions male and female figures at the pavilion's transverse axis, marked by a wide slit in its steel skirt. Scarpa's female figures view the arcosolium through a rectangular metallic piece out of which Scarpa has hollowed a double circle that frames their eyes. In Scarpa's drawings, the eyes of male observers are situated above the metallic joint that takes on the appearance of a predatory mouth. Scarpa had hinted at the ocular symbolism of the interlocking circles in his description of the mosaic-rimmed windows of the propylaeum. We find this motif once more in a planter in the pool, one of four elements placed in each of the pool's quadrants. Another is occupied by the pavilion itself, a third by a decagonal bamboo island, and the last by a second planter, whose shape recalls a sighting-mark that Scarpa aligns with the pavilion and the arcosolium, stressing once more the visual axis he had created between them.

J-F B

Perspective of water pavilion and pool showing the perimeter wall and propylaeum, c. 1970–74. Graphite and colored pencil on paper, 22 x 27.8 cm. Coll. ACS

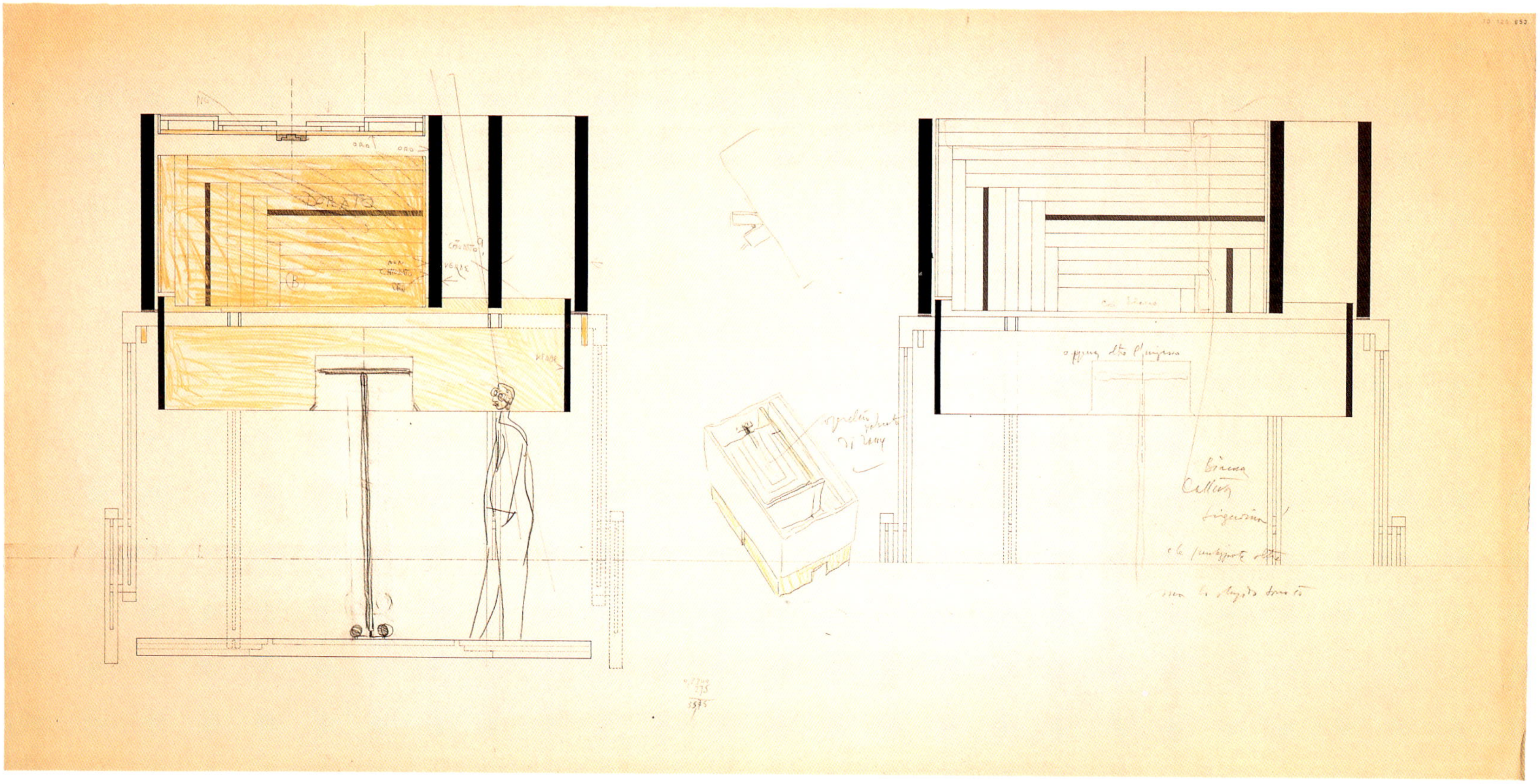

Elevations and axonometric of water pavilion, c. 1970–74. Graphite on paper, 21.8 x 68.5 cm. Coll. ACS

Section-elevations of water pavilion with axonometric of roof, c. 1970–74. Graphite and colored pencil on reprographic print, 42.5 x 59.9 cm. Coll. ACS

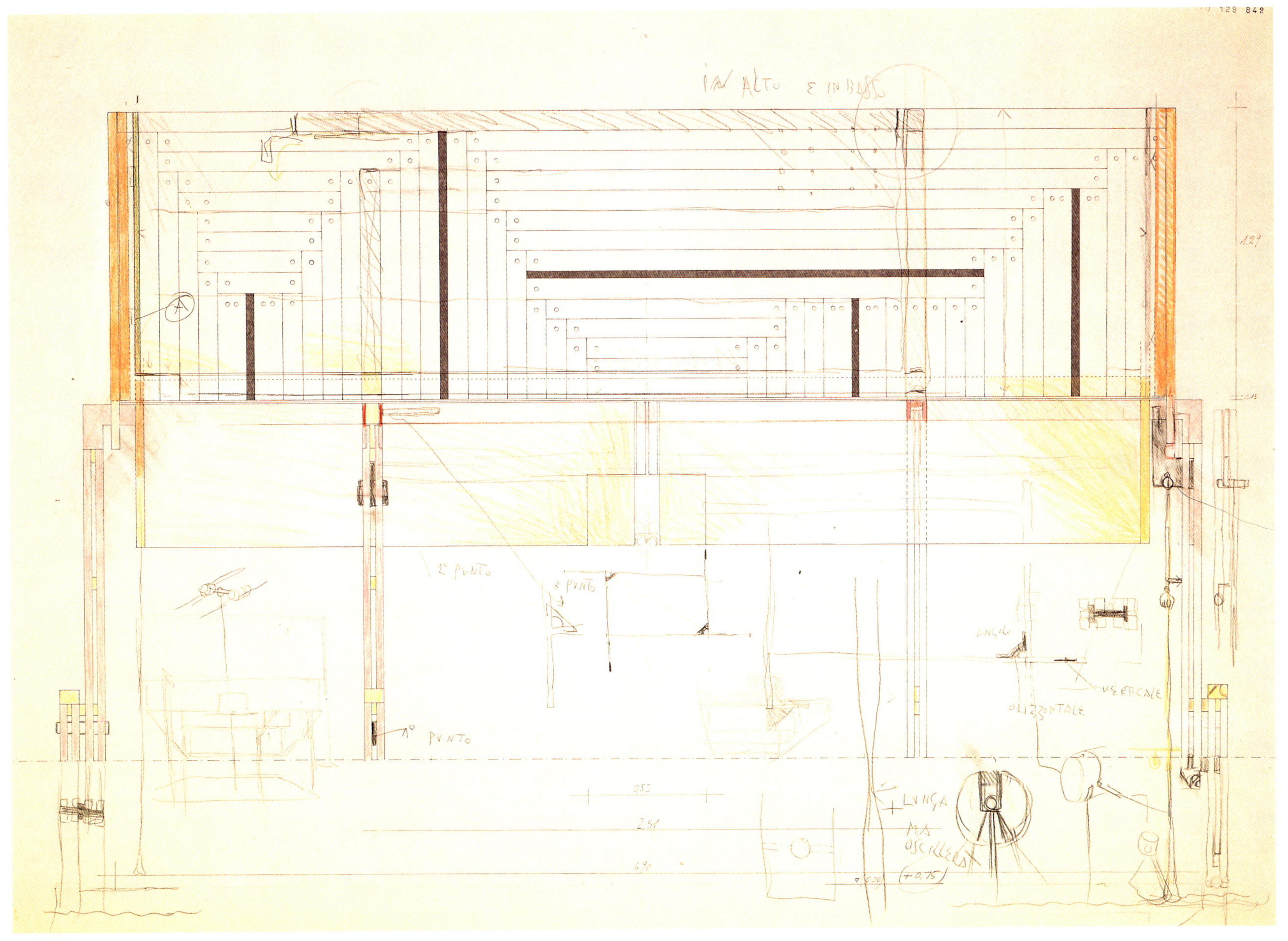

Section-elevation of water pavilion with perspective and detail studies, c. 1970–74. Graphite and colored pencil on reprographic print, 50.8 x 102.6 cm. Coll. ACS

Elevation of water pavilion roof with details of metal fasteners ('eyes'), c. 1970–74. Graphite and colored pencil on tracing paper, 29.6 x 57.5 cm. Coll. ACS

Studies of metal fasteners for columns of the water pavilion, c. 1970–74. Graphite and colored pencil on paper, 25.9 x 83 cm. Coll. ACS

The motif of interlocked rings permeates Scarpa's design for the Brion tomb, from the largest scale of the plan to the smallest scale of the detail. Scarpa's earliest design for the chapel (or *tempietto,* as he called it) was generated from three interlocked rings, each expressed as a distinct volume. A lower cylinder covers a passageway leading to the entrance; two higher, top-lit cylinders shelter the altar in the eastern cylinder; and the congregation is located in the western cylinder. Later, Scarpa modifies this initial design to form in plan a single irregular ovoid intersected by a long rectangle that functions as an entrance.

Scarpa later abandons the circle and its derivations for a simple cube divided into four square quadrants. He rotates the cube 45 degrees with respect to the geometry of the perimeter wall of the cemetery and shifts the altar from its original, traditional, eastern orientation to one facing north. Scarpa emphasizes the quadrant containing the altar by disposing a box (*scatola*) on top of it, which serves as a light source. He then considers covering the altar area with a stepped cupola that he leaves apparent on the exterior – later, as realized, hidden behind a high parapet wall. In the chapel design as elsewhere in the Brion tomb, Scarpa explores the plastic possibilities of his signature steplike motif. "One must have a pattern," he affirmed during a 1976 lecture explaining his design of the Brion tomb; "without a motif one cannot generate special moldings."[19] Scarpa uses bands of this motif to give ornamental emphasis to the edges of the chapel walls: at the door and window surrounds, their point of contact with other materials, and at the cornice, their point of contact with the sky.

J-F B

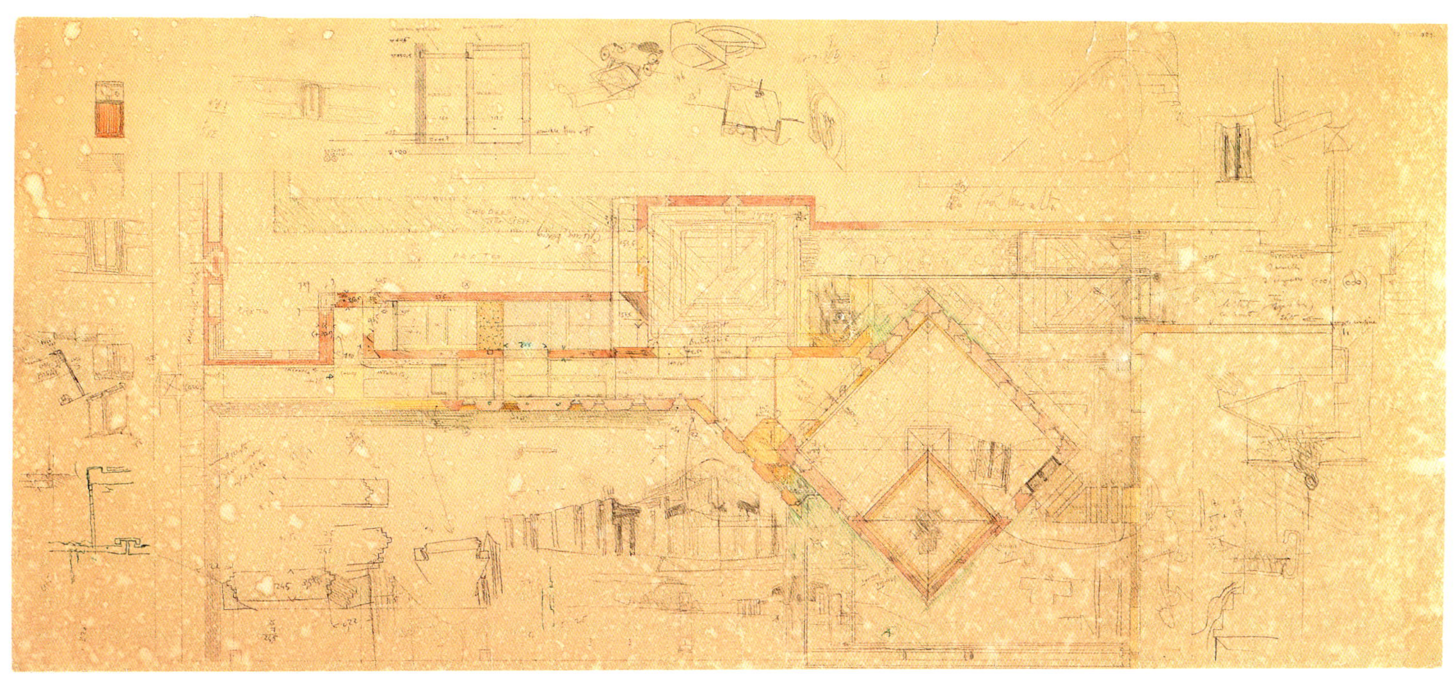

Plan of the chapel and sacristy with studies for facade and details, c. 1970–74. Graphite and colored pencil on reprographic print, 47.6 x 107.2 cm. Coll. ACS

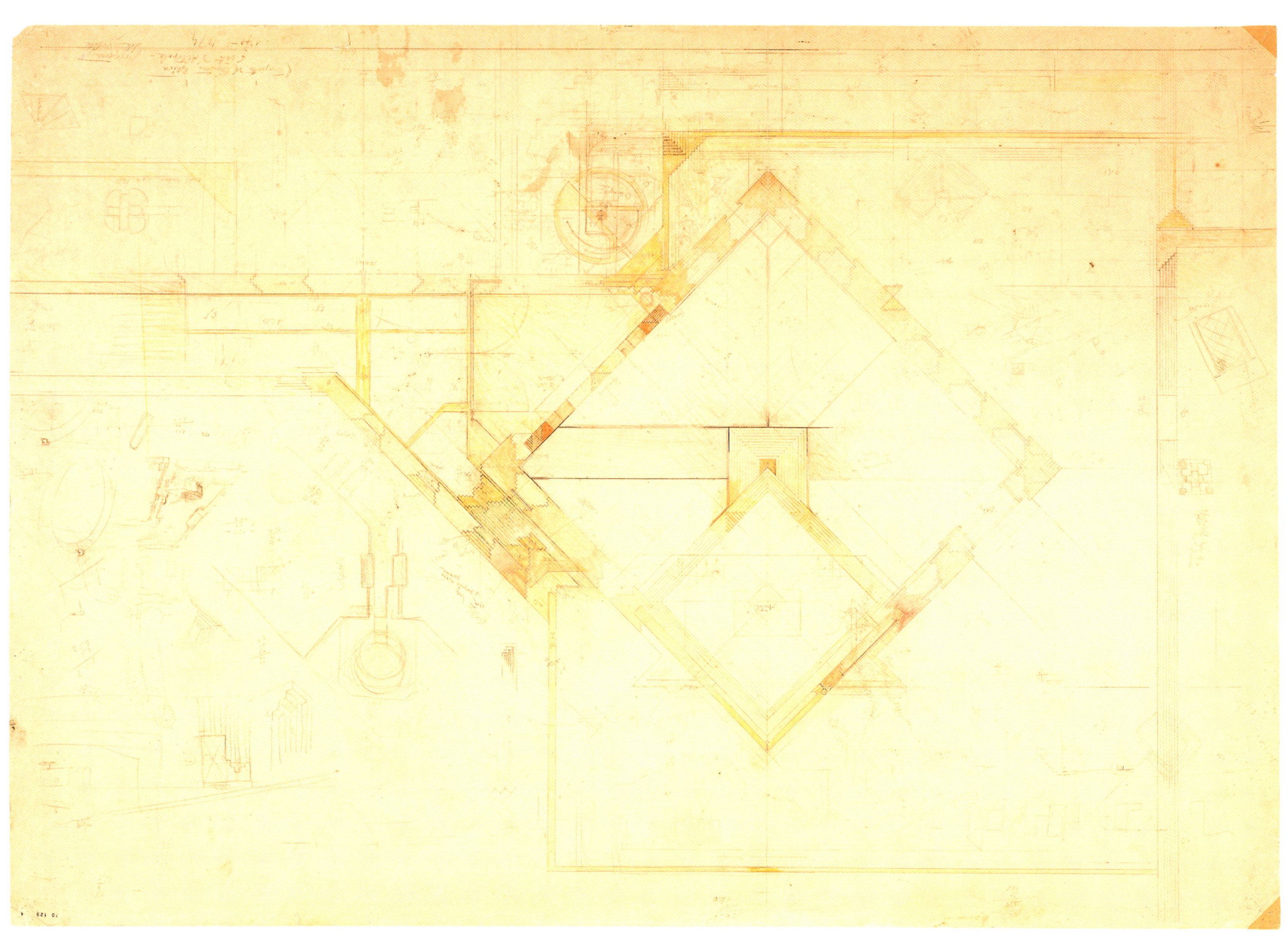

Plan and reflected ceiling plan of chapel, c. 1970–74. Graphite and colored pencil on cardboard, 69.7 x 99.6 cm. Coll. ACS

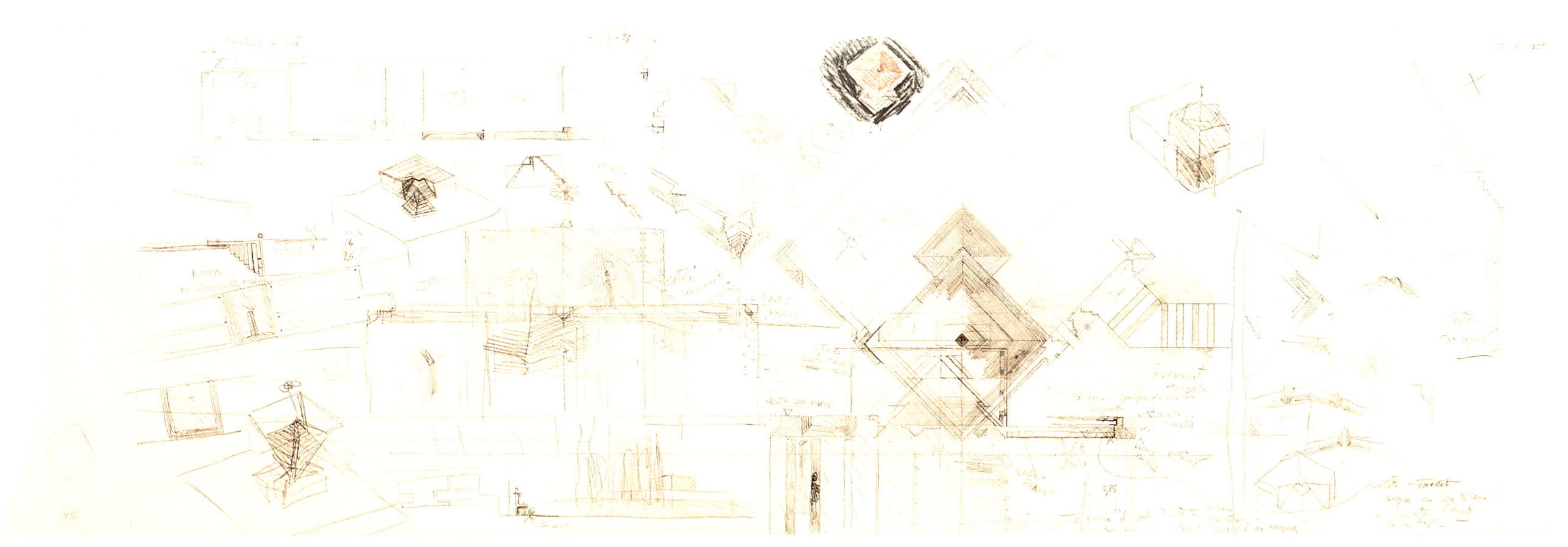

Plan of the chapel roof with studies for the roof and cupola, c. 1970–74. Graphite and colored pencil on tracing paper, 29.9 x 94.5 cm. Coll. ACS

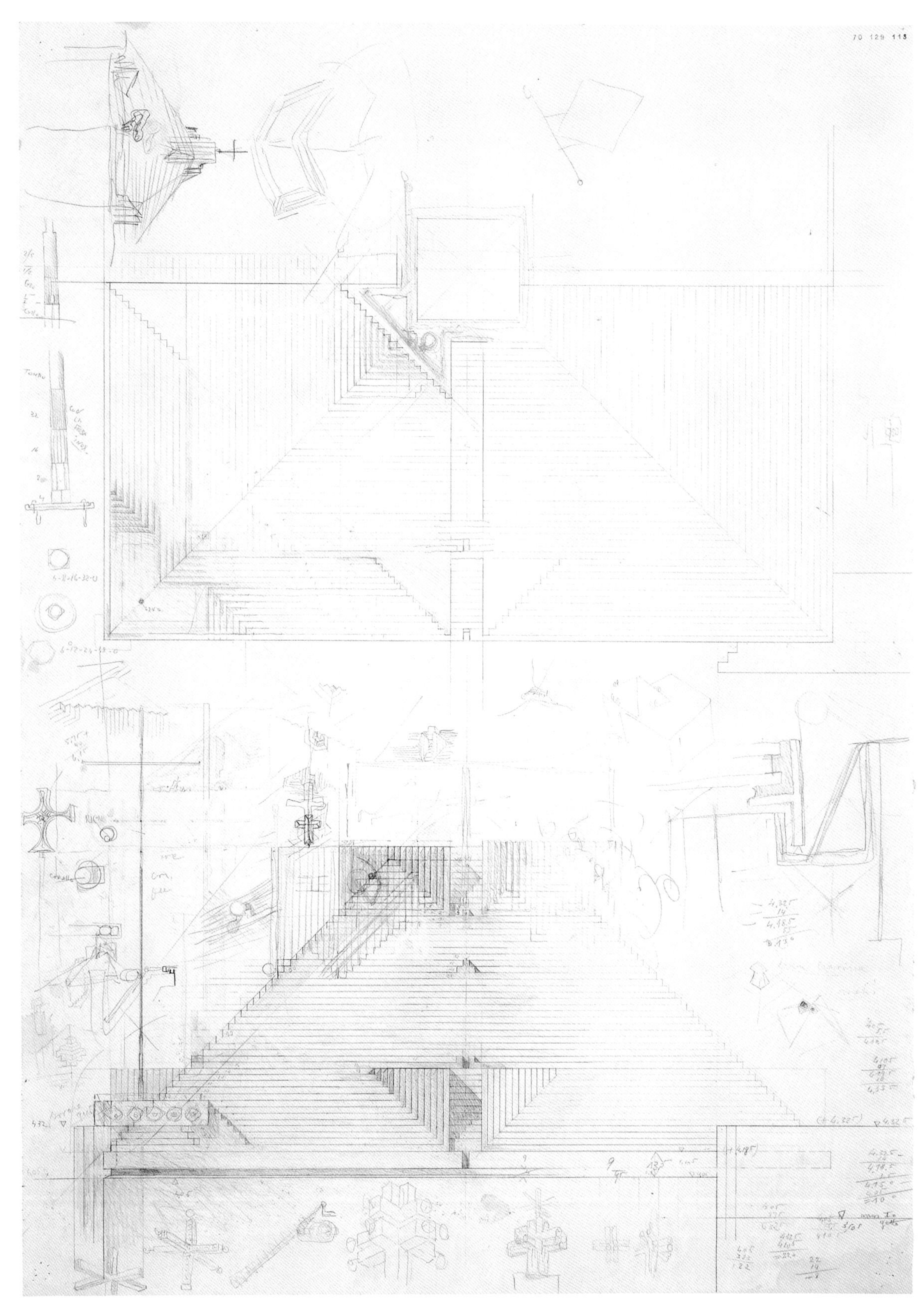

Plan and elevation with perspective sketch of the chapel cupola, c. 1970–74. Graphite and colored pencil on cardboard, 69.8 x 49.9 cm. Coll. ACS

Southwest elevation of chapel, c. 1970–74. Graphite and colored pencil on reprographic print, 30.4 x 54.6 cm. Coll. Marco Fantoni

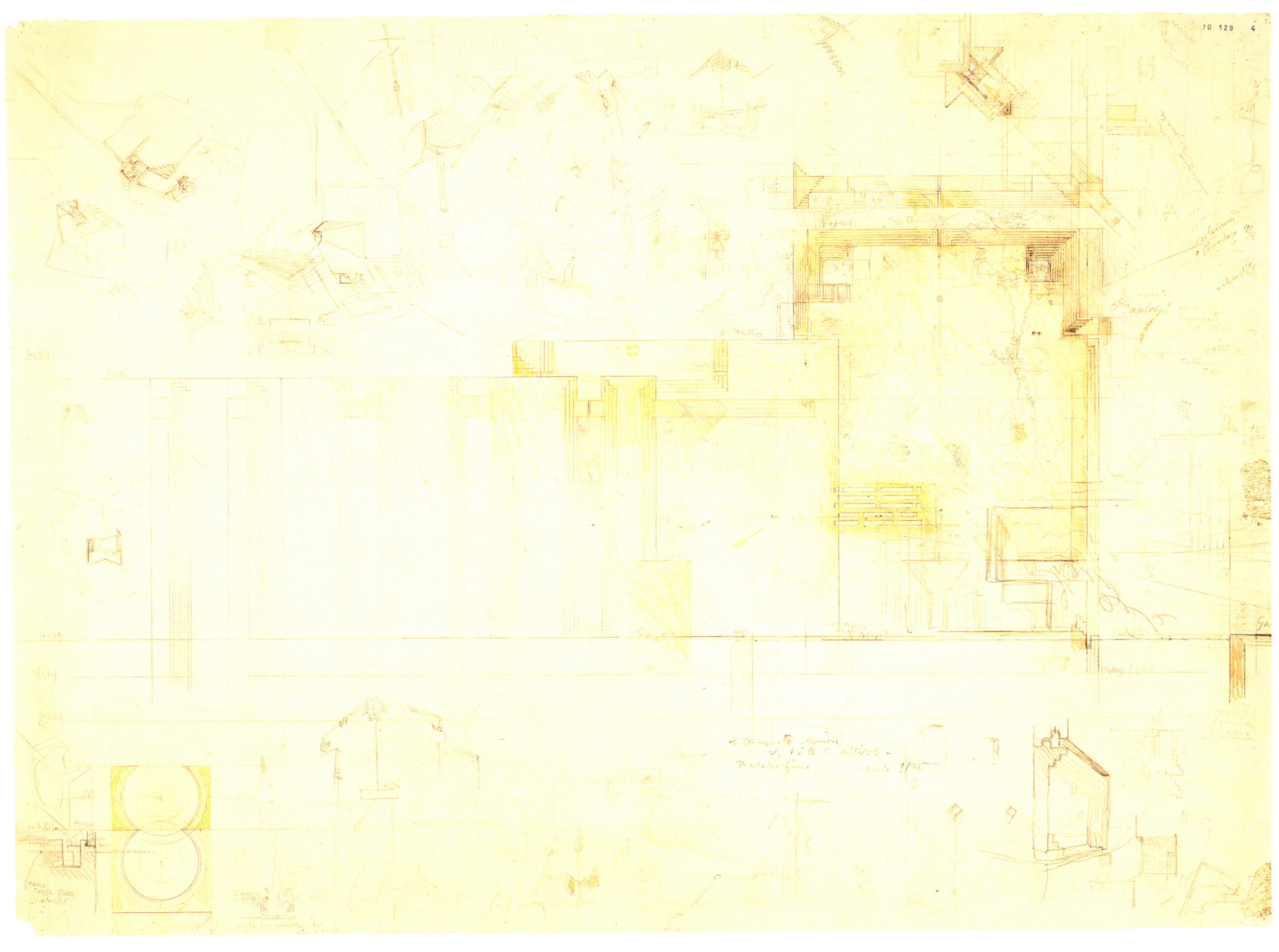

Northwest elevation of chapel with studies for details, c. 1970–74. Graphite and colored pencil on tracing paper, 37.2 x 84.4 cm. Coll. ACS

Northwest elevation and section of chapel with axonometric study for the roof, c. 1970–74. Graphite and colored pencil on cardboard, 43.8 x 99.6 cm. Coll. ACS

Northwest elevation of chapel with studies for details, c. 1970–74. Graphite and colored pencil on cardboard, 49.8 cm x 69.8 cm. Coll. ACS

THE BRION FAMILY TOMB

PHOTOGRAPHS BY GUIDO GUIDI

Portfolio photographs:
chromogenic color prints,
19.5 x 24.6 cm (horizontal),
24.6 x 19.5 cm (vertical).
Coll. CCA

Water pavilion, 21 May 1997.

Pool and perimeter wall, 30–31 January 1997, 3:30–5:20 pm.

Pool and propylaeum, 11 February 1998.

Perimeter wall and family tomb, 22 August 1996.

Perimeter wall, 8 August 1996, evening.

Perimeter wall and family tomb, 30–31 January 1997, 3:30–5:20 pm.

5 December 1996.

Perimeter wall, 5 December 1996.

Perimeter wall and chapel, 5 December 1996.

Chapel, 23 August 1996.

Lych gate, 4–7 September 1996.

Chapel, 30 August 1996.

Lych gate, 23 August 1996.

Chapel entrance, 22 August 1996.

Chapel entrance, 23 August 1996.

Chapel doors: entry to pond, 4–7 September 1996.

Chapel doors: entry to pond,
4–7 September 1996.

Chapel, pond, and cypress grove, 26–27 June 1996.

Chapel, 4–7 September 1996.

Chapel altar and corner doors, 11 July 1997, 12:30–2:15 pm.

Chapel altar and corner door, 4–7 September 1996.

Chapel altar and corner doors, 30 August 1996.

Chapel altar, 4–7 September 1996.

Chapel altar, 4–7 September 1996.

Chapel, 5 December 1996.

Chapel, 23 August 1996.

Pond, 29–30 January 1998, 3:00–5:30 pm.

Chapel and pond, 7 March 1997.

Water pavilion, pool, and propylaeum, 21 November 1996.

Propylaeum, 12 March 1997, 6:10–9:00 pm.

Propylaeum, 12 March 1997, 6:10–9:00 pm.

Propylaeum, 26–27 June 1996.

Propylaeum, pulley mechanism of door, 19 February 1997, 3:00–5:40 pm.

Interior of water pavilion, 20 February 1997, 7:40 am to 2:30 pm.

Perimeter wall and pool, 30 August 1996.

Propylaeum, 30 August 1996.

Propylaeum, 23 August 1996.

Propylaeum, 26–27 June 1996.

Interior of propylaeum, 14 January 1997, 3:00–5:00 pm.

Propylaeum, 30–31 January 1997, 3:30–5:20 pm.

Propylaeum, 30–31 January 1997, 3:30–5:20 pm.

Family tomb, 20 February 1997, 7:40 am to 2:30 pm.

Perimeter wall and family tomb, 22 August 1996.

Arcosolium and family tomb, 19 February 1997, 3:00–5:40 pm.

Arcosolium and perimeter wall, 19 February 1997, 3:00–5:40 pm.

Propylaeum entrance and arcosolium, 6 February 1998.

Guido Guidi

THINKING WITH THE EYES

I BELIEVE THAT IT IS ART THAT MAKES US GRASP THE REALITY OF THE WORLD. IT IS THE EFFORT THAT MAN HAS MADE, SINCE HIS BEGINNING, TO MAKE CLEAR FOR HIMSELF, THROUGH FORMS, HIS OWN EXISTENCE.[1]

CARLO SCARPA, C. 1978

Guido Guidi. Self-portrait by Carlo Scarpa on a wall at Possagno, 1998. Chromogenic color print, 19.5 x 24.6 cm. Coll. CCA

THE SLOW GAZE

Mine is a photography of the incidental, of edges, boundaries, and insertions. I have always focused on margins and peripheries, fragments, and phrases, and never looked for the "central thing." In the same way, Scarpa never has a static composition or a single way to look at anything. He lays out his arguments through circularity, the sidelong glance, the second look, and the process of return. I would like to think that the camera's slow gaze, its patient way of looking, can find in Scarpa's work the dialogue that unites the fragmentary.

There are two ways to go about making images of the real world. One is to use the camera as a telescope, to shoot like an arrow at a critical moment and seize the pregnant particular. This was Cartier-Bresson's approach: the photographer, pointing a finger at a scene, makes a privileged moment of it. The other method is to use the camera like a hunter uses his trap or a fisherman his net, as an implement that patiently absorbs space, light, diffusion, the ambient, the unexpected. These are not just two procedures: they are two ways of thinking. At the Museo di Castelvecchio and the Palazzo Abatellis, where Scarpa dwells on incidents along a given path and invites one to glimpses of surprise, I thought like Cartier-Bresson, and used my camera as a pointer, like a telescope. In the Canova plaster cast gallery at Possagno and the Brion tomb, where Scarpa makes an architecture out of apparently inchoate space and movement, I set my traps like a hunter.

I worked most intensively at Brion, photographing it all many times over, in every season and at all times of day. It was my habit there to work very quickly and then go back to see what I had shot. Using the camera as a gathering tool, I could not know what information I was collecting until I looked again. It was like making soundings in the seabed or sinking a drill into a mine, each time discerning just enough of the submerged to know where to turn next. I realized that this came from a hunger to learn again from Scarpa, who had been one of my favourite teachers, but my admiration for him was forbidding. I scarcely dared speak to him. By the program's third year, I had already turned away from architecture and was not eligible to join his studios, but I went like a pilgrim to see his work, sneaked into his lectures, and crashed his site inspections. Perhaps by coldly and systematically retracing the actual gestures of the master, I could follow him in his own exploratory procedures, enter his mind, and uncover his thinking.

LOOKING THROUGH TIME

"Let's go think," Scarpa used to say, as he moved with his students to the drawing board. The drawing and the photograph are two very different ways of thinking through the same thing, as well as two different ways of describing it, and one can be used to clarify the other. Starting with Scarpa's frontal elevation of the water pavilion, I tried to photograph the same object with a telephoto lens, head on, to get the same point of view as Scarpa. Comparing the master's gesture with my imitation of it, I noticed that the two *tesserae* on the wall behind – one dark, one light; positive and negative; death and life – appear through the peep holes of the pavilion, just at the point in the drawing where the eyes of the young woman appear. I knew the Brion tomb well. I had visited the construction site many times and saw Scarpa's drawings for the project while it was being conceived. But this experiment gave me a clue as to how complex, and how concealed, the symbolic relationships might be. Perhaps the camera could unravel Scarpa's enigmas, thinking with the eyes – the eyes of the water pavilion, the binocular form that urges the visitor to look towards the tomb across the water.

I wanted to photograph not only the objects that Scarpa constructed but also some of the objects that Scarpa 'saw.' In Palermo, at the Palazzo Abatellis, the veil on the brow of Antonello's *Annunciation* takes on the same form as the double circle in the water pavilion at Brion. Because the painting is set on a diagonal, it is possible to trace an imaginary line that runs through the eyes of the Virgin and the corresponding tracery of the door in front of her, to a Nativity on the wall behind her, and on to a Crucifixion in the next room. Thus Scarpa's architectural fragments are not just objects to look at, but places for the gaze to traverse, places from which to 'see.' Bruno Zevi calls Brion "stupendous fragments of an inchoate discourse."[2] I would say 'elusive' rather than 'inchoate.' "The God who is at Delphi does not speak plain, nor conceal, but hints and suggests," says Heraclitus of Apollo. This Madonna is like a veil through which you can see the passages of life. The cycle begins with death, and moves through birth back to death, because for Scarpa this is not a closed circle but a continuous movement. The Virgin's knowing gaze interrupts this passage, and her eyes are reflected in the points of light cast on the floor in front of her, in her bookstand, and in the supports that Scarpa built for the saints at her left. The motif of the eyes is there to remind us of our ability to look, to observe, to think, to 'suffer knowledge.'

TIME AND MOTION

Scarpa always said in class "I can talk about things because I see them." As you wait for a change in the light, or go about the mechanics of setting up a shot, you have the chance to slow down the act of looking. It is said that the camera captures things too fast, and that drawing slows you down. I think the reverse is true. Drawing is a way of recording in haste what might be; the camera is a prosthesis that helps you to think through what *is*. To make photography is not a superficial act. True, the photographer can capture only the surface of things. But he can learn from that simple descriptive gesture the true depth of an object, follow its metamorphosis as the light upon it changes. Scarpa was not very interested in photography. But Arrigo Rudi remembers that for Scarpa, the photograph "had to be static, perfectly axial, rigorous. The photographer had to give back his mental image."[3] Looking at Scarpa's work, I tried to find ways to recapture this mental image. Scarpa demands that we remember what we passed through, hear our footfalls as echoes, look around as we look ahead. I remember that he moved about in an exaggerated sweep (theatrically exaggerated when he was being watched), arms akimbo, bending, stooping, turning from side to side, this way and that, like a chamberlain in the court of the doges. Gary Winogrand said that photographers, too, should move in a zigzag pattern, making the "sign of Zorro" with their feet, switching from shot to reverse-shot. Or as Massimo Cacciari suggests, poetic language, like the gaze of the angels, is a circular vision.

I have tried to capture the sense of movement in Scarpa's works by focusing on fragments, by moving the lens in the same random, patient, and circular fashion in which Scarpa moved his head, by assembling these episodes into sequences or juxtapositions, and by repetition, so as to give a sense of the length of the gaze required to grasp the mutability of the subject.

An astronomer of the early nineteenth century proposed that our whole concept of time should be more circular and the sequence from past to present to future reversed. Scarpa's works have been described as "precarious arrangements" in which the pause and the fragment "reveal the essence of his mode of conceiving a work in relation to time."[4] This overwhelming consciousness of collapsing time and of death marks all Scarpa's strategies and narratives. At the Museo di Castelvecchio I focused on this sense of pause, on the significant spaces between things, on the suspension of time and space, and on Scarpa's generosity toward the action of time. In the galleries at Castelvecchio he leaves great distances between the objects, allowing them to converse with one another solitarily. His job, he believed, was not to show himself but to show the works and to lend them sight, intensifying their resonance with one another and setting up dialogues between them and the architecture. Scarpa finds rhymes here, conversations between the structural forms and the shapes of the objects, between the shape of light and the shape of things. All of these elements – changing light and stable object, corroding paint and eternal glass, old stone and new metal – are in tense but gentle dialogue, and it is Scarpa's virtuosity that puts them at ease with one another.

Scarpa knew how to wait, how to let aging and patina complete their work. The staining and fading that one can see today in the colored gallery panels at Castelvecchio were not unexpected accidents; Scarpa designed with transformation and decay in mind. Sergio Los, who worked with Scarpa in the years when he undertook his first historical investigations,

Guido Guidi. View of *The Annunciation* by Antonello da Messina, Palazzo Abatellis, 1997. Chromogenic color print, 19.5 x 24.6 cm. Coll. CCA

praises his readiness to embrace the inevitability of "re-design," to accept that nature and human needs trace a long and discontinuous line that will change what the architect does as thoroughly as he has changed what others before him had done. Scarpa made works that he watched transform themselves into traces, just one more layer among the accumulating strata of banality and genius that form the fabric around us. The great architect Ignazio Gardella has a lovely image for this: for Scarpa history "was a flower around which he buzzed continually, attracted by its subtle coloration and scent and from which he sucked the essences he transformed into the honey of architecture, knowing well that there were, had been, and would be honey of different kinds."[5] At Castelvecchio I tried to capture the rusting and ruination of his work, the subtle corrosions that Scarpa knew would integrate his interventions with those of others.

Just as at Castelvecchio time is not static, so does Scarpa discourage a static point of view. He moves the viewer around, placing objects so as to make one look sideways. As he demonstrated hilariously in a film for Italian television, he brings one, unexpectedly, back again to the subject matter from another angle. These are circles of seeing within cycles of time. In the great, long sculpture galleries, Scarpa sets up circular relationships among the pieces. I noted, for example, the complex play between the small Madonna and Child (which has a faded blood-red wall as background) and the grieving Mother at the Cross behind the arch in the next room. It is as if the first young Madonna is seen again in the distance, fainting at the foot of the Cross. The fragmentation both isolates and unites. The support for the Madonna and Child suggests a hand holding a sculpture. This 'hand' is echoed by the arm and hand of the Magdalen, which support the fainting mother and at the same time point back to the Virgin and Child. Here the arch that divides the two rooms is continued in the curved form of the grieving mother's body. Everything speaks of the uncertainties of distance and time. This uncertainty is expressed in other ways as well: in the shadows from the window, which recall the existence of the Gothic stone frame and dissolve the new metal one; in the crosses that dance between ceiling, sarcophagus, and crucifix; in the vitrine in the *sacello* anticipating the form that will hold the equestrian statue of Cangrande.

A CONVERSATION WITH LIGHT

It is the framing of the sky above the Cangrande statue – the two geometric forms that the cornice carves out of the void – that held my attention longest at Castelvecchio. In the courtyard, Scarpa emphasizes certain points over which the sculpture keeps watch (the bridge to the north and the steps, for example), while Cangrande, in turn, guards the void behind him (the sky, the river, the countryside). Scarpa designs the light and incorporates it into his forms as a mutable presence. This designing of the sky brought me to Possagno. In the plain space and on the simple surfaces of the plaster cast gallery, the light changes constantly, carving deep but intangible patterns into the architecture of the rooms, while the azure of the skylights that gives the room its color and form stays almost motionless. Artificial light is too still for statuary. Scarpa needed a light that moves, to give depth to the surface of the casts and to lead them into conversation. Natural light is never still. I set up my work by pairing like images, to show the different character of pieces as the fall of light changes – not to show how the light is brought in, but to account for its effects.

Many photograph the sun at sunset, but it is more interesting to show a figure or an object in the sunset's changing light – never the source of the light, but an object that absorbs the light or the shadow of the object that the light designs. And so trying to photograph the sunlight that at that hour comes through the door of the old cemetery at Brion, I had the illusion of having caught the mirror image of a sun with its rays, painted by the sun itself on the north wall, looking like something from the school of Vienna or by Edvard Munch.

That is how light is used at the Brion tomb – as alchemy. Light has a different kind of magic at Possagno. As Scarpa moves away from the gauzy screens that filter the light in the Palazzo Abatellis, he makes it both more pointed and more diffuse. As he explained, plaster is an "amorphous material;" it has no luster, and can gain life only by being "placed in the sun."[6] He talks of the sunlight here as an "element, which, seen in perspective, descends and disappears. A diaphanous light, a light from above."[7] Since photography is above all nothing but the art of seeing shadows, the problem for the photographer is the same as for Scarpa. Scarpa's solution at Possagno is the photographer's: a play of negative and positive, made immensely subtle by casting near-white sculpture against near-white walls. One white object sits slightly apart from another, softening the shadows so that the pieces themselves become shadows. Because of the height of the windows, the tones of the ambient and of the sharp light are very similar; they become two subtle variants of the same thing, making a negative and positive effect out of the slightest differences. It is a play of monochromes in which the sculptures are amplified by the tenuousness of the dialogue between light and shade.

There is a certain eroticism here. As I waited for the light to caress the back of one reclining figure, I realized that Scarpa was making the sun do what his hand wanted – to stroke the soft lines of the torso. Scarpa did not like the exaggerated Neoclassical grace and precision of Canova's hands, feet, and heads. He found them idealized. But "from the neck to below the knee," he said, "it is the true style, 'truth' itself, art which becomes life."[8] Scarpa makes the light full and lets it luxuriate on the plaster. White and bathing in pools of light or sitting among its own shadows, each work becomes solitary, tranquil. But together they engage in a distant conversation, a little distracted, as if in a whimsical salon of Canova's time. They look at one another from their private pools of brilliance or shade and engage in a silent colloquy, each animated in turn as the light falls upon them and brings them to life.

THE SHADOW SIGNS OF THE BRION TOMB: A GEOGRAPHY OF TIME

Joseph Brodsky has famously suggested that geography plus time equals "destiny." "It is not enough to say: I will create a poetic work of architecture," Scarpa said of the Brion tomb. "Poetry arises from things in themselves if the person who makes it has this nature."[9] Sergio Los said that "the architecture of Scarpa works as a symbolic system."[10] At the Brion tomb this metaphorical language becomes immensely complex and layered. I do not think one has to decipher each sign to grasp these metaphors, nor do I think they carry absolute or prescribed meanings. They were simply Scarpa's way of thinking and designing. If the camera found them, it was as clues to the message in Scarpa's mental imagery, not as the unfolding of a definitive emblematic structure. We are told from the start that there will be a kind of magic here, perhaps "alchemy." There is a clear alchemical reference in the double circle that appears as you move through the entrance. Tinged with gold on one side, it provides an initial view of the elements of earth and water beyond. As alchemy is about the mutation of elemental form, and cemeteries concern the mutation of organic form, so the Brion tomb suggests permanence but carries within it a sense of constant growth, decay, and change: the immutable water, with its changing reflections; the mute tombs and walls crowded over with plant life.

Scarpa said that to make architecture "one needs a double mind, a triple mind, the mind of a thief, of a speculator, of a man who wants to rob a bank. One needs what I call sharpness, a nervous readiness to seize upon what happens, or what will."[11] Shadows and beams of light were what Scarpa's 'speculative' eye and thieving mind caught at Brion. As W.H. Fox Talbot observed, "A painter's eye will often be arrested where ordinary people see nothing remarkable. A casual gleam of sunshine, or a shadow thrown across his path."[12]

When he talked about this project, Scarpa compared the religious traditions of Japan, both animist and Buddhist, and the different poetic values of the two. It is as if here he wanted to fuse them, to wed the animist's figurative and narrative view of nature to the Buddhist's contemplative and metaphysical sounding of nature's abstract properties. He admitted that the Brion tomb might be enigmatic, "odd, or perhaps strange," for it was "not easy to ... express oneself freely about highly questionable areas which may exclude modern rational thought."[13]

In Venetian slang, "let's go drink a shadow" means "let's go have a glass of wine," because wine sellers used to set up their stalls in the shadow of the campanile. One can say, with Talbot, that photography is only the art of capturing shadows. Shadow (*ombra*) and beyond the grave (*oltretomba*) have a similar ring in Italian, and at the Brion tomb I glimpsed a crowd of ghosts, the shadows of different cultures. The shadows of Japan have been noted many times, but – perhaps for fear of a curse – no one has yet spoken of Egypt. Notoriously, when asked shortly after the war what he wanted in architecture, Scarpa had replied: a Pharoah for whom I can build a pyramid. He was not speaking entirely in jest. Some time ago I saw photographs of Scarpa riding a camel on a visit to the pyramids, and I noticed that the inclination of the wall surrounding the tomb (the side facing the countryside) is almost the same as that of the pyramids at Giza. Egyptian references appear throughout Brion.

On the morning of 23 August 1996, at 11:30, while I was trying to shoot my first photograph of the interior of the chapel with a wide-angle lens, I followed with the corner of my eye a square of light on the northwest wall, behind the altar. The light came from an opening above, in the truncated pyramid of the chapel roof. At exactly noon, the glowing rectangle, moving halfway along the northeast wall, turned into a triangle – an arrow pointing to the ground, towards the opening on the water. A few days after the summer solstice (11 July 1997), I noticed the same figure of light as it transformed the beak upon the luminous head of an enigmatic bird descending on a section of pavement behind the altar, which seemed exactly designed to capture its fall. In the winter months, when the sun is lower on the horizon (in fact precisely between the autumnal and vernal equinox), a sort of reverse phenomenon is visible: shafts of light coming from the slit windows of the front walls stretch further and further along the pavement until they reach the altar, giving the impression of raising it upwards and helping it to take off in flight.

When I finished the first of these photographs, I paid little attention to the fact that the candelabrum, a wooden pole hanging from the ceiling to the altar was missing (the verger hides it for fear of theft); perhaps the image was better, simpler, without it. But later, looking again at the photograph, I started to see the inside of the chapel vault as a mould, as if it were the negative impression of a wading bird formed by its two interlocking cupolas – the larger, foreshortened, one serving as its body and the smaller one as its head, turned to face south. In the funeral traditions of ancient Egypt, the soul of the dead person sometimes appears as a sacred bird, which is identified with the idea of the phoenix and depicted as a heron. Only then was I able to see that the candelabrum would hang from the roof as if it were the single leg of a great stork-like bird. It is as if Scarpa had used natural elements of the real – light and wood – to help the mind perceive an object from some fantastic and mythical zoology.

I have seen photographs of the vaulting in the Brion chapel, taken from below and looking up into it as Scarpa would have drawn it in plan. But one does not see it this way – only the corpse in the coffin during the funeral service would see it from this viewpoint, and the dead, perhaps, do not see anything. The living, however, look from a normal point of view and see the abnormal: they see the coffin, the vault, the signs made of light – and might somehow 'see,' as a result, the soul rising into the void and taking on the magical form of a legendary bird. It is only thus, by looking from the sober viewpoint of a standing person, that we can see how Scarpa's shaping of the ceiling manages at once to dematerialize and to give form to the space above, bringing to mind drawings by Paul Klee, Leonardo's studies of vortices, and the power of the whirlwind to lift us to the heavens. In this way, as Democritus says, the visible gives us a glimpse of the invisible.

When I photographed the outside of the chapel I looked around extensively, searching for the best places from which to see the openings. Placed high in the wall, these become the eyes of another bird, a kind of falcon, when the whole corner of the chapel is framed properly against the sky. Is this Scarpa's self-portrait as a bird? Or a homage to the sense of sight? Or is it a reference to Horus, the ancient Egyptian sun-god whose two eyes were believed to be the sun and moon, and whose name apparently comes from *hr*, meaning both sky and falcon? In one photograph, I made one of the buttresses of the wall around the cemetery coincide with the north corner of the falcon-chapel, deliberately suggesting the

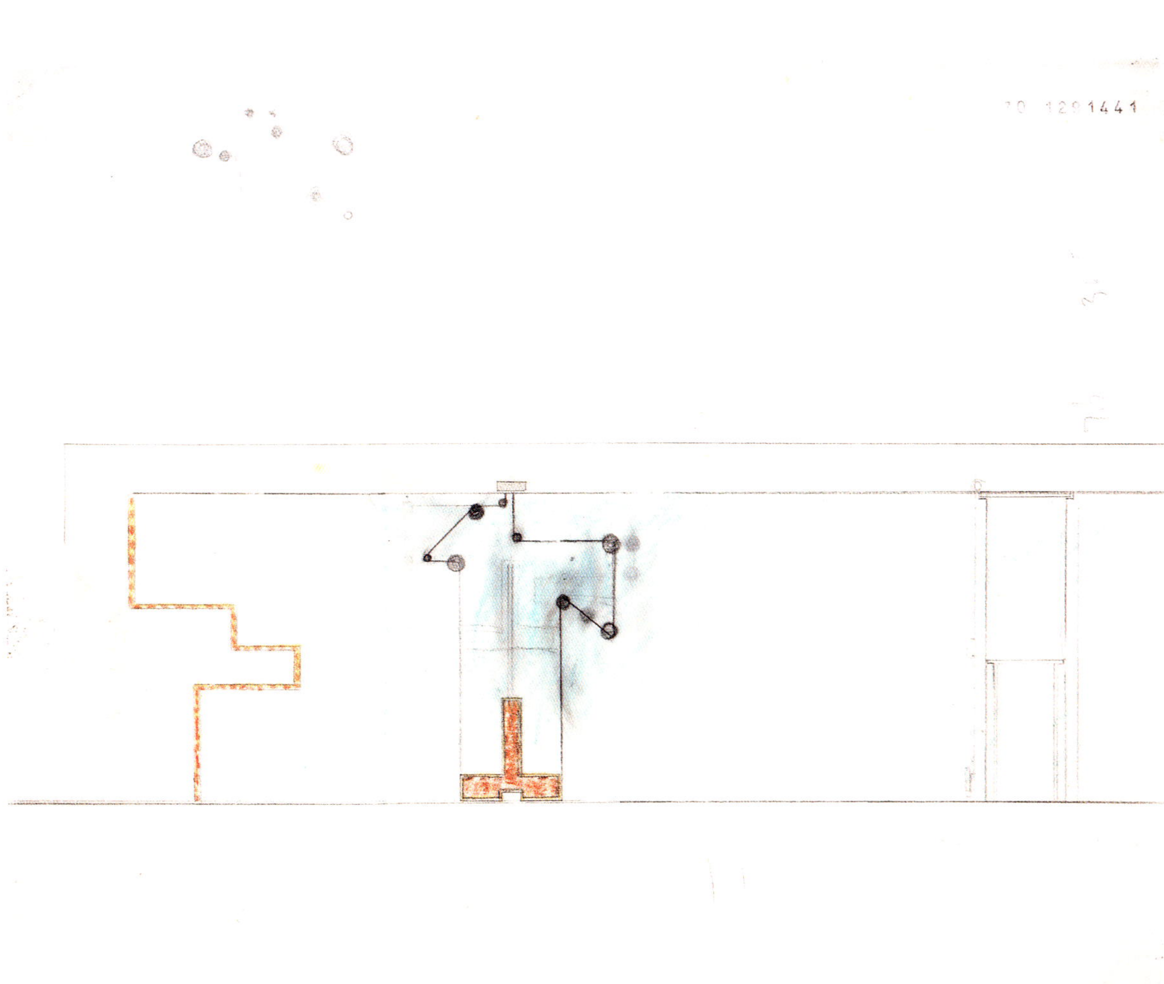

Partial elevation of east facade of propylaeum showing pulley mechanism for the glass door, Brion tomb, 1970–74. Graphite and colored pencil on tracing paper, 21.2 x 25.3 cm. Coll. ACS

massive wings (one horizontal, one vertical) that would appear as the great brid alighted in the cornfield and faced north.

Another type of flying object – a mechanical insect or starry genie – is discernible on the east wall of the pool, where the mechanism for lowering the door out of the propylaeum appears. I tried, but without success, to make the steel cable more visible: the drawing more clearly shows the path of the cable outlining the form of two wings that open or close as the door moves to welcome the visitor in and out of the garden. The cable links fourteen parts of a system of weights and pulleys that serves to raise the glass door immersed in the water behind the wall. According to Egyptian myth, the body of Osiris was dismembered into fourteen parts. Osiris was associated with the constellation Orion, which is visible from within the water pavilion through a rectangular opening. Thus I decided to privilege the theme of light, and on a few mornings I arrived on site before dawn in order to see in the first light of day the steel bolts that, facing east, shine and dissolve like stars. Around nine in the morning, I turned my gaze a little to the left, between the propylaeum and the water pavilion. There, where a narrow passage beyond the glass door slides into the water, unsettling shadow figures cast by the pavilion began to appear. Gradually but inexorably, they transformed themselves into cones or arrows of shadow that, reflected in the water, pointed north, to the main tombs of the site. Shadows and reflections can of course also be seen as a Rorschach test, in which one sees his or her own personal ghosts. Giuseppe Mazzariol remembers Scarpa once saying that the essence of Venice lies "in the play of light, in the reflections, in the doubling of images in the water" – in "the seen and not seen."[14] This memory of Venice, with its sport between visible and invisible, material and illusion, could serve as a sort of contextual reference for the Brion tomb.

Before sunset, a similar optical phenomenon occurs on the other wall of the pool, facing west. These arrows, forming and dissolving, serve as markers mapping this geography of death, mourning, and rebirth. I photographed the great arrow of fluted concrete that appears at the entrance from the old cemetery very carefully, as it is the sign that introduces the visitor to the tomb. I tried to show how the concrete cover at the entrance to the propylaeum also forms a diagonal arrow that, pointing down and to the left, immediately draws one's attention to an opening through which a view of the tomb beyond appears. From this point one sees the arcosolium above the tombs in the way it appears in the drawings, as being composed of two Egyptian eyes that blur into one another, but retain two irises represented by the tombs within. In the parapet above the arch two small, copper "sacred eyes" – again Egyptian – also appear, allowing the nearby hills of Asolo to merge with the structure.

At sunset two further eyes – the interlocking alchemical circles of blue and gold at the center of the propylaeum – blur, becoming, though hot and cold on the outside, reconciled to the same color within. Nearby, five metal cables – a kind of aeolian harp – divide the earth from the water. Many years ago on a windy day I heard and was moved by their mournful sound. This point of interaction between land and water constituted a critical moment in Scarpa's project. "Here," he said, "I would like to express the natural sensation of the water and the grass, the water and the earth, because the water is the fount of life on earth."[15] It is by looking across the water and earth that Scarpa asks us to see the tomb.

Carlo Maschietto recalls hearing Scarpa say, while they were visiting the tomb, that he understood "death to be a moment of life." One spring morning, as I was photographing the northeast side of the chapel and looking at the frosted glass, an overly romantic flowering bush annoyingly appeared in the top left corner of the window, to the right of the chapel and towards the north. I asked my assistant to move it with his hand while I took the photograph. Only at that moment did we realize – a miracle! – that every flower was composed of two small light-colored cupolas, little breasts, on either side of a central, darker form. Another variation of the double lobe, like the circles in the propylaeum and the merging eyes of the arcosolium, but this time in the form of a sacred Egyptian fruit – the fruit that symbolized the universal, the female power of nature and rebirth, sometimes represented as a tree with arms and breasts to nurse the dead.

The first time I entered the propylaeum, many years ago, I had the unnerving and insistent sensation of finding myself inside a skull or a Japanese helmet, with the eye sockets, which my eyes were forced to look through, turned to the east. This image haunted me for a long time, and I kept photographing it and returning to look, questioning myself about the meaning of this enigmatic 'sculpture.' In one photograph it appears as a sort of mummy. I thought of Ka, from Egyptian mythology. Represented as a figure with raised arms, Ka stands for the persona, the id or essence, of the individual – something like a 'double' of the living person, from which the soul becomes independent after death, like the Roman *umbra*. I imagined myself then as a nineteenth-century photographer who, with the pleading gesture of a worshipper in the arcosolium of the Roman catacombs, keeps his hands raised, like Ka, to lift the black cloth and look. I imagined that Scarpa, remembering the orientation of Byzantine basilicas and the crossing of the transept in early Christian ones, had given the propylaeum its T-shaped plan. And I was sure that in this form Scarpa was drawing himself, with his right arm extending over the pool and across the stepping stones to the pavilion, and his left lying in the rill of water that becomes a mere trickle as it nears the tomb. Prostrate, as if worshipping at an ancient propylaeum, one hand on the water and the other on the earth and with his gaze turned to the east, this imaginary figure pays homage with his eyes to what he cannot see. "I believe in a kind of transcendent life, in the hereafter," he said in his last interview. "I believe that one exists, even if I do not try to imagine it."[16]

In memory of Paolo Costantini (1959–1997)

Sergio Polano

THE ART OF DISPLAY

IT IS THE WINTER OF 1952, AND CARLO Scarpa is about to set out on the long rail trip to Messina, where he is to install an exhibition entitled *Antonello da Messina and the Quattrocento in Sicily*. How, one may ask, did this Venetian architect come to receive this commission that will take him to Sicily? It has followed in the wake of a series of major accomplishments in Venice: the artistic direction of the restoration of the university complex of Ca' Foscari (1935–37), unaccountably passed over in the critical literature; the design of the Gallerie dell'Accademia (from 1944); three interiors in the Piazza San Marco area (TELVE, Ongania, A la Piavola de Franza; 1950); the book pavilion at the 1950 *Biennale*; the sculpture courtyard and the ticket office of the 1952 *Biennale*; as well as his installations of the famous Paul Klee gallery for the 1948 *Biennale* and the exhibitions devoted to Giovanni Bellini (1949), Giovan Battista Tiepolo (1951), and finally Toulouse-Lautrec (1952) at the Ala Napoleonica of the Museo Correr on Piazza San Marco.

It was the last of these that created the link with Sicily. Roberto Calandra, the architect originally charged with the design of the Antonello exhibition in Messina, eventually to become Scarpa's main collaborator in all his work in Sicily, had been fascinated by Scarpa's brilliant use of transparent screens to redefine the rigid spaces of the Ala Napoleonica. Calandra enlisted Scarpa as his collaborator on the Antonello exhibition. It was a lucky decision, for the opening of *Antonello and the Quattrocento in Sicily* in 1953 marked a milestone in Scarpa's career as a designer of exhibitions and led directly to another commission in Sicily: the transformation into a museum of Palermo's Palazzo Abatellis.

Built by Matteo Carnelivari in the last decade of the fifteenth century and located in one of the most characteristic streets of the old center of Palermo, the Palazzo Abatellis is organized around a rectangular courtyard, which determines its layout. The street facade is a symmetrical design, with a wide central doorway and a regular sequence of three-light windows in the *piano nobile*. The courtyard features a double gallery with five arches (low arches at the portico level, round-headed arches above), all supported by the slenderest of columns. Heavily damaged in allied bombing raids in 1943, the palace was slowly restored over a period of some ten years – work that was finally taken in hand by Giorgio Vigni, Superintendent of the Galleries of Sicily. As Vigni wrote at the time:

> The problem was thus of the kind so common in Italy: an old building of historic and architectural interest was to be remodelled as a museum.... The building ... must not be allowed to cramp the museum, nor the museum to detract from the aesthetic atmosphere of the building.... For the guidance of the average visitor, a severe selection of works for display is of the utmost importance.... Of course, the severer [the] selection of works, the greater the need for available storerooms, rationally arranged and readily accessible on request.... There remained its adaptation as a museum which meant making the necessary passage-ways and piercing doorways so that all the rooms could be visited in succession, and modifying a certain coldness and emptiness in the restoration of the monument in order to bring the architecture into harmony with the museum as planned. In a sense, the architecture itself was to be on display....[1]

Between the end of 1953 and the museum's opening in June of 1954, Scarpa carried out this transformation of the Palazzo Abatellis in a kind of tour de force that betrayed no sign of the haste of execution. The building that emerged was less a prelude to than a mature confirmation of the genius for museum design that Scarpa would soon display in Verona and elsewhere. Scarpa transformed the palace courtyard by changing the distribution and proportions of several openings and by the application of a light-coloured plaster, divided into alternating bands of subtly varied tint. Inside, his solution to the problem of linking the different areas and allowing visitor traffic to flow through the museum was exceptional, and involved such innovations as a new internal stairway, with steps of hexagonally cross-sectioned stones, supported by steel beams, connecting the ground floor with an ancient stairway leading to the second floor. In his placement of the objects, in his control of light and color relationships, and in the exquisite sense of materials that is demonstrated in each display solution Scarpa gives incontrovertible evidence of his great mastery. A brilliant response to the challenge of display – a challenge demanding the ability to see as well as the ability to make people see – Scarpa's installation is a lesson in the art of using art to display art.

Scarpa's mastery of exhibition design draws not only upon an acute visual sensitivity but also upon a keen awareness of the intrinsic values of the works to be exhibited. Thus he manages to isolate artistic moments in a slow, narrative sequence that winds its way through the silences of Carnelivari's building, moving from the apocalyptic vision of the perturbing *Triumph of Death* to a new "eccentric enucleation" of Antonello's masterpieces.

A deeper understanding of the way Scarpa's exhibition designs work can be had by examining the relationship between the objects and the spaces of the Palazzo Abatellis – by looking closely at the way these come into contact with each other so as to create a kind of "pivot" between time and history. A case in point is the elegant architectural solution Scarpa conceived for the portrait bust of Eleanor of Aragon, in the Sala Laurana on the ground floor. Though description will have to stand in for direct experience, a detailed analysis of this one design solution brings to light some of the implications of Scarpa's approach to design. Scarpa raises the translucent marble bust of Eleanor of Aragon to a carefully calculated height on a platform of polished ebony, upon which it appears to float – the platform's sensuously elliptical curvatures precisely determined by the designer. A thin cushion of air seems to lift the bust from its support, an effect reinforced by the polar contrast of black and white (resonating with the hot-cold dualism of the materials). Supported at the rear by two small cylinders of brass, Laurana's sculpture rests at the front on a blade of lead set in a piece of brass. At the same time, the dimensions of the wooden platform eliminate any suggestion of the decapitation effect that is so typical of busts, and its design complements the shape of the sculpture. Natural light penetrates through a window by a side-lighting that emphasizes the slight inclination of the head and the plastic values of the modeling. Stucco panels in delicate tones project slightly from the walls behind and beside the bust, so that the clear feminine profile is defined against a dense chromatic

Main and side elevations of the display of a *Crucifixion* with *Saints*, Museo di Castelvecchio, 1962–64. Graphite and colored pencil on cardboard, 31.5 x 43.2 cm. Coll. MDC

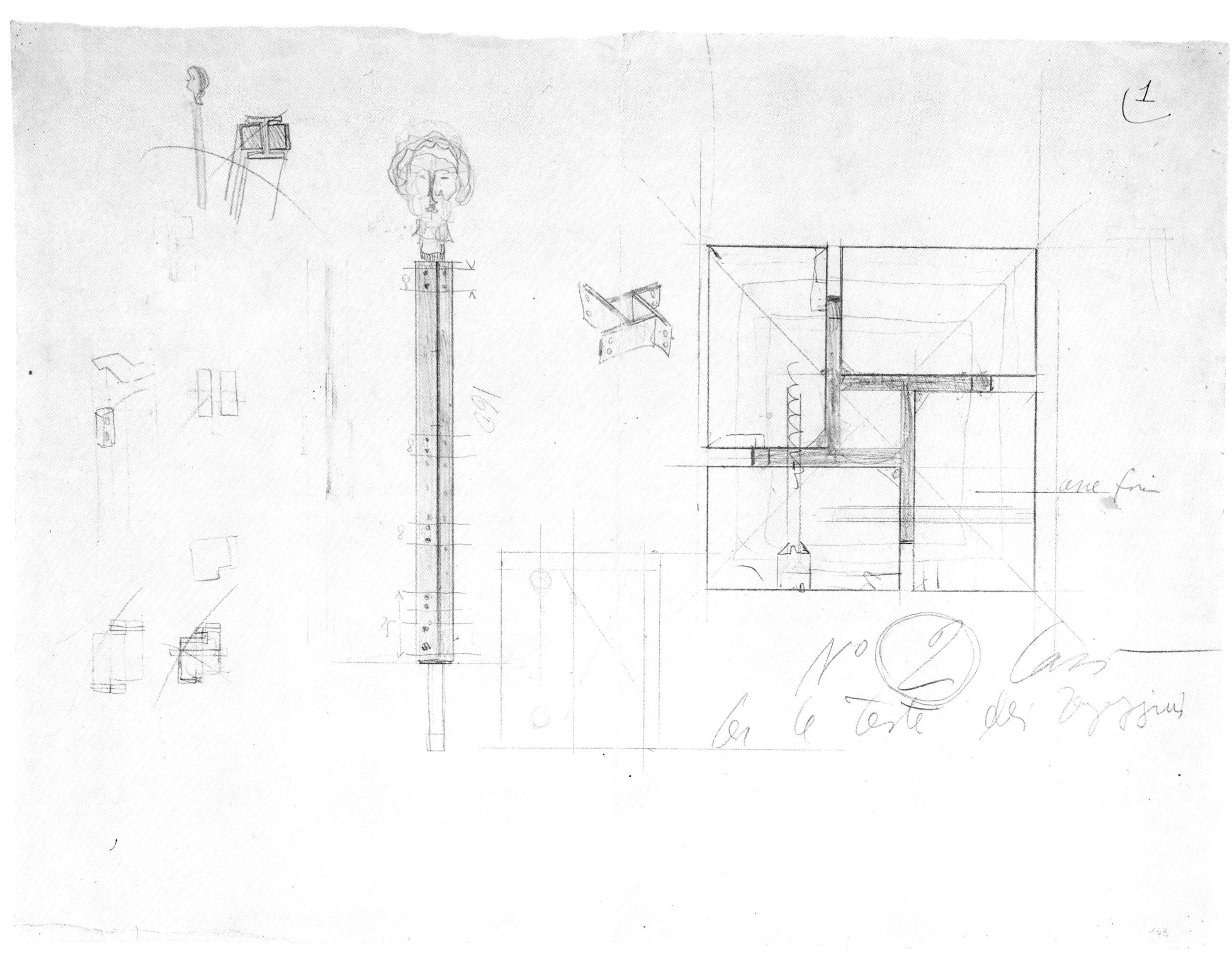

Elevation and plan for support of head by Antonello Gagini with studies for details, Palazzo Abatellis, 1953–54. Graphite on paper, 50 x 70 cm. Coll. GRS

Elevations of supports for *Virgin and Child* by Antonello Gagini and bust of Eleanor of Aragon by Francesco Laurana, Palazzo Abatellis, 1953–54. Graphite on cardboard, 31.5 x 43.7 cm. Coll. GRS

background, the vertical seam between the panels providing a subtle contrasting accent. Anchored in the paving of the floor, the rod supporting both marble and ebony forms an off-center visual fulcrum for the entire display. Entering from the adjoining room, the visitor moves around the display and is first attracted by the play of chiaroscuro on the profile, with its three-quarter lighting. Moving around the bust, gaining a sense of it as a volume, one falls at last under the direct gaze of the figure calmly communicating its power.

It must be understood that *allestimento,* the Italian for 'installation,' is entangled in multiple meanings that, though compatible, are by no means identical. An exploration of these senses helps to articulate several noteworthy distinctions concerning the nature of Scarpa's installations, both in museums and elsewhere. The various senses of installing, preparing, setting up, staging, fitting out, and equipping merge the *process* (creative and material) with the *product* (a concretion or expression we can use or enjoy). The meaning of the word thus encompasses ways of isolating, pointing out, illuminating, dramatizing, and focussing a new manner of perception (more concentrated and less distracted than the usual) on whatever it is we want to show, for the purpose of a kind of heightened enjoyment (by turns critical, interpretative, exemplary, didactic, communicative, promotional, allusive, illusory). It matters little that the occasion is ephemeral and the place anyplace, high-class or mundane. In the end, the important thing is the relationships that are created over the given period of time among place, objects to be shown, installation design, and display apparatus. Whether that period is short (as with displays at fairs) or lasts years (as in a museum) makes little difference, except insofar as the display's physical durability, its resistance to wear and tear, must be taken into account.

Through *allestimento*, the installation of an exhibition, relationships are created with a space that welcomes, includes, and provides hospitality. These relationships can variously deny, hide, conceal, block out, or veil the "container," all the more so as to read that container, comment on it, make it manifest, or include it, but also in order to deform it, modify it, estrange it. No installation can avoid coming to terms with the space in which it must deploy its elements, its own designed artifices, creating an architecture of more or less temporary aggregations of objects through selective instruments of display. These instruments may be endowed with varying degrees of explicitness, with greater or lesser loquacity, with a discreet or an emphatic presence, but they, too, will become objects on display. Negating any notion that their role is neutral, they themselves will be transformed into actors on the stage of the exhibition, eliciting that fatal attraction by which installation is drawn to design.

The Italian contribution to the conception and construction of the contemporary museum, with its characteristic originality and its peculiar mix of approaches generated by an urgent confrontation with history, is certainly one of the highlights of post-war architecture. Italian architects took on the ensemble of problems, in all their complexity, that surround the restoration of historic buildings and the design of museums. The limitation constituted by the use of existing structures for extensive portions of new Italian museums – a condition that was often inescapable – may appear a serious obstacle to formulating an effective and coherent response to the various overall needs of a museum. And yet that challenge was accepted by the most aware and sensitive Italian architects, who saw something positive in a design challenge that combined both the recovery of heritage and the attribution of new meaning, the search for a form of dialogue – subdued or eloquent, but at all times audible – between container and content, invention and permanence.

In his installations, Scarpa's more lyrical and exuberant creations become hieroglyphic extensions of the "decorative" virtuality inherent in the objects to be exhibited; they are precise interpretations that intensify critical perception. The Canova plaster cast gallery at Possagno (1955–57) and the Museo di Castelvecchio in Verona (1956–73) reveal many of the highly refined artifices adopted by Scarpa as he searched for strategies of perception and exposition to arrive at critical assumptions about the works on exhibit.

Perhaps what distinguishes Scarpa's approach centers around the closed dialogue that Scarpa achieves with the works in his installations, the willingness to explore

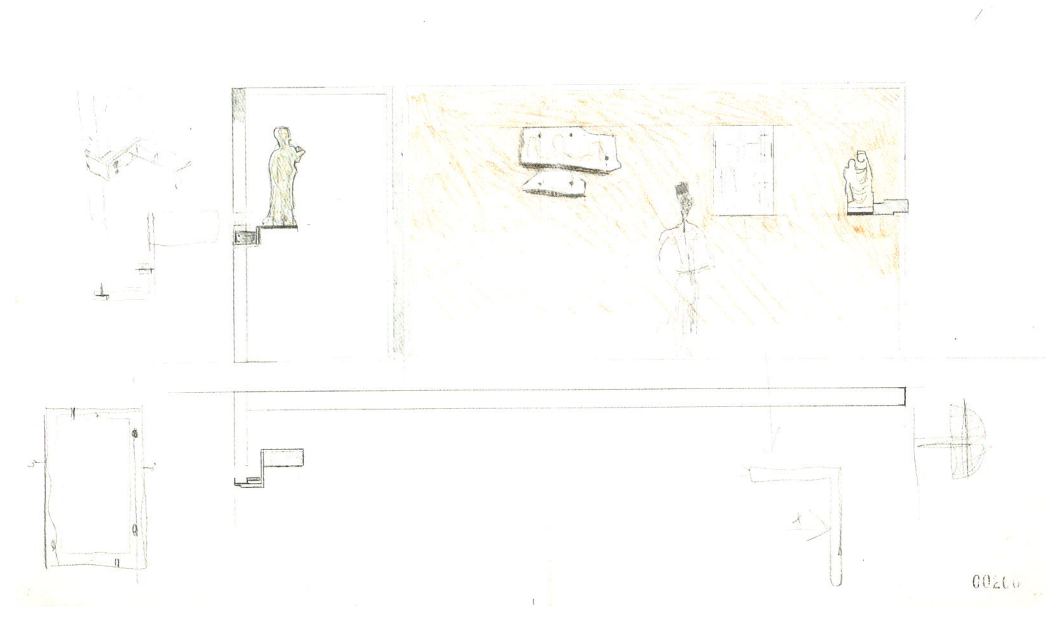

Elevation and plan of plaster screen with studies for the support of the large *Virgin and Child* (left), Museo di Castelvecchio, 1962–64. Graphite and colored pencil on cardboard, 31.5 x 43.2 cm. Coll. MDC

Elevation and axonometric of support for the small *Virgin and Child*, with detail studies, Museo di Castelvecchio, 1962–64. Graphite and colored pencil on cardboard, 31.5 x 43.2 cm. Coll. MDC

an unorthodox conception of display, the skill deployed in Scarpa's solutions. The estrangement of the work from the "here and now" is a necessary condition of returning to question its meaning. Scarpa's "point of view" represents the epitome of sophistication in the thought of what a museum is, a sophistication characteristic of the best in post-war Italian museum design. At the same time, it is what sets it in a historical period we can never go back to, with its connotations of an "applied idealism" and an implicit but strong reference to a public, consisting mainly of an elite, that is a far cry from the mass audiences of today.

Scarpa's skill as a designer of museums reaches its apogee at the Possagno Gipsoteca and the Museo di Castelvecchio in Verona. But his experience in the field of designing installations began earlier on the island of Murano with the restoration he directed as a young man for the master glassmaker Giacomo Cappellin (1925–26) and the displays designed in the late 1920s. Professionally, Scarpa's career as an installation designer began in the 1930s, when he produced such remarkable work as the exhibition *Venetian Goldsmiths* in the Sansovino Loggetta, Venice (1937). But it was not until 1950, when the magazine *Metron* published a review of the book pavilion that Scarpa designed for the *Biennale*, that museum professionals and critics began to take note of his work.

Scarpa's œuvre is not the sum produced by adding together his different activities: architect, restorer, museum planner, designer, decorator, and whatever else one might choose to add to that list. Carlo Scarpa is essentially a craftsman, a maker of artifacts – the author of objects made as art and with art, where *ars* is purely and simply the etymological *augere* or way of acting of an *auctor,* one who makes an 'increase.' For Scarpa, this meant acting on materials and nature, by ornamenting and decorating them, drawing them out of their inert formlessness, assigning them form and meaning – creating artifact and artifice as a second nature to ourselves.

Plan, elevation, sections, and studies for the *paragoni*, Museo di Castelvecchio, 1962–64. Graphite and colored pencil on cardboard, 50 x 70 cm. Coll. MDC

Alba Di Lieto

THE RENEWAL OF THE CASTELVECCHIO

A room in the Reggia wing before interventions showing the decoration of the 1920s. Photograph: Maurizio Brenzoni. Coll. Maurizio Brenzoni

MASSIVE IN SCALE AND MARKED by its imposing towers, the Castelvecchio still dominates the skyline of Verona today. Built by the della Scala dynasty between 1354 and 1356, this fortified castle incorporated several existing structures dating from Roman and medieval times, including the church of San Martino in Aquaro, dating from the eighth century, and a portion of the twelfth-century city wall.

The castle's strategic position assured the della Scala family control of Verona and facilitated their escape north to Germany and the safety of the Holy Roman Empire, where they had strong political allies. The fortified bridge that eventually permitted their flight north across the river Adige was a rather daring feat of engineering for its day; destroyed in the Second World War, it was promptly rebuilt.

The fourteenth-century castle has two courtyards: the frescoed 'Reggia' courtyard (the probable residence of the della Scala family) and a main courtyard enclosed on three sides by a 'curtain' wall with battlements and shielded corner towers, its fourth, north-facing side overlooking the river.

Over the centuries the Castelvecchio underwent numerous transformations, especially under Napoleonic rule, when two large barracks were built by military engineers (1802–06) along the north and east sides of the main courtyard. The castle lost its military function at the beginning of the twentieth century. Deeded to the city of Verona, it was restored between 1924 and 1926 following nineteenth-century French and Italian models:[1] the towers that had been lopped off in the previous century were reconstructed, the battlement walkways and swallowtail crenellations recreated, and the drawbridges replaced. A Romantic image of Verona's medieval castle was restored to the city.

A leading figure behind the reconstruction was Antonio Avena, director of Verona's museums. Avena proposed to move the city's art collections to the Castelvecchio from their home in the Palazzo Pompei.[2] For the facade of this new museum, the Napoleonic barracks were modified with the insertion of Gothic and Renaissance windows taken from Veronese buildings that had been demolished during the transformation of the city in the late nineteenth century. The barrack interiors were entirely renovated: the walls were decorated with frescoes, vaulted ceilings were replaced with coffered ceilings, fireplaces built of recycled elements were installed, and

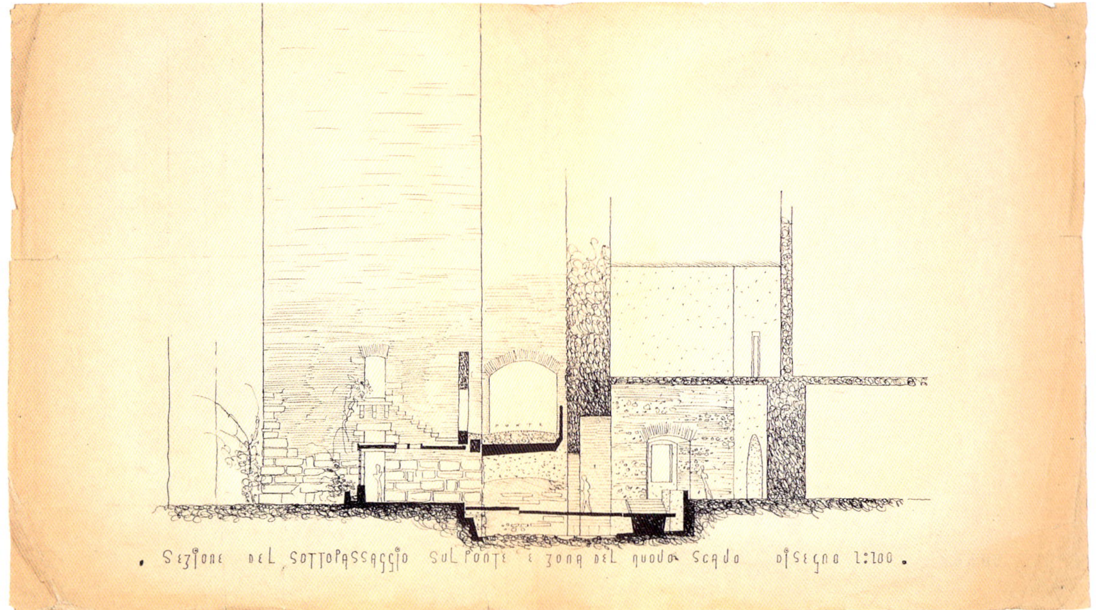

Carlo Scarpa, designer and draftsman; Angelo Rudella, draftsman. Section of the Porta del Morbio and the underground passageway leading to the bridge, 1958. Pen-and-ink on cardboard, 31.2 x 57.3 cm. Coll. MDC

the halls were finally filled with furniture, sculptures, paintings, and various other objects. In the midst of all this decor, the works of art were often reduced to mere components of the decoration.

THE PORTA DEL MORBIO AND THE REGGIA WING

When Licisco Magagnato assumed the post of director of Verona museums in 1956, the dimly lit, jumbled installations of the Museo di Castelvecchio – unchanged since the 1920s – led this young man with fresh ideas to search for a specialist capable of devising a new and original architectural design for the ancient structure, while at the same time respecting the museum's historical setting and significance. Magagnato had undoubtedly seen some of Carlo Scarpa's museum work, including that for the Gallerie dell'Accademia[3] (from 1944) and the Museo Correr (1953–57), both in Venice, and the Palazzo Abatellis in Palermo (1953–54).[4] Magagnato participated in the work not merely as the museum's director but equally as an historian, furnishing Scarpa with a series of notes clarifying the different eras to which the various structures of the Castelvecchio dated. He would make many such valuable contributions, not only enriching the project with ideas but also complicating it considerably.

The first phase of reconstruction (1957–64) began quietly late in 1957, with underground excavations that revealed the Porta del Morbio and the road linking the castle to the bridge built by the della Scala. Scarpa's first drawings for the project address this crucial area, proposing a link between the two sections of the castle via an underground passageway running beneath a public street, at the same time revealing the historic and architectural stratifications that had emerged by April 1958.

In August of 1958, the exhibition *From Altichiero to Pisanello*, which was also designed by Scarpa, opened in the museum's Reggia wing. Magagnato's decision to award its design to Scarpa was calculated to demonstrate the architect's abilities to the Verona city council. The centerpiece of the exhibition was Pisanello's fresco *St. George and the Princess*, lowered from the Gothic vaults of the Pellegrini chapel in the Church of Sant'Anastasia.[5]

By the time of the exhibition, work on the Reggia wing had advanced considerably: the ground floor, the second story of the keep, and the two floors of the Reggia (linked by a newly designed staircase) were also opened, although not yet completely finished. Scarpa had connected the Reggia to the Torre del

View of the moat and bridge, 1960–62. Coll. MDC

Second-floor gallery in the Reggia wing, 1958. Coll. MDC

Mastio (the keep) by a daring hanging bridge and to the galleries in the Napoleonic wing by the underground passageway of the Porta del Morbio. Drawings by Scarpa are rarely dated, but several are clearly linked to the work done in this period, among them plans featuring various solutions for the floors[6] and sketches for the frames of paintings hung in the 1958 exhibition. The renovations to the Reggia preserved the fourteenth-century masonry, though it was necessary to demolish the old plaster in the search for original frescoes; these were then restored and highlighted by neutral colored panels of new unfinished plaster composed of lime and sand. The floors of the second floor were redone in Clauzetto marble, while those of the third were replaced with mansonia walnut surrounded by limestone moldings. The wooden ceilings with their exposed beams were left untouched.

Although in the restoration of this wing of the museum Scarpa used traditional materials and an understated color scheme, his approach to the installation is truly innovative. Simple limestone shelves served to support the polyptychs, and Scarpa conceived special frames for the paintings, displaying some pictures on rotating structures and suspending others from the ceiling. Crosses were set on limestone parallelepipeds.[7]

The visitor's path through the museum was completed at the beginning of 1964 with a covered outdoor passageway made possible by the demolition of the Sala Albertini. According to the construction logbook, two small rooms on the third floor of the Reggia were also completed in 1964 with floor and wall treatments similar to those seen there today.

THE GALLERY WING

Work proceeded intensively during the first eight months of 1958 leading up to the Pisanello exhibition; between 1959 and 1961 it continued more sporadically. During this period, the work of uncovering and identifying the castle's original structures continued. At the same time, the collaboration between Scarpa and Magagnato broadened to include an exhibition of Murano glass that opened in March of 1960 in Verona's Palazzo della Gran Guardia. Scarpa also designed a temporary sculpture gallery for the ground floor of the Napoleonic or gallery wing; all that survives of that renovation are a few archival photographs and a publication by Roberto Aloi,[8] but from these it can be determined that the walls were stripped of plaster and the false frescoes and false fireplaces removed, while the *terrazzo* flooring and the coffered ceilings remained those from the 1920s.

This initial phase of experimentation allowed Scarpa and Magagnato time to give further thought to the significance of the restoration and the type of exhibition system and lighting they would use. In the gallery wing, they monitored the effect of natural light on the sculptures during the course of the day and over the seasons, and determined the ideal location for each sculpture by setting them on temporary supports made of the local Prun stone and moving them around, a technique that allowed a full exploration of their relation to the space. Despite the ongoing construction the museum remained open, a temporary wooden walkway having been built over the moat to allow visitors entry. The sculptures remained in place and were removed only when construction made it necessary.

Scarpa's plans for the permanent installation of this sector of the museum were based on an overall system involving orthogonal elements, which appear in both the architecture itself (for instance floors and ceilings) and the installation of the works of art. Seeking a simultaneous graphic depiction of all aspects of the project, Scarpa overlaid his basic ground-floor drawing with tracing-paper plans of the upper floors or drew the floors superimposed on the same drawing. The grid became both a point of reference and a leitmotif. The square shape of the rooms is echoed in the ceilings, divided into four quadrants by a concrete cross element. The bays thus created are treated with matte stucco in a shade of gray that shifts to green on sunny days, due to light reflected from the lawn. At the intersection of the crossbeams, a steel "carriage" assembly transfers the load to a further steel beam that spans all the rooms along the longitudinal axis of the building. This beam plays an important role not only structurally but visually; a long, continuous axis, it functions to underscore the perspectival progression of the galleries. Structurally, its addition was necessitated by the decision to reduce the excessive thickness (80 cm) of the floor above, which was lowered relative to the windows, thus shifting the light source higher up above the works of art. The result is a more diffuse and satisfactory illumination, brighter and different in quality than the natural light in the halls.

The floors of each room are also squares, internally divided into long bands: a series of dark 'carpets' of polished cement bordered in white Prun stone. There was a technical reason for this division, as cement in large surfaces tends to crack, while in narrow strips it remains intact and even acquires a certain gloss. The sculptures were set on elevated platforms treated with colored lime paste, raised so as not to interfere with the geometric composition of the floor. More than mere furnishings, these platforms achieve a major presence.

While in the ground-floor gallery the Napoleonic wall structure was left intact, radical modifications were made on the upper floor, with the construction of new floors, the sealing and opening up of doorways, and the removal of fireplaces. In order to display the works of art on the transverse partition walls that segmented the gallery, it was necessary to remove the sixteenth-century doors added at their centers by Avena. A set of plans of the second floor illustrates, in sequence, the general layout, the masonry of the partition walls, ideas for the floors and false ceilings, and designs for the lighting system. A lateral passageway leads to the courtyard while an oblique corridor, floored in Prun stone, runs along the side overlooking the river. Parallel to one another, the partition walls are slightly staggered on the river side, dramatically accentuating their perspective. A series of screen-like panels finished in glossy stucco closes off the riverside corridor and marks the boundaries of the individual galleries.

Here Scarpa intensified the architectural language he employed. With the same spirit and rigorous design as that used in the gallery on the ground floor, the chromatic range was adjusted to mark a pictorial contrast with the works of art, which here dated from the sixteenth to the eighteenth century. The flooring is an expanse of terracotta tile bordered in white stone. Above hang the quadrants of the false ceilings, in dark gray stucco except for the next-to-last room, finished in black, and the Sala Avena, in cobalt blue – a schema evoking Mondrian, an artist for whom Scarpa felt a particular fondness.

Throughout the museum, natural lighting was supplemented with artificial lighting. An array of upright floor lamps was installed on the ground floor, while on the upper floor fluorescent lights were suspended from the panels of the false ceilings, forming strips of light.

THE STATUE OF CANGRANDE DELLA SCALA

The work surrounding the placement of the equestrian statue of Cangrande I della Scala was carried out in two phases, the first involving the selection of the site and the design of the hanging and vertical links, the second focusing on the design of the structure supporting the statue itself. The initial phase involved a long period of study and exploration, while the second proceeded rapidly, both in conception and in construction, between January and October of 1964. The few months prior to the opening of the museum was a time of feverish activity.

The earliest plans place the statue at what is today the entrance to the museum, at the east end of the gallery wing – an idea that was discarded because the sculpture would have been seen immediately by all visitors; it seemed better to have this symbolic work "discovered" along the tour. Another early idea had been to display the statue in an exhibition hall, but with the decision to demolish a stretch of the Napoleonic barracks, Scarpa and Magagnato considered the idea of placing the statue outside.

Archival research and archeological explorations in 1958 had afforded a thorough understanding of the building phases of the Castelvecchio. Magagnato's knowledge of the castle's history had led him to suspect that a large arch within one of the blockhouse walls might be an ancient passageway; the excavation of the surrounding wall in fact revealed a road dating from the della Scala period linking the twelfth-century Porta del Morbio with the bridge over the Adige. This passageway was, and remains today, the only connection between the building's two wings. After lengthy study, it was decided finally to demolish two Napoleonic rooms and a nineteenth-century staircase.

The historical importance of the Porta del Morbio made it the ideal location for the equally significant statue of Cangrande I, both a symbol of the museum and an important example of European Gothic sculpture. It had originally been installed outdoors atop the Church of Santa Maria Antica. After weighing the dangers, Scarpa and Magagnato decided finally to place it once again in the open air, positioned high up. A system of walkways and aerial supports would allow visitors to view the work at close range. To shield it from the elements, Scarpa designed a covering that functions much like an enormous umbrella, while leaving the statue visible from all angles, illuminated by the constantly changing natural light. This ingenious covering was designed as an extension of the existing roof, but in different materials. Its interesting and irregular composition is formed of wooden beams recovered from the demolition of the old roof and its double-pitched structure has stepped edges that cut away completely from the Comune wall. The massive timbers at its apex rest on the steel support of the wall's battlements, the only remnant of the original junction. Strips of copper, green from exposure, contrast with the red of the traditional roof tiles.

Demolition of Napoleonic stairs, 1960–62. Coll. MDC

The design and renovation of the area that was to receive the statue took place between the end of 1961 and July of 1962. The construction logbook records explorations of the original structures, the removal of columns and cornices from the three-light window of the Salone Cangrande, the demolition of both the facade wall (to the height of the joisted second floor), and the dismantling and reconstruction of a wooden truss structure. These notes continue right up to a month prior to the museum's opening. The statue was installed on 1 November 1964.

The first ideas for the structure supporting the sculpture of Cangrande were developed at the beginning of 1964. Scarpa began with the intention to reuse a pedestal that may have come from the tomb of Cangrande, but in a second phase shifted to the idea of a completely new structure suggestive of columns: six or seven large tubes, perhaps to be made of steel, topped with a slab that would support the sculpture – a plan that was pursued as far as a wooden model. In the next phase the support took on a new and unusual form: a curving bracket that on the same sheet of paper rapidly changed to an inverted L, the form finally adopted. The L-shaped structure, built, for technical reasons, with three castings of concrete, stands nearly five meters tall, its verticality further emphasized by the vertical imprint of the formwork boards. Only the first of the seven drawings that develop the design of the support is dated; less than eleven months would elapse between it and the completion of construction.

SALA BOGGIAN, SALA AVENA, LIBRARY, AND NORTHEAST TOWER

The second phase of Scarpa's work (though only partly completed by him) concerned the Sala Boggian on the second floor of the east wing, the Sala Avena, and the northeast tower, and took place between 1967 and 1973.

Destroyed by bombing but rebuilt between 1948 and 1950, the Sala Boggian had been used as a concert hall in the 1920s. Scarpa intended it to retain that function, and made several studies for the stage and the conductor's podium; one small sketch even called for the installation of an elevator. However, the space that was originally meant for the stage was converted into the Sala Avena, the last hall in the museum to be constructed (begun in 1967 and completed ten years later), while the Sala Boggian became a space for temporary exhibitions. A series of rapid sketches calling for a suspended, covered, and glassed-in passageway give evidence of Scarpa's intention to link the upper floor of the museum and the Sala Avena with the northeast tower. Several studies from the same period explore ways to free the fourteenth-century tower from the Napoleonic-era wall, so as to emphasize the historical distance between these two structures.

During the second phase of the renovation Scarpa was asked to renovate the art library, located in a space adjacent to the tower. The incision made by Scarpa between the Napoleonic wall and the tower thus had a practical function as well, which was to bring light to the library reading room. The studies for the large bank of windows in the reading room and for the wood facing of the wall overlooking the river all date from 1966. The restoration of the northeast tower, which was adapted to contain offices and a restoration workshop (it now houses a collection of prints and drawings), dates from the same period.[9]

FACADES AND GARDEN

For the facades on the courtyard of the gallery wing, Scarpa chose to preserve the 'collage' of architectural fragments, but redesigned the interior divisions of the windows, which are punctuated by rigorous Mondrian-like rhythms and proportions that contrast with and at the same time emphasize the surrounding Gothic frames. The old plaster and the false decoration on the facades were replaced by a rougher plaster with a vibrant grain and texture. This second skin is cut away in several places to reveal the underlying masonry structure.

In his very first drawings for the facade, Scarpa planned to isolate the gallery wing from the enclosure wall dating from the time of the Comune, intending to locate the statue of Cangrande at the Porta del Morbio. Scarpa retained the facade established by Antonio Avena in 1923 and structured the space meant for the Cangrande as a partly open room.

It is interesting to follow the process that led Scarpa from his first hesitant ideas for the window frames (reminiscent of those built

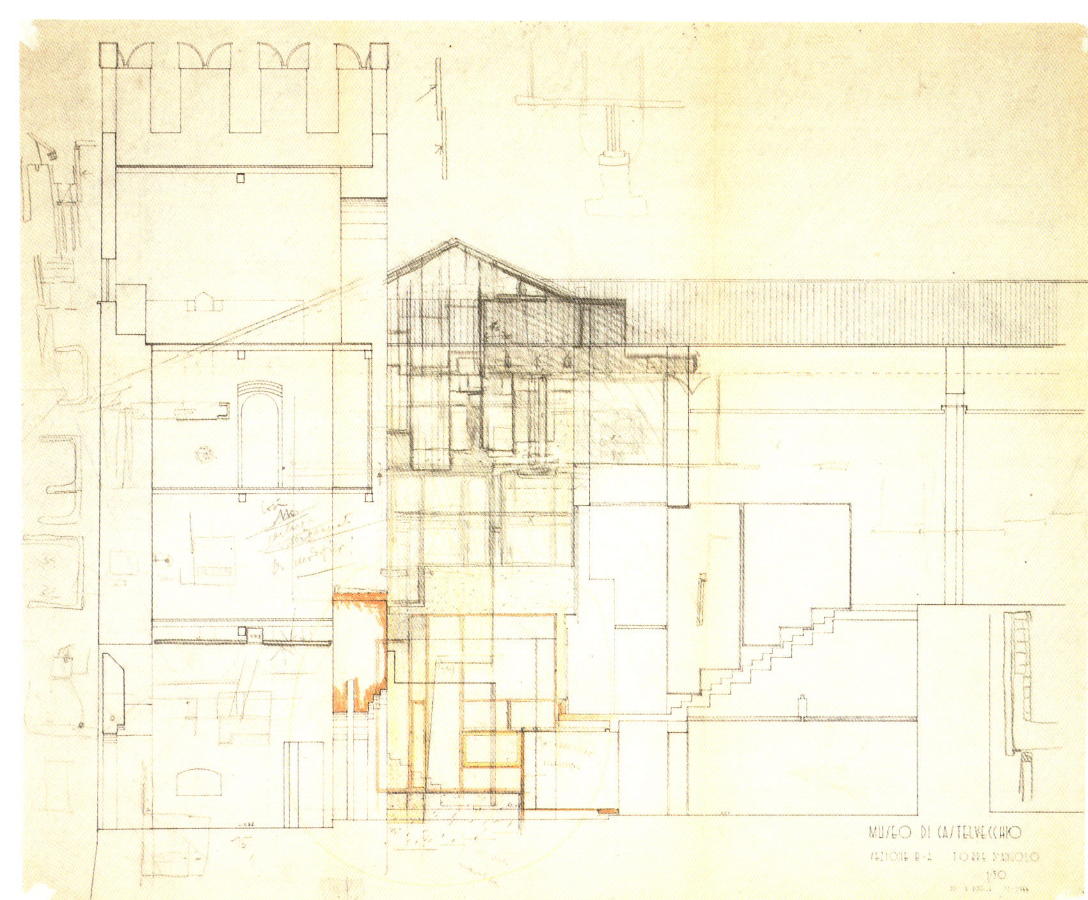

Carlo Scarpa, designer and draftsman; Angelo Rudella, draftsman. Elevation of gallery wing, 1962. Graphite and colored pencil on reprographic print, 30 x 97 cm. Coll. MDC

Carlo Scarpa, designer and draftsman; Angelo Rudella, draftsman. Section of the northeast tower and elevation of new wall of the Sala Avena and the library, 1966. Graphite and colored pencil on reprographic print, 50 x 60.2 cm. Coll. MDC

in the 1930s for Ca' Foscari) to his decisive, final creations suggestive of Mondrian. The genius and innovative quality of Scarpa's renovation is revealed also in the treatment of the central hall, another solution showing the absolute perfection of the chromatic, material, and spatial equilibriums achieved by Scarpa. Having moved the museum entrance to the northeast corner of the courtyard, the architect used the original Gothic loggia at the center of the ground floor to great advantage by erecting behind it a rigorous geometric window, neoplastic in origin, that accentuates the elaborate workmanship of the triple arcade, while at the same time constituting a filter between exterior and interior. A door serves as a passage from this sculpture gallery to the garden, inviting a dialogue with the outside, where a number of additional sculptures are on display.

The *sacello* is the sole protruding element of the facade: a cube sheathed in a mosaic of Prun stone in shades ranging from white to pink and from violet to red. From the interior, this cube is a small space housing precious objects dating from Longobard times, which otherwise would have been lost in the immense space of the sculpture gallery. A clear shaft of light penetrates from the skylight, illuminating the objects that rise from the floor and stand out against the dark, bottle-green stuccoed walls. It is a perfect instance of a small room with a very specific formal equilibrium.

The master plan of the museum includes a definitive scheme for the garden, whose design Scarpa also based on an orthogonal system – one axis represented by the hedges and another, intersecting axis formed of the path leading to the museum entrance. The two hedges, fundamental components of the garden geometry, run parallel to each other, separated by a narrow passage that was originally to be paved in stone or concrete. When viewing the main facade, these hedges delimit an initial partition; they are pruned at an angle to align with the windows and correct the slight slope of the lawn. Scarpa created a second region beyond them: a large green rectangle bounded at the south by a hedge and at the north by a concrete curtain wall that partially isolates the facade and allows only a glimpse of the *sacello*. The presence of water softens the rigidity of the composition and serves to mediate between the architecture in greenery and the architecture in stone.

The garden was the last element of the project to be completed, even though it constituted the prologue and spatial antecedent to the whole. The land in the courtyard was leveled in November 1964 and the greenery was planted during the fifteen days prior to the opening of the complex.[10] Scarpa personally chose the plants.

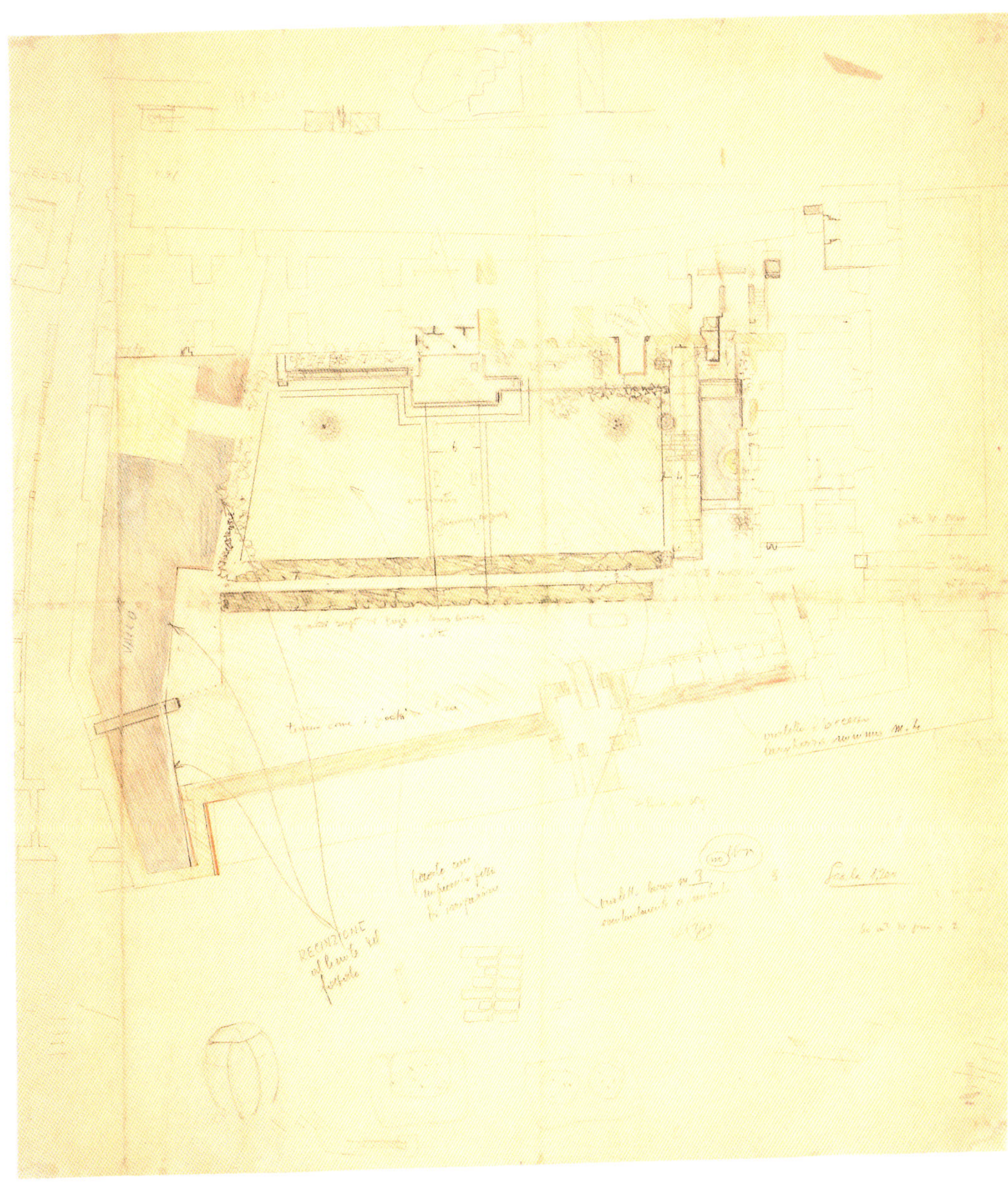

Carlo Scarpa, designer and draftsman; Angelo Rudella, draftsman.
Plan of courtyard, showing first proposal for garden, 1961–62.
Graphite and colored pencil on reprographic print, 61 x 55.5 cm.
Coll. MDC

Mildred Friedman

SCARPA TODAY

BECAUSE WE FEEL CONFIDENT IN OUR PERIOD WE CAN LOOK AT THE PAST AND DERIVE INSPIRATION INSTEAD OF FALLING INTO IMITATION.

EERO SAARINEN

CARLO SCARPA, NEVER AN ACCEPTED member of Italy's architectural brotherhood, stood apart from the long post-war debate about the future of modernism, and concerned himself instead with the culture of his region, the Veneto: its colors, its materials, its crafts, its sensuality, and, above all, its spirit. His closest friends were artists and writers, and so his work reflected the poetics of his time rather than its reason. Thus, in the 1960s and 1970s, Scarpa's focus on the specificities of place and his revival of such poetic concerns as narrative, time, personal symbolism, and the senses engaged him in a subtle, discreet, and sometimes subversive debate with prevailing architectural models and attitudes. Throughout his later career, there was widespread admiration, and equally evident discomfort, with his obsessive craftsmanship and his passion for the act of making. His last works, notably the Brion tomb and the Banca Popolare di Verona, were seen by some as self-indulgent and overwrought, and by others as pioneering examples of a startling new poetics of place.

Scarpa was never an enemy of modernism or an advocate of historicism. He believed that architecture must, above all, be an expression appropriate to its time.[1] That point of view is perhaps the primary reason that so many of today's architects express a profound interest in Scarpa's work. But beyond the philosophical, is there something in his drawings or in the built work that relates to their own? Is Scarpa's collaboration with artisans a method they wish to emulate? Has his ability to bring new life to historic buildings become an even more relevant skill today? Did his close relationship with artists and his admiration for ancient and contemporary works of art inspire a similar interest among contemporary designers?

Interviews conducted with a wide spectrum of a new generation of architects suggest that the lessons of Scarpa for current practice reside in his manner of working within design and craft traditions.[2] His revival of a sense of architecture as a public vehicle for private expression and his ability to provoke a dialogue between old and new are significant to this generation. Further, Scarpa's importance stems from his ability to adapt ancient local traditions to current and global concerns, from his skill in making a historic fabric absorb a modern vocabulary, and from his use of ancient techniques of building and design to produce radically new, highly personal forms. Young architects, moved and inspired by Scarpa's accomplishments, feel a kinship with him in their own resistance to the neutral and their growing search for individuality.

Three years after Scarpa's death, Nory Miller writing in *Progressive Architecture* recognized that Scarpa had moved the once confrontational dialogue between past and present to a new level: "He achieved an extraordinary coexistence involving architecture of different centuries ... without the crutches of 'neutral' glass linkages, uniform materials, or historical 'references.'"[3] In this fusion of past and present Scarpa found the freedom to develop a private imaginative language that would still carry common meaning, a point the eminent Japanese architect Fumihiko Maki raises in evaluating the relationship of Scarpa's work to Japanese traditions. Scarpa was an ardent admirer of Japanese art and architecture, and when he finally journeyed to Japan he began to understand their mysteries. One finds echoes of a Japanese sensibility in the translucency of his woven screens and gates, which suggest the transmission of light and shadow through traditional shoji screens. Maki locates the subtle but critical relationship between working within a common tradition and finding private expression in this sympathy between Scarpa's work and Japanese architectural sensibilities. For Scarpa, like the Japanese, Maki explains, "Architectural creation is not invention but discovery; it is not a pursuit of something beyond the imagination but the externalization of the collective imagination of an age. Scarpa's works always recall for me the variegated designs of the early Edo period Katsura Detached Palace, because the two cultures are both characterized by a strong tendency to become private in character."

From the first years of Scarpa's design practice he received commissions to install painting and sculpture exhibitions and to reorganize old master galleries. He stocked his library with books on art, and found a private iconography in the artists he loved – Antonello and Titian, Piet Mondrian and Paul Klee. Their influences and those of many artists of his generation whose works he came to know through his installation designs for the *Venice Biennale* are subtly felt in the luminosity and textural complexity of Scarpa's use of colors and materials. For example, we can sense a clear relationship between the rich reds of Venetian painting, the palette of Mark Rothko, and the interior colors of Verona's Banca Popolare. And the rhythm of the patterning in such works as the stone facade of the *sacello* at the Museo di

Kaze-no-oka Crematorium (Fumihiko Maki, Architect; 1997), Nakatsu City, Oita Prefecture

Castelvecchio shows a painter's compositional hand, a quality that has been admired by architects such as Steven Holl, Brigitte Shim and Howard Sutcliffe, and the Hariri sisters. In his unique installations of the permanent collections at the Palazzo Abatellis, the Canova plaster cast gallery, and the Museo di Castelvecchio, he uses the works of art as organizing elements for the design of the space. It is this revolutionary approach toward making space through the allocation of discrete forms rather than through spatial planning that attracts many architects today. For example, the buildings were made to accommodate the objects, sometimes in idiosyncratic ways, as in his daring view from above to the lower floor of the Palazzo Abatellis chapel, where the great quattrocento fresco *The Triumph of Death* is displayed. His individualized approach to the installation of each work of art stands in total opposition to the neutrality of approach characteristic of so many museums today. Scarpa's associate on the Castelvecchio and Banca Popolare projects, the Veronese architect Arrigo Rudi, has pointed out how curators were enriched after working with Scarpa, gaining a new freedom in their thinking and a new technical versatility. Rudi believes that museum practice for curator and architect alike has been changed forever by Scarpa's work.

There is a dichotomy in current architectural circles regarding the evaluation of Scarpa's methods and emphases. At one extreme are the conceptualists, such as the Los Angeles

Blades residence (Thom Mayne, Morphosis, Architects; 1995), Santa Barbara, California. Photograph: Kim Zwarts

Machado Silvetti Associates, Inc. Model of Getty Villa; section of café and bookstore, 1997. Basswood, 106.7 x 40.6 x 60.9 cm. Photograph: Anton Grassl. The J. Paul Getty Museum, Malibu, California

architects Thom Mayne and Eric Moss, who, although they admire Scarpa's eye and hand, believe it impossible to emulate his method, today's issues being so different from those that he faced. "When I was young, in the '60s and '70s," Mayne recalls, "I was more interested in the work of Aldo Rossi and James Stirling. There's a formal aspect to Scarpa's work that is somewhat problematic to me. As I get older I am finding myself more interested in its spirit and what it is attempting to do. Scarpa was committed to artistry, to nuance. He worked in an episodic, localized way. The whole is an accretion. He represents the end of a way of thinking. He deifies the materials. Now I'm more committed to organization and concepts. I'm more interested in the realities of life in a broader sense: metropolis, scale, infrastructure. So I have to give up some of the artistry."

On the other hand, there are those practitioners of a more romantic, even poetic sensibility, exemplified by the New Yorkers Leslie Gill and Steven Holl, Los Angeles architects Craig Hodgetts and Ming Fung, and Jorge Silvetti of Machado Silvetti in Boston, who find much to identify with in Scarpa's persistent search for expressive, appropriate new forms. Holl, who, like Scarpa, is deeply concerned with the detail of his buildings, believes that there is a degeneration underway in the construction process today, and that Scarpa "stands for what is now missing": the ability to craft a building patiently, modifying details as the need arises, and the freedom to continue designing to the end. "Today we have a gun against our heads: it is called the contract, the bid document, the price."

Scarpa's admirers have so often been preoccupied with the eloquent detailing of his projects that the deeper significance of his architecture – the restructuring of historically important buildings – is often overlooked in analyses of his accomplishments. Many major cities in America and Europe today contain vast sections of historically consequential buildings requiring extensive renovation merely in order to function. As today's architects cope with the aging of existing urban realms, Scarpa's singular ability to absorb and to accommodate a vernacular with a contemporary sensibility will surely be viewed as increasingly significant. Thus, for New York architect and critic Michael Sorkin, Scarpa's influence lies "in his easy way with the historic fabric of cities." Sorkin still finds his methods "exemplary and instructive," not only in his ability to relate modern circumstances to historical settings, but also in his weaving together of disparate new ideas. "He has a family of thoughts that he develops into something masterful and beautiful." Leslie Gill explains, "Scarpa's work assimilated itself particularly well to its historic milieu where it seamlessly grew upon that which it inherited, while clearly maintaining its own identity. This integrated approach has been particularly influential in my own work."

Richard Murphy, who practices architecture in Edinburgh and has written brilliantly on the renovations of the Museo di Castelvecchio

Royal Terrace Mews (Richard Murphy, Architects; 1995), Edinburgh. Photograph: Allan Forbes

and the Palazzo Querini Stampalia, admires Scarpa's uncanny talent for revealing, without emulating, the past. He maintains, for example, that uncovering the complex history of the Castelvecchio and responding to it in an architectural sense involved not just designing a museum, but unraveling and clarifying the history that preceded the intervention. In exposing the building's historical layers – literally "deconstructing" it – Scarpa revealed and enhanced its nineteenth- and twentieth-century banalities along with the powerful medieval beginnings of this extraordinary structure, which has long played a vital role in the public life of Verona. In so doing, Murphy shows, Scarpa turned the building itself into an exhibition.[4] Silvetti agrees that Scarpa's handling of the boundary between his interventions and the old was unequalled. The spaces 'in between' possess particular force: "The slab of travertine that he adds next to a medieval stone wall acts as an emblem of his architecture. Such a sliver of space joins them ... yet at the same time it literally separates them, puts air in between, and ... makes unequivocal what is new and what is old; that slice of space is also the space of his signature."

Holl states that in many works by others where restoration and a respect for the old are involved, "a loss of nerve takes over, and then you see it's a kind of bowing down, and not a hope for another generation." "He was saying something new about something old," Hodgetts agrees. "It's hard to see where Scarpa's interventions start and finish, because they have such an incredible empathy for what is there. His work was a layer of pure reason laid over an old, decaying structure." His sensitivity to the significance of each place and his boldness in realizing its resuscitation are Scarpa's primary legacies to a younger generation of architects. One sees these influences beautifully realized in such recent historical interventions as those by Piñon and Viaplana in Barcelona and Sverre Fehn in Norway.

Another eloquent aspect of Scarpa's work that fascinates young architects is the intensity with which he drew his way to design solutions. Scarpa's drawings were never conceived as sales tools, as contract drawings, as works of art, or even as finished working drawings as we know them today. In the words of Tod Williams, of the New York firm Williams/Tsien, "Scarpa's drawings were not technically working drawings, rather they were 'thinking drawings.'" Michael Sorkin describes Scarpa's method as "layer after layer, drawing and redrawing, a passionate intent to get it right. Doodles in the corners, wine stains – the drawing is alive for him." Seeing Scarpa's drawings as fractured – floating and dispersed elements rather than a visible whole – Diane Lewis associates this drawing technique directly with Scarpa's strategy of intervention, and sees the parts of the drawing as "elements in a field, an historic field, which is the city."

The hands-on studio method of Tod Williams and Billie Tsien is analogous to Scarpa's. Williams explains that their work was influenced by the sensuality of Scarpa's expression. "We don't use computers. We think

Neurosciences Institute (Williams/Tsien, Architects; 1996), La Jolla, California. Photograph: Michael Moran

Cordioli residence (Anna Maria Padovani, Architect; 1997), Verona. Photograph: Sergio Benaglia

the hand has a lot to do with the work. Our working method is more like his than it is like most offices today. However, our circumstances are very different from Scarpa's. We recognize that the essence of modernism is to somehow be in the present. The authentic can't emerge unless one is specific to the moment. We agree with him in that. We want to be profoundly affected by the present, the circumstances of the moment. Our work has been influenced by Scarpa because we saw something expressive in his work that we had never seen before. We believe deeply in the issue of the senses."

Scarpa's own sense of the value of drawing was apparent in his teaching methods, mocked by many in his day. The studio began with a lesson in sharpening pencils and might end, as Anna Maria Padovani, now an architect in Verona, remembers it, with the presentation to each student of an exquisitely made ebony straightedge. Massimo Vignelli remembers that his experience in Scarpa's drawing class united draftsmanship with the study of detail, sensitivity to materials, and, perhaps most intriguingly, the development of a sense of the accidents of time. Students would go with Scarpa to a *campo* in Venice where they were asked to measure and draw every surrounding building, invited to study the coloration and texture of the walls, the buildings' details, the intentional and unintentional results of the passage of time. They learned how chance plays a critical role and how the gradual change that was inherent in the nature of the materials could be calculated. Scarpa thus saw drawing as the essential tool of the eye.

Like Scarpa, Leslie Gill came to architecture through painting and readily recognized the sensitivity to the plasticity of materials and to color displayed in Scarpa's drawings. "He considered the entire piece of paper and didn't ignore the boundaries. Every space on the paper is activated. In studying Scarpa I learned how to convey material sensibility on a working drawing, how to use the page, and how to hook that into the computer. The computer helps. What you have lost in pencil lines you've gained in the flexibility of being able to reshuffle the information, much as he did in the layering of his drawings." She points out that "Scarpa is always thinking large-to-small and doesn't separate the details into one sort of category or sheet of development. The sequence of narrative details tells the whole story. The layers create an aggregate." Murphy explains that "his drawings are generative rather than descriptive. Just as his architecture is layered, his drawings are also layered. He often uses color to distinguish the many different ideas going on."

Although Scarpa's drawings are unique and represent his singular effort to build solutions in dialogue with craftsmen, in an unexpected way his drawings predict the computer software systems that are becoming the dominant tools used by today's architects to convey construction information. Frank Gehry – whose broad, sculptural gestures are as complex as Scarpa's contained ones – has computer experts in his office who are, in a way,

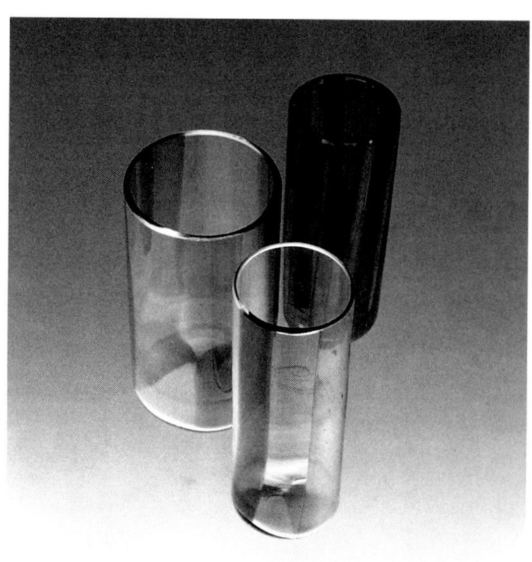

Venini tumblers (Vignelli Designs, Inc., New York; 1957). Blown glass. Coll. Vignelli Designs, Inc., New York

Watrous/Weatherman residence (Leslie Gill Architect/Bryce Sanders, Architecture/Design; 1997), Brooklyn, New York. Photograph: Jeff Goldberg. Coll. Esto Photographics Inc.

Teiger residence (Michael Rotondi, RoTo Architects; 1996), New Jersey. Photograph: Jeff Goldberg. Coll. Esto Photographics Inc.

St. Ignatius Church (Steven Holl, Architect; 1997), Seattle, Washington. Photograph: Paul Warchol Photography.

the contemporary equivalent of Scarpa's artisans. With the computer, images can be layered, reshuffled, compiled in a way that describes the history of the architect's thought patterns, much as Scarpa was able to describe them with his hand-drawn depictions.

"How do we bring the juices of craftsmanship into the connections – where edges come together?" Charles Eames asked. "What is missing is craft, the quality of hand." Scarpa's revival of the sense of hand – not in drawing only but in the realized work as well – continues to appeal to young architects. With his drawings, Scarpa would go directly to the artisans who were his collaborators, to the work under construction, and then back – modifying and clarifying as he proceeded toward the realization of an idea. The Los Angeles architect Michael Rotondi, former director of the maverick school SCI-Arc, points out that "Scarpa almost single-handedly resurrected the notion of the architect as master builder," because he understood the craftsmen's techniques and working methods. It was the give and take, the understanding between designer and artisan that made his work possible. "Instead of working only on paper, he worked full size and in real time," notes Rotondi. "We often think that drawing and modeling is the complete way to test an idea. But it isn't. The ultimate test of an idea is to build it." For Rotondi, "the aesthetic decisions Scarpa made came out of understanding the techniques of the artisans. They learned from him and he from them."[5]

Today, in northern Italy, in Japan, and to some degree in the rest of Europe, it is still possible for architects to emulate the Scarpa method with local artisans. Steven Holl believes, however, that this type of collaboration does not exist in America, and the kind of work it generates is open only to architects willing to take on the artisanal role directly, carrying out the fabrication of certain architectural elements themselves. Holl's St. Ignatius Church, perhaps his most Scarpaesque work, includes many handmade elements created under the architect's immediate supervision.

The question of detail and materiality in Scarpa's work is a complex one. While some still find his work too precious, too indulgent, too rich, there is growing recognition that what might once have been taken for decoration or cast aside as ornament was in fact a sophisticated and radical new design strategy. It was a way of making space through miniaturization, of making architecture through the joint and using materials not just to vary surfaces but to articulate a whole.

While in architecture school at Cornell, Gisue Hariri's investigations at the Center for Islamic Art (the "integration of something Eastern in a Western culture") brought her to Scarpa, who famously referred to himself as Byzantine. "I was born by San Marco church," Scarpa noted, "so I loved the Byzantine and the Islamic.... An Arab house is built like Venice:

you walk in narrow corridors and there is pleasantness of water and space."[6] That memory recurs in the color and sheen of his plaster walls and in his intricate combinations of stone, metal, and wood. Gisue's partner Mojgan Hariri describes Persian and Islamic architecture as "having a connection to nature and beauty represented in architecture via geometric forms. Scarpa is unique, an aberration. His work is like Mughal architecture. It's not decorative, it's detailed."

Eric Moss agrees that Scarpa's work "is not about space – it is about erogenous joints." Out of his relentless research into the application of new materials and the inventive ways he combined them with traditional ones, Moss sees Scarpa as a maker of something that is indeed precious, but in the best sense: something exquisite and "rare." "His work says there is only one of these. You can't copy it or reproduce it." The encounter with this architecture startles one, notes Moss, into "an insight you never had before, a new attitude toward making things." For Moss, Scarpa was not a planner, as he was rarely inventive in terms of the envelope; his strength lay precisely in the perfect disposition of details. For Jorge Silvetti, that strategy of detail was ultimately about managing space. Silvetti sees Scarpa as "one of the few original designers in this century ... relying on joining, detailing, and assembling rather than on the spatial planning strategies so predominant in modernism as the generators of space."

Scarpa's fascination with craft and detail carried over into every aspect of his life. This sense of the unity of design, of an architectural approach to all aspects of life, exercises a powerful appeal today. Scarpa began his career in 1929 as a designer of art glass for Giacomo Cappellin. In 1931 Scarpa was hired by the Murano glassmaker Paolo Venini, a relationship that would continue for many years with Scarpa's exhibition designs for the company. Whether working with traditional glassmakers or in architectural interventions, Scarpa created new forms with old techniques. Undoubtedly, his mastery of the color and surface characteristics of the glass objects he designed for Venini carried over into his work in other materials and other disciplines. This understanding of a material and its possible applications – a skill not widely prized in the 1960s and the 1970s – has returned as a significant consideration in many practices.

Michael Rotondi reminds us that in the 1970s "most of the work we knew had more to do with the intention of architecture than with the execution of it. Scarpa was able to take us all the way down to the fasteners on a building, and that was the first time we'd ever seen anybody do work like that. The sensuousness of the work impressed us. Modernism, for the most part, lacked that quality. I wanted to touch his buildings: it felt like a sin!" Another aspect of the work that seemed to him sinful at the time was Scarpa's use of detail as a generative force, and the luxury of time that Scarpa sometimes had to develop his solutions. "We don't know about the length of time Scarpa worked on these buildings. There is a relationship

New Canaan residence (Hariri & Hariri, Architects; 1990), Connecticut. Photograph: John Hall

between that duration and the amount of detail you can put into a building. The detail is like the DNA of the building."

Diane Lewis, who today teaches architecture at Cooper Union, visited Scarpa in 1976 when she was a young graduate architect living in Italy. The maestro invited her to the Villa Arnani and when she arrived early in the morning and rang the bell, a man with a toothbrush in his mouth leaned out of a tiny attic window to greet her. Once inside, she was met by Scarpa and his wife Nini, both in their kimonos. Nini spread the breakfast table with cheeses. A few minutes later, Scarpa emerged from an adjacent room with an object exactly the size of one of the cheeses. It was bronze – a drain fitting for the Verona bank. He put it on the cheese board, and in a sense, she recalls, "everything became bronze." Later they talked in Scarpa's office, which was not an office in our understanding of the term, but an atelier – an atelier in the Renaissance sense. Lewis believes that "the continuity of making the art of architecture was in that room." That kind of continuity, knowledge, and diversity is found in the work of the Williams/Tsien partnership, Steven Holl, Hariri and Hariri, and Hodgetts and Fung – architects who design everything from table utensils to exhibition installations to buildings, much as Scarpa did.

"Few architects have dealt with the kind of luminosity, reflection, and sheen of materials as that which preoccupied Scarpa," Leslie Gill maintains. "Here, where we work so much with a material as banal as sheet rock, we're

Samitaur Building (Eric Owen Moss, Architect; 1987–96), Culver City, California. Photograph: Tom Bonner

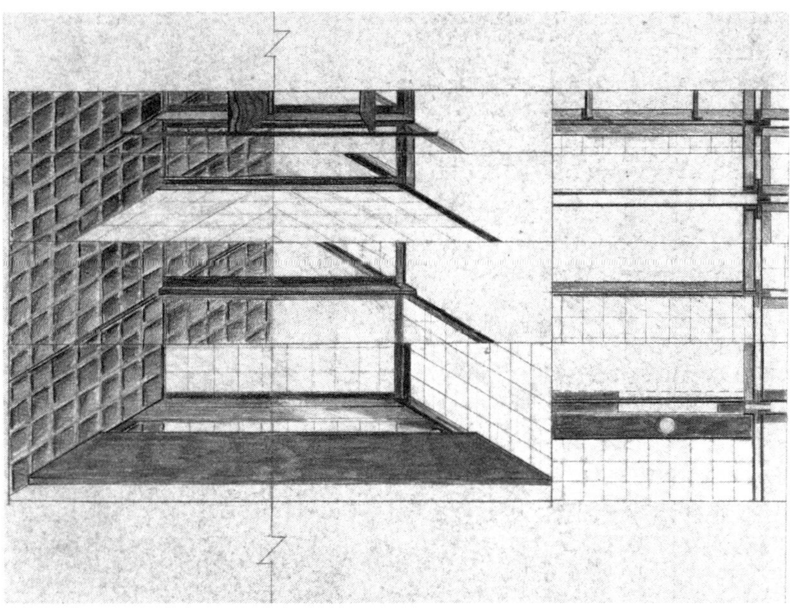

Diane Lewis, Architect. Studies for an Order. A plan view and section perspective at the eye-level of the inhabitant. Structure serving the most internal activities of the home, 1976. Graphite, colored pencil, and ink, 22.8 x 30.5 cm. Coll. Diane Lewis, Architect

Gagosian Gallery (Craig Hodgetts/Ming Fung, Architects; Robert Mangurian, Designer; 1979), Los Angeles. Photograph: Jayme Odgers

Memorial Landscape (Shim-Sutcliffe, Architects; 1997), North York, Ontario. Photograph: James Dow. Coll. Shim-Sutcliffe, Architects

constantly trying to reaffirm materiality." Some have noted that Scarpa extended his revelation of material surfaces into the realm of nature, composing with light and water, both of which were recognized as design materials that play with and upon the made surface. The Toronto architects Brigitte Shim and Howard Sutcliffe have been chiefly impressed with Scarpa's ability to incorporate water, as a powerful life force, into his built work. At the Brion tomb, they explain, "Scarpa turned farmers' fields into a 'sea' in which he built an island oasis. Perhaps he was recalling the island cemetery of Venice." At the Museo di Castelvecchio, Scarpa works into his design the waters of Verona's Adige River, the moat of the castle, and the sky above the statue of Cangrande. At Brion he composes space with reflection. And at the Palazzo Querini Stampalia, Scarpa lets the reflection of light on the canal enter the building and retains the traditional celebratory entryway via gondola, while at the same time creating a new footbridge across the canal. Fumihiko Maki explains that "Scarpa's use of light was very special. In Castelvecchio he painted the walls gray instead of white in order to modulate the light. He could calculate the kind of color the wall should be in relation to the amount of natural light he wanted for a particular object in a room; he was a master at that."

Ultimately, there is not just a renewed admiration for Scarpa's sense of history, materiality, and craftsmanship, but also a kind of respectful jealousy for the small scale that the nature of Scarpa's strategies and interventions suggests. Mayne points out that as architectural scale goes up, the relationship to craft diminishes, and that Scarpa's ability to sustain his distinctive artistry was a function of the relatively small scale of his work. In that regard, Steven Holl advances a theory about Scarpa that turns upon the difference between the miniature and the gigantic. "If meaning is conveyed in a small gesture it has more meaning than in a large gesture. The miniature has in it the hope of accessibility to many, a hope that many people could make something like it. Thus, the renovation of an apartment could be as important as the construction of a skyscraper. The intensity of the miniature is as meaningful as the grand gesture. Scarpa did not have the large scale." Billie Tsien also comments that the "Castelvecchio is so powerful because of the size of the gesture; a small but very strong gesture against a very big background." Much of Scarpa's time was spent creating exhibition designs and adding onto, altering, and adjusting existing spaces; such small projects afforded him the time and opportunity to experiment in ways that would not have been possible with larger, more complex programs.

Perhaps the most significant aspect of Scarpa's working method, one that many architects today would like to emulate, is the artistic impulse – the breadth of imagination, the depth of expression. Scarpa came to each situation with a blank slate, gradually filled in as fresh ideas flowed from his heart onto the drawing board. Holl believes that what matters in Scarpa's work are the experiential essences: "It is these – the thorn on the rose, the drop of water on the leaf – that must be reinstated in our daily lives." Scarpa possessed what Fumihiko Maki called "a superior power of appreciation, a private hedonism." Collaborating with skilled artisans, he brought his ideas to a level of realization of unique aesthetic merit. This quest for expression distinguishes all of Scarpa's work, which in its transcendence of rationality and function continues to provide inspiration for young practitioners. "All great architecture is rational," said Scarpa, "but great art is created only when spiritual and imaginative elements appear in it – the irrational, which constitutes its inspired, creative function."

NOTES

INTRODUCTION

1 Carlo Scarpa in "Incontri a cura di Gastone Favero: Un'ora con Carlo Scarpa," Radiotelevisione Italiana documentary, c. 1970.

2 Scarpa, "Un'ora con Carlo Scarpa."

3 Carlo Scarpa, "L'architecture peut-elle être poésie?" in *Les cahiers de la recherche architecturale* 19 (1986): 12.

4 Scarpa's first encounter with images of Wright's work clearly predates Bruno Zevi's extraordinarily influential introduction of Wright to an Italian audience in *Verso un'archittetura organica* (Towards an Organic Architecture, 1945).

5 Scarpa, "Un'ora con Carlo Scarpa." Bruno Zevi, in his 1952 history of modernism, *Storia dell'architettura moderna*, was among others in Italy to call for the return of "individual expression" to the modernist agenda, after the example of Wright.

6 Carlo Scarpa, "Furnishings" in *Carlo Scarpa: The Complete Works*, ed. Francesco Dal Co and Giuseppe Mazzariol (Milan: Electa, New York: Rizzoli, 1985), 282.

7 In a critique of the Seagram Building, which he greatly admired, Scarpa pointed out that its surface, as we approach it, conceals the structure by engulfing the visitor in reflections of the surrounding context and arousing a delight in the glass itself rather than what the glass reveals. It was perhaps in response to it that he orchestrated the framed reflections in the facade of the Banca Popolare.

8 Scarpa, "Furnishings," 282.

9 Scarpa, "Un'ora con Carlo Scarpa."

10 Scarpa, "Un'ora con Carlo Scarpa."

11 Scarpa, "Un'ora con Carlo Scarpa."

12 Carlo Scarpa, "Leçon sur la gypsothèque," *Les cahiers de la recherche architecturale* 19 (1986): 100.

13 Rafael Moneo, "Representation with the Eye," in *Scarpa: Complete Works*, 236.

14 Manfredo Tafuri, "Carlo Scarpa and Italian Architecture," in *Scarpa: Complete Works*, 77.

15 Scarpa, "Un'ora con Carlo Scarpa."

16 Francesco Dal Co, *Villa Ottolenghi* (New York: Monacelli Press, 1998), 51, 56.

17 Mario Brusatin, "The Architect in Asolo," in *Scarpa: Complete Works*, 196.

18 Unpublished interviews.

HISTORY, CRAFT, INVENTION

1 Cited in *Carlo Scarpa* (Vicenza: Accademia Olimpica, 1974).

2 Sergio Los, *Carlo Scarpa: architetto, poeta* (Venice: Edizione Cluva, 1967), 19.

3 Carlo Scarpa in "Incontri a cura di Gastone Favero: Un'ora con Carlo Scarpa," Radiotelevisione Italiana documentary, c. 1970.

4 Scarpa, "Un'ora con Carlo Scarpa."

5 Carlo Scarpa, "Interview conducted by Martin Dominguez in May 1978, in Vicenza," in *Carlo Scarpa: The Complete Works*, ed. Francesco Dal Co and Giuseppe Mazzariol (Milan: Electa, New York: Rizzoli, 1985), 297.

6 Scarpa, "Interview by Martin Dominguez," 297.

7 Scarpa, "Interview by Martin Dominguez," 298.

8 Scarpa, "Interview by Martin Dominguez," 298.

9 Scarpa, "Interview by Martin Dominguez," 297.

10 Scarpa, "Un'ora con Carlo Scarpa."

11 Scarpa, "Interview by Martin Dominguez," 297.

12 Carlo Scarpa, "Carlo Scarpa: Cours donné le 20 février 1975," AMC: *Architecture, Mouvement, Continuité* 50 (December 1979): 23–24.

13 Scarpa, "Interview by Martin Dominguez," 298.

14 From an interview with Carlo Scarpa videotaped in October 1978 by Barbara Radice only one month before Scarpa's death.

15 Scarpa, "Interview by Martin Dominguez," 299.

16 Carlo Scarpa, "Furnishings," *Scarpa: Complete Works*, 282.

17 Carlo Scarpa, "Can Architecture Be Poetry?," in *Carlo Scarpa: The Other City/Carlo Scarpa: Die andere Stadt*, ed. Peter Noever (Berlin: Ernst & Sohn, 1989), 17, 18.

18 Scarpa, "Can Architecture Be Poetry?," 18.

19 Françoise Véry, "La tombe de monsieur Brion," AMC: *Architecture, mouvement, continuité*, 50 (December 1979), 23–24.

THINKING WITH THE EYES

1 The epigram is from notes, possibly for a lecture, in the Scarpa archive, Trevignano.

2 Bruno Zevi, "Beneath or Beyond Architecture," in *Carlo Scarpa: The Complete Works*, ed. Francesco Dal Co and Giuseppe Mazzariol (Milan: Electa, New York: Rizzoli, 1985), 272.

3 "Interview with Arrigo Rudi in Venice on 28 May 1984," Radiotelevisione Italiana documentary.

4 Francesco Dal Co, "The Architecture of Carlo Scarpa," in *Scarpa: Complete Works*, 27.

5 I. Gardella, "The 'Gamin'," in *Scarpa: Complete Works*, 214.

6 Carlo Scarpa, "Leçon sur la gypsothèque," *Les cahiers de la recherche architecturale* 19 (1986): 97.

7 Scarpa, "Leçon sur la gypsothèque," 97–98.

8 Scarpa, "Leçon sur la gypsothèque," 102.

9 Carlo Scarpa, "Can Architecture Be Poetry?," in *Carlo Scarpa: The Other City/Carlo Scarpa: Die andere Stadt*, ed. Peter Noever (Berlin: Ernst & Sohn, 1989), 17.

10 Sergio Los, *Carlo Scarpa: An Architectural Guide* (Venice: Arsenale Editrice, 1995), 11.

11 Scarpa, "Leçon sur la gypsothèque," 100.

12 Beaumont Newhall, *The History of Photography: From 1839 to the Present* (New York: Museum of Modern Art, 1982), 43.

13 Scarpa, "Can Architecture Be Poetry?," 17.

14 Carlo Scarpa in "Incontri a cura di Gastone Favero: Un'ora con Carlo Scarpa," Radiotelevisione Italiana documentary, c. 1970.

15 Translated from Carlo Scarpa, "L'architecture peut-elle être poésie?," *Les cahiers de la recherche architecturale* 19 (1986), 17.

16 Scarpa, "Un'ora con Carlo Scarpa."

THE ART OF DISPLAY

1 Giorgio Vigni, "Recollections of Working with Scarpa: New National Gallery of Sicily, Palermo" in *Carlo Scarpa, Il progetto per Santa Caterina a Treviso* (Treviso: Vianello libri, 1984), 37–39.

THE RENEWAL OF THE CASTELVECCHIO

The author wishes to express her gratitude for the assistance of a friend who wishes to remain unnamed and to thank Pada Marini and Arrigo Rudi for their invaluable advice.

1 See Marisa Dalai Emiliani, "Musei della ricostruzione in Italia, tra disfatta e rivincita della storia," in *Carlo Scarpa a Castelvecchio*, ed. Licisco Magagnato (Milan: Edizioni di Comunità, 1982). There are clearly references to the Castello Sforzesco in Milan, restored by the architect Luca Beltrami between 1892 and 1911. Beltrami had strong links with Verona, where he was a respected member of the Commission for the Preservation of Monuments. See the essay by Alberto Grimoldi, *Restauri a Verona: cultura e pubblico 1866–1940* (Verona: Editori della Banca Popolare di Verona, 1994), 154, and Luca Beltrami in *Milano tra Ottocento e Novecento*, ed. Luciana Bolddrighi (Milan: Electa, 1997).

2 For a history of the castle and the collections, see Sergio Marinelli, "Il castello, le collezioni" in *Carlo Scarpa*

a Castelvecchio, 133–48, and Lino Vittorio Bozzetto, "L'architettura di Castelvecchio dal Trecento all'Ottocento" in *Castelvecchio e il ponte scaligero* (Verona: Headquarters of the Allied Ground Forces in Southern Europe, 1995), 75–105.

3 It was probably Vittorio Moschini, director of the Gallerie dell'Accademia in Venice, who suggested Scarpa to Magagnato. In a review of the exhibition at the Triennale devoted to the subject of museum design, Magagnato wrote appreciatively of the renovation of the galleries, where "in room after room, we see examples of the styles and new concepts of exhibition design, resulting in some noteworthy instances of display." *Comunità* 53 (1957): 70–72. After a thorough analysis of the situation, Magagnato wrote a letter to the mayor of Verona recommending Scarpa for the renovation of the Castelvecchio. Licisco Magagnato, "Il Museo di Castelvecchio e la continuità dei criteri museologici" in *Museo oggi*, ed. Giovanna Rezzonico (Milan: Giessea edizioni, 1996), 122–29.

4 At the congress of Italian museum directors that took place in Palermo in 1954, Scarpa had been praised for his restoration of Palazzo Abatellis by none other than Roberto Longhi. Paolo Morello, *Palazzo Abatellis: il maragma del Maestro Portulano da Matteo Carnilivari a Carlo Scarpa* (Ponzano: Vianello Libri, 1989), 55; Sergio Polano, *Carlo Scarpa a Palazzo Abatellis: L'allestimento della Galleria Nazionale della Sicilia, 1953–54* (Milan: Electa, 1991), 25–39.

5 The fresco was returned to its original location after being once more exhibited at the Castelvecchio in the Pisanello exhibition of 1996. See Paola Marini, ed., *Pisanello* (Milan: Electa, 1996).

6 The ground plans for the renovation of the Reggia are signed not by Scarpa but by Verona's chief engineer. Scarpa's chief collaborator throughout the project was Arrigo Rudi, who continued to work with Scarpa at the Istituto universitario di architettura di Venezia. Rudi completed the construction of the Banca Popolare after Scarpa's death. Angelo Rudella, surveyor for the museum, executed numerous drawings and supervised the construction. Arrigo Rudi, "Le contestazioni e i processi a Carlo Scarpa," *Architetti Verona: materiali su Carlo Scarpa* 4/5 (1980): 34–59.

7 The plans for the exhibition appear to have been lost; the only evidence for the arrangement and selection of the exhibited works are archival photographs and the exhibition catalogue, *Da Altichiero a Pisanello*. Most of the works listed there (such as many panel paintings from the fourteenth and fifteenth centuries, polyptychs, detached frescoes, the *Madonna del Roseto* by Stefano da Verona, the *Madonna della Quaglia* by Pisanello, and various crucifixes) are still on display in the Reggia wing as presented in the exhibition.

8 Roberto Aloi, *Musei, Architettura-Tecnica* (Milan: Hoepli, 1962), 253–67.

9 Restoration of the northeast tower was completed between 1994 and 1996 under the supervision of Paola Marini, following plans by Alba Di Lieto and Maurizio Cossato. The work was financed entirely by the Association of Friends of Castelvecchio and of the Civic Art Museums.

10 The chronology of the reconstruction of the courtyard is given in notes by the surveyor, Angelo Rudella, in the Castelvecchio archives. Arrigo Rudi recalls that it was Scarpa who selected the planting. For economic reasons, *Piracantha* was proposed for the hedges, an alteration that was quite acceptable to the architect, although his drawings had specified that the two hedges should be composed of *Thuja*, *Laurus cerasus*, or *Taxus baccata*. Along the footpath running from the Prun-stone paving to the fountains, a row of *Portulache* was planted.

SCARPA TODAY

1 With reference to Scarpa's approach to design, it is interesting to note the parallel between his career and that of Charles Eames (1907–1978), equivalent in time and not dissimilar in character. Eames was another maverick who plowed a unique course through several diverse fields.

2 These interviews with architects concerning the architecture of Carlo Scarpa were conducted in 1997 and 1998.

3 Nory Miller, "The Legendary Castle [Castelvecchio]: Critique," *Progressive Architecture* 62:5 (May 1981): 122.

4 For a brief history of Scarpa's renovations of Verona's Castelvecchio museum, see Alba Di Lieto's "The Renewal of the Castelvecchio" in this volume.

5 It is conceivable that the traditional *stucco lucido* method perfected by Eugenio de Luigi for his work with Scarpa, in which many coats of integrally colored plaster create shimmering wall surfaces, may have inspired the many-layered wall drawings in ink created by the American artist Sol LeWitt, who has long spent part of each year in Italy.

6 From an interview with Carlo Scarpa, videotaped in October 1978 by Barbara Radice only one month before Scarpa's death.

SELECTED BIBLIOGRAPHY

GENERAL WORKS

ALBERTINI, Bianca, and Sandro BAGNOLI. *Carlo Scarpa: Architecture in Details*. Cambridge, Mass.: The MIT Press, 1988.

——. *Scarpa: i musei e le esposizioni*. Milan: Jaca Book, 1992.

BAROVIER, Marina, ed. *Carlo Scarpa, i vetri di Murano, 1927–1947*. Venice: Cardo, 1991.

CRIPPA, Maria Antonietta. *Carlo Scarpa: Theory, Design, Projects*. Cambridge, Mass.: The MIT Press, 1986.

DAL CO, Francesco. *Villa Ottolenghi: Carlo Scarpa*. New York: Monacelli Press, 1998.

DAL CO, Francesco, and Giuseppe MAZZARIOL. *Carlo Scarpa: The Complete Works*. Milan: Electa, New York: Rizzoli, 1985.

FONATTI, Franco. *Elemente des Bauens bei Carlo Scarpa*. 2nd ed. Vienna: Akademie der bildenden Künste, 1985.

FRASCARI, Marco. *The Body and Architecture in the Drawings of Carlo Scarpa*. Cambridge, Mass.: Peabody Museum of Archeology and Ethnology, Harvard University, 1987.

HOH-SLODCZYK, Christine. *Carlo Scarpa und das Museum*. Berlin: Ernst & Sohn, 1987.

LOS, Sergio. *Carlo Scarpa*. Cologne: Benedikt Taschen, 1994.

——. *Carlo Scarpa, architetto, poeta*. Venice: Edizioni Cluva, 1967.

LISTS OF BUILDINGS AND PROJECTS

LOS, Sergio. *Carlo Scarpa: An Architectural Guide*. Venice: Arsenale Editrice, 1995.

POLANO, Sergio. "Catalogue Raisonné." In *Carlo Scarpa: The Complete Works*: 97–149. Ed. Francesco Dal Co and Giuseppe Mazzariol. Milan: Electa, New York: Rizzoli, 1985.

RUDI, Arrigo, ed. "Carlo Scarpa, Frammenti 1926–1978." Special monographic issue of *Rassegna* 7 (1981): 6–81.

SCARPA BIBLIOGRAPHY

HEZEL, Dieter, ed. *Architekten, Carlo Scarpa*. IRB-Literaturauslese 1350. Stuttgart: IRB Verlag, 1995.

WORKS ON THE EIGHT PROJECTS

Palazzo Abatellis, Palermo (1953–54)

FRASCARI, Marco. "Carlo Scarpa in Magna Graecia: The Abatellis Palace in Palermo." *AA Files* 9 (1985): 3–9.

POLANO, Sergio. *Carlo Scarpa a Palazzo Abatellis: l'allestimento della Galleria nazionale della Sicilia, 1953–54*. Milan: Electa, 1991. Originally published as *Carlo Scarpa: Palazzo Abatellis, La Galleria della Sicilia, Palermo, 1953–54*. Milan: Electa, 1989.

VIGNI, Giorgio. "Recollections of Working with Scarpa: New National Gallery of Sicily, Palermo." In *Carlo Scarpa: il progetto per Santa Caterina a Treviso*, 34–43. Treviso: Vianello Libri, 1984.

Canova Plaster Cast Gallery, Possagno (1955–57)

"Carlo Scarpa: Ampliamento della Gipsoteca Canoviana a Possagno (1956–57)." *Casabella-Continuità* 222 (1958): 8–14.

SCARPA, Carlo. "Leçon sur la gypsothèque." Trans. Françoise Brun. *Les cahiers de la recherche architecturale* 19 (1986): 94–103.

Museo di Castelvecchio, Verona (1956–73)

DI LIETO, Alba. *Analisi dei materiali usati da Carlo Scarpa nel restauro di Castelvecchio*. Verona: Museo di Castelvecchio, 1993.

MAGAGNATO, Licisco, ed. *Carlo Scarpa a Castelvecchio*. Milan: Edizioni di comunità, 1982.

MURPHY, Richard. *Carlo Scarpa and the Castelvecchio*. London and Toronto: Butterworth Architecture, 1990.

Veritti House, Udine (1955–61)

ALOI, Roberto. "Casa Veritti a Udine – Carlo Scarpa/ Veritti House at Udine – Carlo Scarpa." In *Ville nel mondo*, 1–12. Milan: Ulrico Hoepli Editore, 1961.

"Carlo Scarpa, Casa Veritti a Udine, 1960." *Casabella-Continuità* 254 (August 1961): 3–11.

Olivetti Showroom, Venice (1957–58)

"Il nuovo negozio Olivetti a Venezia." *Domus* 362 (January 1960): 9–14.

RAGGHIANTI, Carlo L. "La 'Crosera de piazza' di Carlo Scarpa." *Zodiac* 4 (1959): 128–47.

SCARPA, Gigi. "Un negozio in Piazza San Marco, a Venezia." *L'architettura Cronache e Storia* 1:43 (May 1959): 18–27.

Palazzo Querini Stampalia, Venice (1961–63)

MAZZA, Marta. *Carlo Scarpa alla Querini Stampalia: Disegni inediti*. Venice: Il Cardo, 1996.

MAZZARIOL, Giuseppe. "Història i gènesi de la intervenció a la Fundació Querini Stampalia /Storia e genesi dell'intervento nella Fondazione Querini Stampalia." *Quaderns* 158 (July–September 1983): 52–63.

MURPHY, Richard. *Querini Stampalia Foundation*. Architecture in Detail. London: Phaidon, 1993.

Banca Popolare di Verona, Verona (1973–81)

DUBOY, Philippe. "Carlo Scarpa: Banca Popolare di Verona Head Offices, Verona, Italy, 1973–1981." *Global Architecture* 63 (1983): 1–47.

RUDI, Arrigo. "La Banque Populaire de Verone: Le siège central de la banque." AMC: *Architecture, Mouvement, Continuité* 50 (December 1979): 78–88.

RUDI, Arrigo, and Valter ROSSETTO, eds. *La Sede Centrale della Banca Popolare di Verona nel progetto e nella realizzazione di Carlo Scarpa e Arrigo Rudi*. Verona: Banca popolare di Verona, 1983.

Brion Family Tomb, San Vito d'Altivole (1969–78)

DUBOY, Philippe. "Locus Solus, Carlo Scarpa et le cimetière de San Vito d'Altivole (1969–1975)." *L'Architecture d'Aujourd'hui* 181 (September–October 1975): 73–86.

NOEVER, Peter, ed. *Carlo Scarpa: The Other City/Carlo Scarpa: Die andere Stadt*, Berlin: Ernst & Sohn, 1989.

SCARPA, Carlo. "Can Architecture Be Poetry?" In *Carlo Scarpa: The Other City/Carlo Scarpa: Die andere Stadt*, 16–20. Ed. Peter Noever. Berlin: Ernst & Sohn, 1989. See also "L'architecture peut-elle être poésie?" in *Les cahiers de la recherche architecturale* 19 (1986).

STERN, Michael A. "Passages in the Garden: An Iconology of the Brion Tomb." *Landscape Journal* 13:1 (spring 1994): 38–57.

INDEX

ABBREVIATIONS

Coll. ACS
Collection Archivio Carlo Scarpa, Trevignano

Coll. CCA
Collection Canadian Centre for Architecture, Montréal

Coll. FQS
Collection Fondazione Querini Stampalia, Venezia

Coll. GRS
Collection Galleria Regionale della Sicilia, Palermo

Coll. MDC
Collection Museo di Castelvecchio, Verona

Illustrations are noted in boldface.

This book has been typeset in Adobe Jenson and Thesis TheSans and printed on Lustro Dull paper. Six thousand copies were printed in Montréal in May of nineteen ninety-nine by Litho Acme.

Senior Editor: Lesley Johnstone
Production Manager: Denis Hunter
Editing: Edward Tingley and Marcia Rodriguez
Translation: Vittoria di Palma,
Paola Ludovici MacQuarrie, Antony Shugaar
Design: Glenn Goluska
Reproduction rights: Jocelyne Gervais
Word processing: Lynda Lefebvre